The New Americans
Recent Immigration and American Society

Edited by
Steven J. Gold and Rubén G. Rumbaut

A Series from LFB Scholarly

Russian Immigrants in the United States
Adapting to American Culture

Vera Kishinevsky

LFB Scholarly Publishing LLC
New York 2004

Library of Congress Cataloging-in-Publication Data

Kishinevsky, Vera, 1953-
  Russian immigrants in the United States : adapting to American
culture / Vera Kishinevsky.
    p. cm. -- (The new Americans)
  Includes bibliographical references and index.
  ISBN 1-59332-056-6 (alk. paper)
  1. Russian Americans--Social conditions. 2. Russian Americans--
Cultural assimilation. I. Title. II. Series: New Americans (LFB
Scholarly Publishing LLC)
  E184.R9K57 2004
  305.891'71073--dc22

2004012667

ISBN 1-59332-056-6

Printed on acid-free 250-year-life paper.

Manufactured in the United States of America.

Table of Contents

Acknowledgments

I wish to thank wonderful women who made this book possible — Iris Fodor, Elizabeth Kosky and Korine Fitzpatrick for their support and inspiration. I am also grateful to Lynn Glassman for her pertinent comments about a large part of the manuscript and for the considerable time she spent in discussing with me many of the topics that are treated in the book. I am indebted to Jean Cheng-Gorman for providing many valuable contributions to this work from its inception.

CHAPTER 1

Why the Russians?

PROLOGUE

It is a hot day in late July. Natasha is sitting on a couch in her sunny apartment overlooking the ocean. She is in her mid-forties. Large dark eyes with long lashes beam with warmth on her round face. With her small chiseled nose, bottomless eyes and curved lips, she resembles a Renoir portrait. The phone rings. "Yes, mama, I am OK, and Tanya, too. Yes, she had breakfast. I made sure, I know. Don't worry, she is coming home for dinner." Bedridden after a massive stroke, Natasha's mother regularly checks that Natasha's daughter Tanya, a college senior, eats three full meals every day. Natasha hangs up and gets off the couch with a visible effort. She is walking to the kitchen, and I become acutely aware of her swollen ankles and heavy, dragging sounds of her feet. She returns with a bowl of fruit and a platter of homemade pastries. Natasha tells me that she has been seriously overweight since a year after she arrived to the United States. She tried many diets, but none helped. Once she managed to lose forty pounds, just to gain fifty during the following year. "I went to the doctor last week," says Natasha, returning to the conversation interrupted by her mother's call. "He insisted that I lose weight to avoid serious health problems. I know I have to do it, I will try again, I promise. Look, I bought an exercise bicycle and I plan to work out for an hour every day." Natasha sounds frightened enough to make the necessary changes.

Tanya walks in and talks about her latest achievement—she slimmed down from 172 lbs. to 140 lbs. She proudly lists her routines, "I have been exercising in the gym and running four days a week, honest! I eat healthy—no fat, chicken, grains, vegetables. I knew I had to do it—I am five feet two inches tall. And I don't want to be like my friend Olga—she looks great, miniskirts and all, but I know that she throws up after dinner. I followed her to the bathroom."

Last spring, Natasha and Tanya agreed to be interviewed for the pilot research project. During the interviews, Natasha told me how much she enjoyed tasting new foods and preparing large meals for her family when they first came to America. Taking home loads of affordable delicacies and eating them with her family and friends was so pleasurable, comforting and reassuring during the initial, stressful period of her adjustment in the United States that she did not notice her significant weight gain. She realized how much heavier she became when she started watching television and buying fashionable magazines, but no matter how hard she tried, she could not return to her pre-emigration weight.

A year after, Natasha looked heavier than before and Tanya was back to 176 pounds. Natasha said with resign, "My weight will eventually kill me, I know." Her mother was doing better—Natasha said that she was able to walk around the house. She also said that she was concerned about her mother's "dangerously high" weight, blood pressure and cholesterol level.

Natasha and Tanya are not unique in their struggle. Millions of American women live in the society that operates on two contradicting sets of messages about their bodies and food consumption. Double standards permeate the media—luscious images glorify food on magazine pages, TV screens, and gigantic billboards. The same magazines and TV programs deliver a constant stream of "absolutely sure" methods of losing weight and looking "great," equalizing thinness and beauty. Every year, American women spend billions of dollars on the elusive pursuit of looking reed-thin. For immigrant women who grew up in the culture of permanent scarcity of food, this struggle must be even more stressful. Coming from the country where women's roles are in large part defined by food to the culture that glorifies appearance, they are tempted by the abundant affordable provisions and pressured to look thin. How do they deal with this cultural clash? What is their experience of adjustment in the United States?

PERSONAL STANCE

I remember growing up in a culture where food and feeding were symbols of love and care. Being a "good mother" was primarily to feed the child and being a "good daughter" meant licking every plate clean. Summer camp started with registering every child's weight. At the end of the season, a weight increase was reported with pride to happy parents. Mean skinny witches and plump beauties with rosy cheeks populated fairy tales of my childhood. Popular actresses and singers did not mind looking voluptuous or outright heavy. Russian language has one word for "to improve" and "to get fat"; the same is true for "bad" and "thin."

I came to the United States 26 years ago. During the stressful period of initial adjustment, tasting new foods, cooking and inviting friends over for dinner were therapeutic for me, helped me feel more secure in the new world. My mother and close friends indulged in the same "medicine." Meanwhile, my daughter was growing up and Americanizing fast. When she became a teenager, she started criticizing me for being overweight and insisted that I go on a diet. My mother was annoyed by my struggles. She mused, "We couldn't eat well there [in the former Soviet Union] because of food shortages, we cannot eat well here because tasty food is fattening. What is the sense of immigrating then?" My daughter grew up to become a slim young woman, and my mother often worries that she is "too thin to be healthy." Nevertheless, my daughter has retained some Russian cultural standards, including those regarding food and eating. She loves well-prepared and beautifully served dishes, especially desserts, and her friends admire her elegant dinner parties with beautiful china and flatware.

As a Russian immigrant mother at midlife, I was interested in the stories of other women who came to the United States from the former Soviet Union. I wanted to learn how other mother-daughter dyads deal with body image issues and how acculturation influenced this process. When I turned to the literature, I was surprised to find, given the size of the Russian immigrant community, almost a total absence of studies examining the subjective experience of female Russian immigrants. As I realized that the literature could not provide me with the information I needed, I decided to turn to the former Soviet women for the answers. I wanted to know how beauty standards changed along the acculturation line, what cultural attitudes were carried over from the old country and passed to the daughters. I wondered about the daughters' attitudes toward them. How did Russian cultural experience influence eating habits and attitudes of immigrant mothers and daughters? What changes in body attitudes and eating habits came with their acculturation?

PILOT STUDY

In a pilot project, I interviewed seven mothers, who immigrated from the former Soviet Union, and their teenage daughters. The interviews revealed that former Soviet women become progressively more indoctrinated by American beauty norms as the length of their stay in the USA increases. All the participants talked about their desire to lose weight. In particular, the daughters' self-esteem seemed to depend notably on their weight. One girl demonstrated signs of disordered eating, and two girls, significantly overweight by American standards, reported feeling better when their weight decreased. Both overweight girls had overweight mothers. These mothers also talked about their desire for a slimmer figure, but their body ideal seemed to be more relaxed. One mother said, "A woman should enjoy what G-d gave her" and described reed-thin American models as "pitiful and sickly."

Listening to the participants, I realized how close they were to their grandmothers and how meaningful this relationship was for them. Every participant stressed her grandmother's role in her upbringing. The grandmothers were reported to be the most accepting of a rather fleshy beauty ideal. Even those who reportedly took pride in their relatively slimmer bodies did their best to force abundant fatty meals on their children and grandchildren. I came to realize that the study of Russian immigrant women would be incomplete without listening to the grandmothers' voices.

INTRODUCTION

In this study I explored the experience of immigrant women from the former Soviet Union, their mothers, and their teenage daughters using qualitative research method—observing, and conducting extensive semi-structured interviews with these women. My original interest was in the changes in their attitudes to their bodies and to food as they acculturated in the United States. I wanted to explore the influence of American obsession with thinness on their lifestyle and to learn how they responded to its pressures.

Immigrants from the former Soviet Union have been a growing presence in the United States since the middle of 1960s. Chiswick (1993), citing the U.S. Department of Justice, Immigration and Naturalization Service (1990, unpublished tables), estimates that

> Over one quarter of a million persons living in the United States... can be described as Soviet Jews, that is, individuals born in the former USSR (or their U.S.-born children) who consider themselves Jewish by religion or ethnicity and who immigrated to the United States from the Soviet Union since the mid 1960s. (p. 260).

By the late 1990s, these numbers have significantly increased. As the political and financial situation in the former Soviet Union has worsened since the fall of the Communist system, various unofficial estimates agreed that the numbers of people who relocated from the former Soviet Union to the United States approach one million. Cass (1997) estimated the size of only one area populated by former Soviets:

> The number of Russians [non-Jews] permitted to emigrate rose steadily as the Soviet Union, nearing its collapse, began to ease travel and emigration restrictions... It is reasonable to suggest that the number has doubled since the turn of the decade. The largest Russian émigré area, "Brighton Beach, is currently home to about 30,000 Russian émigrés. (p. 181)

Bellafante (2001) cited the 1999 New York Housing and Vacancy Survey that indicated that the numbers of former Soviets more than tripled in Brooklyn during the 90's and reached 148,000. Immigrants from the former Soviet Union have attracted little attention of social researchers probably due to their "rapid linguistic and economic mobility" (Chiswick, 1993) and low level of political activism that make them almost invisible in the American society. Their acculturation to American life was primarily studied by Jewish communal organizations and, therefore, the focus of these studies was on Jewish issues, such as participation in Jewish communal institutions, engagement in Jewish religious practice, and interaction with other

Jews on a personal basis. As a result, other needs and problems of this "silent minority" are to a large degree overlooked by research.

THEORETICAL BASIS

Upon arrival in the new country and during the initial stages of adaptation, immigrants usually experience confusion, deprivation, anger, and even mourning, commonly referred to as "culture shock," resulting from the need to cope with the new culture and its demands (Taft, 1977). The need to make substantial psychological changes can be stressful, and an individual may pursue different strategies to reduce this pressure. Some choose to withdraw into the comfort of the familiar ethnic enclaves formed by their "fellow-countrymen" and to resort to the old familiar behavior patterns. Others, with a passage of time attain a reasonable level of inner comfort to move on and to open themselves to the influences of the larger "host" society.

After overcoming the initial shock, immigrants usually come to terms with the predominant culture and gradually get integrated into a new society. Interacting with the "host" society, they start adopting its attitudes, beliefs, and values, thus acquiring cultural competence, defined by Taft (1988) as a potential for acculturation. Eventually, they achieve a full or partial acculturation, or actual convergence with the behavior and attitudes of the "host" society.

Acculturation has been defined as the adaptive process of cultural adjustment and adoption of new competencies, which occurs as the result of contact and interaction between two distinct cultures (Berry, Trimble, & Olmeda, 1986; Mendoza & Martinez, 1981). The model, proposed by Berry, Trimble, & Olmeda (1986), added psychological change to cultural and behavioral change as components of the process. Szapocznik, Scopetta, Kurtines, and Aranalde (1978) described acculturation as the modification of a person's customs, habits, language usage, life style, and value orientations because of contact with a different culture. In related literature, some authors use the term acculturation interchangeably with "assimilation" and "integration" (Taft, 1988, p.152). Thus, Taft (1988) equated acculturation to assimilation by describing "fully acculturated" immigrants as people who alter their dress, eating habits, home decoration, and spoken language to such a degree that they would be perceived as members of the dominant group. He added, however that "this is probably a rare occurrence in persons who emigrate as adults" (Taft, 1988, p. 163). Others (Berry, Kim, & Boski, 1988) clearly distinguish between these terms based on several differing characteristics they find in these two processes of cultural adaptation. Immigrants entering the United States during its "melting pot" period were subjected to assimilative pressure of the dominant culture, which necessitated rapid and radical changes and often led to the abandonment of original culture and language. In a detailed analysis of this particular form of acculturation, Gordon (1964) defined assimilation as a process of relinquishing one's cultural identity and moving into the larger society. He discerns two subvarieties of the process. One is cultural or behavioral assimilation, in which individuals match their behavior and perceptions to those of the collective. The other is structural assimilation, in which the nondominant groups participate in the social and economic systems of the larger society. In the case of structural assimilation, "individuals and groups may select the domains (for example, language, food, dress, religion) in which they will change and those in which they will not change" (Berry, Kim, & Boski, 1988, p. 65).

Berry (1984a) proposed a model founded on two major decisions individuals and groups must make. One involves retaining ethnic distinctiveness, including the language, cultural identity and customs. The other decision entails the contact with the larger society, its value and extent. Depending on what decisions are made, four options are available to immigrants in pluralistic multicultural societies, such as Canada (Berry, 1984b) and the present-day United States: assimilation, integration, separation, and marginalization. Complete cultural transformation with attendant loss of original culture is defined as assimilation. O'Bryan, Reitz, & Kuplowska (1976) examined heritage-language knowledge, use, and support among ten major ethnic groups residing in Canada. The most dramatic finding was that heritage-language knowledge virtually disappears after two generations. Integration refers to retaining of some cultural specificity while advancing toward the inclusion into a larger society. When limited relations with the larger society are coupled with adherence to ethnic identity, language, and traditional values, either separation or segregation takes place. The difference between those is defined by the power relationship: separation is voluntary, while segregation is separation imposed by the dominant group. The fourth option, marginalization, is defined as a loss of cultural and psychological contact with both original and "host" cultures. Feelings of alienation, loss of identity, and anger against the larger society, typical for the initial period of acculturation or "acculturative stress" (Berry & Annis, 1974), may lead to marginalization of individuals who, due to various reasons, failed to recover from its impact.

Conducting a cross-cultural study in Canada, Berry, Kim, & Boski (1998) concluded that the integration option was clearly favored by all participant groups. In Australia, researchers of acculturation abandoned the assumption of linear progressive assimilation (Taft, 1986) and adopted a multifaceted model, similar to the one described above. Multiple studies of various ethnic groups acculturating in the United States, produced similar results favoring integration (Hurh & Kim, 1984, Mendoza & Martinez, 1981), or closely related "cultural pluralism" (Newman, 1973), "acculturation without assimilation" (Rosenthal, 1970), and "accomodative pluralism" (Kurokawa, 1970). These authors posited that assimilation is not the only possible way of acculturation.

The modes of acculturation, delineated above, evolve from the choices immigrants make during the course of their acculturation. These choices may be predicated upon the interplay of various external and internal conditions. External conditions include the size of immigrant groups, political atmosphere, and the availability and level of social supports in the "host" society. Internal conditions, among other factors, include age, family status, education level, and acculturation attitudes. Since former Soviets typically achieve linguistic and job market parity with other European immigrant groups (Chiswick, 1993), marginalization is clearly not a threat for them as a group. Increasing numbers of former Soviets cause and support the existence of numerous radio- and television stations, newspapers, magazines, and other cultural institutions. They appear to have become numerous enough to create a sizeable cultural enclave in the United States. In the environment of multiculturalism, younger generations of former Soviets seem to opt for varying levels of assimilation or integration while people of retirement age tend more toward separation with an admixture of integration.

PARTICIPANTS

In the process of selecting research participants, I used the following two criteria: the first criterion was that all participants have been living in the United States for at least five years. This meant that I chose women who had sufficient time to overcome the initial culture shock (Taft, 1977) and to be substantially exposed to the mainstream American culture. The second criterion was that the participants belonged to different socioeconomic groups and came from different geographical areas of the former Soviet Union. The participants of this study included a former factory worker, two teachers, a musician, a bookkeeper, and an engineer. They came to the United States from large and medium size cities in Ukraine, Belarus, Caucasus, and Middle Asia.

Initially, I did not worry about finding a sufficient number of interested families to participate in the study. I distributed recruiting leaflets near cultural institutions and business establishments frequented by former Soviets and collected a large group of volunteers of the mothers' and daughters' generation, but none of them was able to convince the grandmother to participate in the study. Finally, I realized that I had underestimated the fear the older generation of former Soviets harbor for the perceived authorities. To correct that, I made necessary adjustments to my recruitment campaign, starting with reaching out to the grandmothers first. I painstakingly explained to potential volunteers that I was not connected with the government or with any structured social service. I also promised that they might refrain from signing the consent form with their last names. Finally, the grandmothers agreed to participate in the study after I personally assured them of their complete anonymity and convinced them that my interest lies only in research. Their attitude, paranoid by mainstream American standards, had its roots in the period of Stalin's terror when a flippant remark or a stray written word could cost a person a long prison sentence or life.

In my reporting the results of the interviews, I was challenged by the need to define the participants as a group. At different times, various researchers used different terms to describe my participants' cultural background. From the beginning of the 1970s, a steady stream of people has been moving from the former Soviet Union to the United States of America. As it consisted mainly of Russian-speaking Jews with the admixture of ethnic Russians and representatives of numerous other nationalities from the former Soviet Union, the confusion of terms used to describe them reflected the multilingual and multicultural nature of the immigrants from the former Soviet Union. Cass (1997) indicated:

> By Russian émigrés we mean individuals in the United States who were born in the region formerly known as the Soviet Union, and their children. This definition includes not only Russians, but others with a variety of ethnic identities including Armenian, Chechen, Ukrainian, Azeri, and Jewish. (p. 142)

Brodsky (1982) used the term "Soviet Immigrants", and Chiswick (1993) chose to name members of the same group "Soviet Jews" even though he wrote about high rates of intermarriage among them. The breakup of the Soviet Union added more confusion to the already complex problem. Emigrating from Russia, Ukraine, Caucasian regions, etc. the new arrivals could be identified by the name of their country of origin (Russians, Ukrainians, Armenians, etc.), their language (usually Russian), or religion. Since the participants of this study were Jewish or of mixed origin from Russia and other parts of the former Soviet Union, I will use the term *Russians* only to refer to the ethnic, non-Jewish population of Russia proper. To simplify the matter, I will refer to the participants of this study as to *former Soviets or immigrants from the former Soviet Union.*

For the readers' convenience, names used for concealment of the participants' identities were coordinated by their generations: all grandmothers' names start with a "G", all mothers' names start with an "M", and all granddaughters' names start with a "D".

All the interviews were conducted in the participants' homes, as this setting is probably the most conducive to openness and sharing of feelings and opinions. This was particularly important for Soviet immigrants whose upbringing included deep distrust of anything that reminds official structures. A number of observers wrote about the separation between private and official life in the Soviet Union. (Brodsky, 1982; Bunyon, 1983; Smith, 1976).

CHAPTER 2

Relevant Literature

Cultural background of participants of this study is a result of an interplay of Russian and Soviet elements, so information on both sources sheds some light on their inner reality. A section on mainstream American culture gives a brief description of its major attitudes toward body image issues and addresses its influence on acculturating immigrants and on the population of Westernizing countries. Since some immigrant women develop eating disorders in the course of their acculturation in the United States, this review includes information on eating disorders and their occurrence.

RUSSIAN EXPERIENCE

Many observers noted that in the Russian society women play a more important role than is often found in other nations. "Russian women have traditionally been the backbone of the nation." (Binyon, 1983, p. 34). They found that mothers in Russian culture have a traditionally strong role and a life-long influence on their children (Hubbs, 1988; Engel, 1986, Remennick, 1999). They described a typical family unit there as consisting of a married or unmarried daughter, her children, and her mother—married or widowed by the World War II. In the family where a grandmother takes care of small children and does all the housekeeping, men's role becomes less significant. If "that great destroyer, male alcoholism, hanging over virtually every couple" is added to the picture, Russian women's negative attitude toward men becomes easy to understand (Binyon, 1983, p. 45, Cockerham, 2000). Other authors also noted the secondary role of men in the Soviet Russian society. Du Plessix Gray (1990) quoted one of her respondents, "Here is the way our order of priorities goes: one—career, two—a child. As for a man, that's irrelevant. He can go on his way as soon as the child is conceived" (p. 51). Rotkirch and Haavio-Mannila (1996) reported similar conclusions:

> In the private sphere, the man is often a quite invisible figure. Men more easily join and leave the family. Whereas the mother is a stable person who keeps things going and stays with the children. As the father is perceived as an absent person, he is not expected to learn how to care for the home or to take responsibility for it.

Most observers noted that strongly matrilineal structure was typical for most of the Soviet families. Du Plessix Gray (1990) found that many Soviet women blame WWII for their "matriarchal" orientation and are concerned with its self-perpetuating quality. A mother of an adolescent daughter said, "Thirty, forty years after the war we seem to continue this all-woman tradition through sheer force of habit... I fear that my daughter will follow my example, take me as a model, our matriarchal ways have become chronic, infectious..." (p. 61). Several women du Plessix Gray met in Moscow had divorced because their mothers did not get on with their husbands; they never doubted their choice, "Mother always comes first"(p. 153). Du Plessix Gray (1990) compared mainstream American and Soviet families, "In Russia, very strong women hold many families together... Whereas in our white households, husbands and fathers often have far stronger roles." (p. 84). The author concluded that filial and maternal attachments in the former Soviet Union are far more "precious" than romantic ones and that in Russia, as compared to the U. S., men are given lower priority in family life.

Pilkington (1996) had similar findings in her study conducted in a town of Piatigorsk, "Most [students] agreed that they had spent far less time with their fathers than their mothers because their fathers had been so involved in their work. In all but four cases their mothers had also worked" (p. 148). When Mamonova (1994) asked her respondents about their childhood, they invariably described their mothers and grandmothers. Strong, emotionally loaded words, such as idolize, worship, treasure, and enormous significance were used in these descriptions.

Soviet women of various backgrounds and socioeconomic status stressed their close intergenerational bonds. "Above all, throughout my life I want to maintain close bonds with my daughter and my mother— my grandmother and my mother were very close and lived together, and that's how it should remain from generation to generation, mother-and-daughter bonds must remain intact." (du Plessix Gray, 1990, p. 153).

Several researchers pointed to the payoff side of the mothers' involvement in their adult daughter's households. "In a society which has the reputation for cradle-to-the-grave welfare but which has only a limited and not very attractive institutional system for the caring for the aged, families care for their own elderly at home (Smith, 1976, p. 139, Remennick, 1999, p. 349). Du Plessix Gray (1990) cited one of her respondents to illustrate similar findings, "I live alone with Mama, who is a wonderful eighty-nine years old. I get up at six and prepare breakfast for Mama. All her life she got breakfast for me and my children, so I do that for her" (p. 88).

Reviewing children's preschool literature, Rotkirch and Haavio-Mannila (1996) found that the family circle of a child consists mainly of women—mother, sister, grandmother. In one study, a boy observes: "Isn't it good to be able to read for yourself! You don't have to bother the mother (!), you don't have to disturb the grandmother (!)... to read for you." (Rosenhan, 1977, p. 394). The grandmother was present as an especially important socialization agent, "Grandmother taught Nina how to dress, how to wash—and even how to write letters." (Rosenhan, 1977, p. 398).

European-American and Western European researchers of family dynamics focus on nuclear family as a basic unit of the society. They stress the growing paternal involvement in the childrearing (Sanderson & Sanders Thompson, 2002, Bulanda, 2004) and point to the limited involvement of grandmothers in their grandchildren's upbringing. Van Ranst, Verschueren, & Marcoen (1995) found that 80 percent of Belgian grandmothers meet their grandchildren once a month. Observers of Soviet life found that a Russian maternal grandmother often lives with her adult children and assumes the major role in taking care of grandchildren. Hedrick Smith (1976) stressed the importance of the grandmother in the Russian household unit, "A *babushka* may add to the crowding and squabbling in the family apartment, but she is an indispensable aide to the working mother and a very few families willingly get along without her" (p. 139).

Western observers noted that in the Soviet Union many married children shared apartments with their parents because of housing shortages (Smith, 1976, Binyon, 1983). In such families, the grandmother usually did almost all food hunting and cooking. If a family had its own apartment, it was not unusual for a grandmother to visit with dinners in tow or to have grandchildren come for dinner on a regular basis. As a result, grandmother's attitudes and habits were influential in families and made an impact on their grandchildren's lives.

Brodsky (1982) pointed to the central role a grandmother continues to play in the Soviet immigrant families:

> With the elderly members usually remaining a viable part of the household unit after immigration, family work with Russian immigrants often includes the presence of one or two generations more than is used in working with [Anglo-] American families. Because of their typical role of caretaker for their grandchildren, problems involving children in a family are often unable to be resolved without the babushka's attendance in the session. (p. 18)

Cooking, serving, and feeding were traditional expressions of love in Russian culture. Greeting a visitor with bread and salt is an age-old custom practiced until today in official receptions. The communist revolution of 1917 introduced the population of the country to permanent food shortages. Since then, Soviet citizens have always had to struggle to obtain even basic staples, such as bread, sugar, meat, potatoes. Fresh fruit and vegetables were almost never available in government stores, so people had to pay exorbitant prices on farm markets or do without them for a larger part of the year. As a result, Soviet citizens' everyday diet consisted mainly of starches with a small percentage of meat and milk. In his highly embellished 1979 report, Leonid Brezhnev had to admit this fact:

> Almost half of the average Soviet intake is through grain products and potatoes. In North America almost 70 per cent

[of protein] comes from animal products, while in the Soviet Union the figure is just over one half of that. (p. 4)

In the nineties, these numbers became even more depressing. The authors of The National Statistical Compendium (1992) have admitted that "People started consuming 25% less milk products than in 1991, 15% less meat, 17% less fish, 30% less fruit. The food consumption structure is dangerously moving toward an increasingly carbohydrate-based model." Koval (1995) reported a similar trend. "Two-thirds of energy intake among the Russian population is from the consumption of bread and bakery products, potatoes and sugar." (p. 6). Long food lines have been an everyday reality of the Soviet and post-Soviet life, and too many people spend too much time in them. In his chapter, *The Art of Queing*, Hedrick Smith (1976) noted that due to the shortage of consumer goods, a Soviet woman spent an average of two hours daily waiting in lines to do her food shopping. Another way of obtaining food was through connections, so many friendships had a "useful" bartering side.

In the Soviet Union, quality restaurants (nightclub type) with lots of vodka and loud music were not family-friendly. After the collapse of the Soviet Union, new privately owned restaurants started opening in Moscow and larger cities. These restaurants serve elegant French or Caucasian delicacies at such high prices that only wealthy "new Russians" (nouveau rich) can patronize them (Kuh, 1997). Cafeterias at factories, schools, and other public establishments served notoriously bad food. In this situation, home cooking and baking was crucial for health and survival and, therefore, was highly valued. (Koval, 1995).

Many observers noted that Soviet women feel proud about being a good hostess and consider it one of the most important feminine virtues. Du Plessix Gray (1990) cited Sofiko Chiaureli, one of the Soviet Union's most beloved film stars, who compared American and Soviet women's attitudes, "We always spread the table at home for a guest, it's unthinkable to take a visitor to a restaurant. American women seem to *live* in them" (p. 36). Other authors described the same traditional norm, "Despite soaring prices, Russian women have kept up traditions of hospitality, which include treating guests to a lavish array of dishes." (Koval, 1995, p. 48).

Festive eating in the Soviet society has been highly valued for its social meaning and psychological comfort. Western authors were impressed by the abundance and variety of home-cooked delicacies adorning the tables even during the times of frequent food shortages. Binyon (1983) stressed the joys and hardships of organizing a typical Russian-style feast:

There is nothing a Russian likes better than getting together with friends and relatives for a good meal... The Russians organize lavish parties... The table groans with whatever food the enterprising host or hostess can procure. It takes a lot of ingenuity to find all the ingredients for such a feast. But for a special gathering Russians spare no expense or effort to get enough to make their table a proud sight. ... A Russian festive dinner, as a rule, starts with a rich variety of appetizers. Pickles, salads, cold cuts, and other rather fatty culinary creations are a necessary accompaniment to the copious amounts of vodka consumed by each guest. Hot meat, fish, and poultry dishes follow in several servings. Tea with rich home-baked cakes and fruit preserves was served well into the wee hours of the morning (p. 70)

The observers found several reasons for this cultural norm: home life has always been the only island of warmth and happiness in the ocean of Soviet misery and bleakness (Smith, 1976). A big, groaning table has become a proud display of the hostess' domestic talents, so important for the household's general prosperity. Having a circle of friends had a crucial survival value—the warmth of each other's company gives people reassurance of future support in times of need. A lavish table has been a rare treat in the culture of constant shortages, a compensation for scanty, monotonous daily meals. Dinner parties were an important source of entertainment in a society that provided almost no other pleasurable leisure activities. (Binyon, 1983, Mamonova, 1984).

A traditional populist beauty ideal in Russia, as noted by many authors (Binyon, 1983, du Plessix Gray, 1990, Rotkirch & Haavio-Mannila, 1996), was a full-bodied, strong woman with rosy cheeks and a round face. "Throughout Russian history the mother has been the focus of the Russian family, and her image is that of a large, warm, strong woman, almost enveloping her family in her ample bosom." (Binyon, 1983, p. 34). Since the communist revolution, women's participation in the work force was a social and financial necessity. As Binyon (1983) reported, "Women make up 51 per cent of the labor force, and 92 per cent of all working-age women either work or study." Health and strength necessary for the fulfillment of a double role of a mother and a productive worker have been promoted by the Communist government and glorified in mass media since the early days of the Soviet regime. Social Realism, the one and only artistic style allowed by the Communist government depicted robust peasant and worker women in sculptures, paintings, and movies. Most of the Kremlin wives, as well as popular singers and actresses were of various degrees of plumpness bordering on serious overweight (Vasilieva, 1992/1994). With the lifting of the Iron Curtain and the slow introduction of Western goods and media, thinness as a beauty component started making its way into the culture of Russian capitals—Moscow and St. Petersburg. Nevertheless, Russia has not yet fully subscribed to the Western-style thinness as the beauty ideal. A significantly overweight "new Russian" mother and her plump teenage daughter look comfortable and contented on a photograph in the feature magazine story (Kuh, 1997).

Since the Communist revolution, Russian women were "liberated" to do hard work on factories and railroads. They never had an American-style feminist movement and aspired to be as feminine as they could. For them, fashionable hairstyles, clothing, and makeup were an aesthetic and emotional outlet in the bleak and dreary reality. Many observers found that Soviet women pay great attention to outward appearance and spend significant amounts of their income and energy trying to "look decently", following fashionable Western magazines, focusing on hair, manicure, and clothes. (Smith, 1976). French influence has always been the strongest, and Russian women's femininity is mostly of the French type—their enjoyment of sex, cooking, and dressing up does not diminish with weight increase.

WESTERN BEAUTY IDEAL AND DISORDERED EATING

Adolescence is an exciting time for girls as their bodies start changing and acquiring specific feminine proportions. Instead of rejoicing their developing womanhood, American adolescents view these changes with alarm and become preoccupied with their bodies. Studies of mainstream American culture suggest that a substantial proportion of adolescents are concerned about being overweight (Walker et al., 1982). American young women live in a society where the thin ideal is a driving force in most aspects of social life. They are constantly bombarded with messages equating extreme thinness with beauty and success. Thus, given media messages and society values, many adolescent girls start developing a negative attitude toward their bodies if these bodies do not fit the culturally prescribed thin ideal (Killbourne, 1994, Rothblum, 1994, Wooley, 1994). Sobal and Stunkard (1989) reviewed several studies (Sobal, 1985, 1987; Sobal, Klein, Graham, & Black, 1988) and presented the following picture of health concerns in American adolescents:

> Over half of adolescents are concerned about being overweight; adolescents are more concerned about being overweight than about many other health issues, such as drinking and birth control; and girls are consistently more concerned about overweight than are boys. (p. 267).

Negative feelings towards their bodies (body dissatisfaction) place female adolescents at high-risk for the development of disordered eating (anorexia nervosa—AN, and bulimia nervosa—BN) which in turn spawns unhealthy weight control practices, such as taking diet pills, vomiting, using laxatives and diuretics. According to American Psychiatric Association, Diagnostic and statistical manual of mental disorders (4th edition), "Anorexia Nervosa is characterized by a refusal to maintain a minimally normal body weight" (p. 539). And further, "Bulimia Nervosa is characterized by repeated episodes of binge eating followed by inappropriate compensatory behaviors such as self-induced vomiting; misuse of laxatives, diuretics, and other medications; fasting; or excessive exercise" (DSM-IV, 1994, p. 539). In the United States, 0.5 to 1.0% of females in early adolescence and late childhood meet full criteria for Anorexia Nervosa (DSM-IV, 1994, p. 543). The prevalence of Bulimia Nervosa among adolescent and young adult females is approximately 1%-3%. (DSM-IV, 1994, p. 548). Roughly similar rates of occurrence for both disorders have been reported in industrialized countries, including Canada, Europe, Australia, Japan, New Zealand, and South Africa. "Few studies have systematically examined their prevalence in other cultures, but all the available information suggests that eating disorders appear to be "far more prevalent in industrialized societies, in which there is an abundance of food and in which, especially for females, being considered attractive is linked to being thin" (DSM-IV, 1994, p. 542).

Since the prevalence of eating disorders varies among different cultural groups, these disorders, unlike most other psychological disorders, must be greatly influenced by sociocultural factors. The importance of these factors can be tested by studying populations which differ in customs regarding food, standards for physical beauty, family values, social roles for women, economic status, etc., as well as what happens when women move from one culture to another.

Until recently, nearly all research on body image and disordered eating focused on young Anglo-American women. Sociocultural factors have been noted to play a significant role in the development of disturbed self-perception which in teenagers is associated with a wide variety of dieting behaviors and disordered eating (Garfinkel & Garner, 1982; Johnson & Connors, 1987). Some theorists and social critics have suggested that disordered eating is largely a sociocultural phenomenon (Bordo, 1993; Gordon, 1990). Levine, Smolak, & Hayden (1994) propose that body dissatisfaction and weight concerns reflect the adoption by women of a socially approved female role. They proposed that "some young [White American] adolescent girls live in a subculture of intense weight and body-shape concern that places them at risk for disordered eating behavior." They list four basic components to the sociocultural argument:

1. Since the 1950s, the ideal woman, as portrayed in fashion magazines for example, has gotten thinner, despite the fact that real American women have gotten heavier (Garner, Rockert, Olmsted, Johnson, & Coscina, 1985, Silverstein, Perdue, Peterson, & Kelly, 1986).

2. The thin shape has become a symbol, not only of beauty but also of professional success (Silverstein & Perdue, 1988).

3. Women and especially adolescent girls have been led to believe that the thin "look" is obtainable through dieting, exercising, and other weight management techniques. The normative nature of weight and shape dissatisfaction, as well as dieting, among [Caucasian] American girls and women reflects the internalization of these messages (Polivy & Herman, 1987).

4. Direct exposure to subcultures emphasizing the importance of body shape, slenderness, and perfectionist achievement greatly increases the risk of unhealthy weight management behavior and of eating disorders (Hamilton, Brooks-Gunn, & Warren, 1985, pp. 471-472).

Smolak and Levine (1994) suggested that in addition to the media, other influential sources of the sociocultural message that thinness is very important for girls and women are parental and peer pressure. Approximately 50% of the 9th-grade American girls surveyed by Desmond, Price, Gray, & O'Connell (1986) said they received information about weight control from their friends. Some researchers (Levine and Smolak, 1992; Levine et al., 1994) found that 41.5% of the middle school girls they surveyed reported talking with their friends about weight, shape, and dieting at least sometimes.

Studies of body attitude across different cultural groups report patterns, somewhat different from those in the mainstream American culture. Anglo-American girls report more concern about weight and eating than African-American or Asian-American girls (Wardle & Marsland, 1990). African-American girls hold more favorable body-image attitudes than Whites on both global and weight-related body-image affects, cognitions, and behaviors (Rucker & Cash, 1992), African-American women report more satisfaction with and positive feelings toward their bodies than Euro-American women (Harris, 1995). Yet we are now seeing the increase of eating disorders in this population, as well. Pumariega (1986) views acculturation as an important factor in the development of eating disorders among American minorities.

In a number of studies, SES (socioeconomic status) is also associated with the overall weight concern. Sobal and Stunkard (1989), in their review of 144 published studies of the relationship between SES and obesity, found that the higher the SES and the more developed the society, the more likely rounded forms and higher body weight are stigmatized. Striegel-Moore and Smolak (1996) demonstrated that distribution of eating disorders varies across American cultures or subcultures and directly correlates with the SES.

Body image as a research area is mostly absent for Soviet psychologists (Mandel, 1970) and there are no studies of body image of Russian or former Soviet immigrant women in the USA.

Several studies of immigrants to the United States point to the negative impact that Western culture could have on ethnic minorities as they acculturate to American society (Nasser, 1988; Osvold & Sodowsky, 1993). The rate of eating disorder symptoms was reported to be extremely low among women in Greece and in the Middle East compared with immigrant women from the same countries who were living in Western Europe (Nasser, 1988). In a comparative study of body image of Latinas and non-Latina White women, Lopez, Blix, & Blix (1995) found length of residence to be a significant variable associated with the development of ideal body image for adolescent Latinas. The age of immigration to the United States was an important factor in shaping the ideal body image. Bulik (1987) described two young Eastern European immigrants who developed bulimia and anorexia nervosa within two years after their arrival in the United States. "They began to evaluate their self-worth on the basis of their body and the ability to control their appetites" (p. 138). Other researchers found Western cultural influence to be a significant factor in the development of body dissatisfaction among people moving from one culture to another and among the populations of westernizing countries. In one study in Zimbabwe (Hooper & Garner, 1986), 399 Black, White, and mixed-race schoolgirls were compared on the EDI (Eating Disorder Inventory). The White group showed the highest "drive for thinness, body dissatisfaction, and sense of ineffectiveness," and indulged in more episodic dieting than the other groups. On most of the scales, the Black group scored lowest, with the mixed race group falling in the middle. The authors indicated how acculturation into Western society affects changes in values, "the African adolescent seeks after Western ideals including its ideals for feminine beauty."

Another study compared two similar groups of Arab undergraduate female students from upper- and middle-class backgrounds, one group attending a university in Cairo, the other attending a university in London (Nasser, 1986). London Arab students, who were similar to European students in dress and level of Westernization, demonstrated significantly higher level of unhealthy attitudes toward their bodies and eating than more traditional Cairo students.

A longitudinal study, conducted by the Harvard Eating Disorders Center of Harvard Medical School, found that three years after the introduction of television programs from the United States, Britain, and Australia, Fijian adolescent girls showed a significant increase in disordered eating behaviors (Goode, 1999). 15 percent of surveyed 63 Fijian secondary school girls reported that they induced vomiting to control their weight as compared to 3 percent in the 1995 survey conducted one month after television signals became available to the consumers of the region. 29 percent of the surveyed girls scored highly on a test of eating disorder risk as compared to 13 percent three years before. Popular TV personalities, like Heather Locklear, were found to make a significant influence on Fijian adolescents' body image.

CHAPTER 3

Family Portraits

Participating Families

Grandmother's Name	Mother's Name	Granddaughter's Name
(Age) (Time in USA)	(Age) (Time in USA)	(Age)
Greta Golder (70) (5)	Maya (40) (7)	Daniela (16)
Gita Kaplan (72) (5)	Marlena (40) (7)	Dina (16)
Golda Weiss (72) (10)	Minna (34) (10)	Dora (15)
Genya Arber (70) (6)	Margarita (39) (6)	Dosia (14)
Galina Levin (60) (7)	Marina (39) (9)	Dana (14)

All names and other identifying information have been changed.

THE ARBERS

The Arber family consists of Margarita, age 39, and her daughter Dosia, age 14. Margarita's mother, Genya, age 71, and father, Greg, live two blocks away from her, in Brooklyn, N.Y. All four of them came to the U.S. 6 years ago from a medium size city in Crimea, a fertile peninsula in the Black Sea, famous for its mild climate and beautiful coastal resorts. Formally a part of Ukraine, Crimea was populated by Tartars, Jews, Greeks, and many other national groups. During World War II, a part of the Tartar population collaborated with the Nazis. After the Soviet regime was reestablished in Crimea, all

23

Tartars were interned into Siberia as punishment for being "traitors." They were allowed to return to Crimea during the late 1970s/1980s.

Genya

When I came to interview Genya in her apartment, she looked pale and gaunt. Her short straight gray hair and stern face without a trace of makeup reminded me of cold and impersonal Soviet bureaucrats I had to endure in my life in the former Soviet Union. My first impression was misleading—Genya's face, as I learned later, reflected her futile attempts to hide intense physical and emotional suffering . She apologized for not introducing me to her husband who was in bed in the other room and led me to her small bedroom, sparsely furnished with a narrow bed with a frayed bedspread, a rickety Formica dresser, and a kitchen chair made of metal tubes. She invited me to sit on the chair and sat on the bed, leaning against the headboard. Genya's voice, gait, and posture suggested fatigue and strain caused by the plethora of ailments she reported in the course of the interview. My questions seemed to be far from her area of interest, so they became a backdrop against which she could delve into her memories, argue with herself, and unburden her long-suffering soul. When she turned the conversation to her favorite subjects—music or teaching, her gray eyes acquired a vivid gleam and she spoke with inspiration and pleasure. At times, she interrupted herself and apologized for "talking a lot of nonsense for too long a time." Genya's worn cotton dress was plain and loose on her body; she wore no jewelry, nor any other adornments. Cracked walls with peeling paint and mismatched furnishings suggested tight finances. The only decoration in Genya's room was a large, nicely framed portrait of her daughter Margarita in full blossom of her sultry beauty. Talking about Margarita, Genya got up with visible effort, slowly limped to the dresser, dragging her feet in tattered corduroy slippers, and picked up the portrait. She demonstrated it to me, saying, "Look how beautiful she was before she went to college" and sighed, almost moaned, deep in her own thought. During the rest of the interview, she kept the portrait on her lap, clutching it in her wrinkled hands with short nails and bulging veins.

Genya's Story

Music saved my life more than once, and it keeps me alive even now. My first memories are about my parents, and they are connected with music. Every day, after I finished practicing, my father locked the piano. I was not allowed to play by ear, only by the notes, so that I wouldn't spoil my playing. According to the new theory, it is OK, but he did what was considered right then. He wanted me to have good education, academic and musical. In school, I was an "A" student, with a very serious attitude, probably because my father was very strict. I liked fun, I was more easygoing than my granddaughter; she is even overly dedicated to her studies. She devotes her whole life to learning, and I did get distracted once in a while, but he would force me, he did everything to make me a good student.

We lived in bad conditions—one room in a communal apartment in an old neighborhood; we had to go to the backyard to use the water pump and the outhouse. It was my fate to live in horrible old houses all my life. We shared a corridor with several neighbors, so my mother cooked on a kerosene burner there or on a tiled stove in the room. She was a great cook. She used to make such wonderful meat pies, Crimea style, the way her people made them.

My mother got married very late because she was not good-looking, and I always felt uncomfortable because of my long crooked nose. Her body was also like mine, not fat, not thin. I have been in the same shape for many years; I never gained or lost much weight. I consider that I am in good shape, normal. If my parents lived longer, my life would have been different.

My parents lost their lives too young during the WWII, before they turned 42. My father was drafted in the first days of war, and I remember how we went to see him off. The clouds are low, the railway station is full of people, everybody is crying. And my mother started crying and kept crying all the time as long as I remember her. She died of malaria and malnutrition when I was 12 and my sister was 4 years old. We were separated then, my sister was placed in an orphanage, and I got into a hospital with malaria. I was emaciated, with frostbitten feet. I had high fever, like my mother, I almost died there. After three months in the hospital, I was like a shadow; so weak I could not climb two steps. They discharged me into the orphanage where I almost died of malnutrition. The nurses were very anti-Semitic; they called me "a little kike." They often took my dinner away for a tiny misbehavior or just for nothing; they enjoyed torturing me. It was music that saved my life at that time and times again.

One day, I was washing the floors in the unheated entrance hall. Frozen dirt was hard, and I crouched to scrub it off so that these nurses would not yell at me. The hall was poorly lit, so I had to move slowly, carefully, and then I hit something with my back—it was the piano! Even though I am an atheist, I believe it was G-d's help. Memories of my mother, my family, and me playing classical music filled me, so I lifted the cover, wiped my hands off my clothes, and started playing with my half-frozen fingers. Adults and children started coming into the room looking at me with surprise, listening, but I was oblivious of all that, I was like in a trance. I was playing and feeling my fingers and my soul thaw. Somebody brought me a chair, everybody looked happy. The piano was silent for a long time in the orphanage, and I was playing Bach, Clementi, the entire program I learned in the musical school. Before the war, I completed my third year there.

After that event, they started treating me a little better, punished me less and gave me better clothes, some even from the American aid supplies. For being a straight-A student, I was getting a "Stalin stipend"—a hundred rubles a month. That was great—I could go to the market and spend it all on a loaf of bread, so my sister and I could have our fill of bread that day. I still remember these thick warm slices smelling of human body—the workers at the factory would sneak them under their clothes to pass the factory checkpoint.

I found my sister by sheer luck. When we got a new principal, I felt she liked me, so I begged her to help me find my sister. She agreed to look her name up in the city office that was in charge of orphanages. One day, she took me home, her mother gave me something to eat, and the principal went to wash her hair in the backyard. I will never forget how she unwound her towel, and the scorpion jumped out of it—she could have died on the spot. Then we went to my sister's orphanage, and she did not recognize me. I still remember her biting into a tomato I brought for her, and she recalls this scene, too, how the juice was spurting from her little teeth.

In the orphanage, we were always hungry, never having enough to eat. We were growing up, we needed nutrition, and the portions were so miserably small. We could not get any second helpings, so we used tricks not to starve, all kinds of tricks. There was a cook's aide there, she liked it when I was on kitchen duty—I used to scrub the tables real clean, and the pots, too, so she would let me come more often. She allowed me to collect the leftovers from the pots into two bowls and to give one to my sister. My sister ate under the bed; this is how she and I got some meat onto our bones. I was growing up, going through the body change, but there was nobody to explain things to me, so I was just looking at myself and wondering what was going on. By that time, I looked better, not so horribly thin.

When we returned to our town after the war, our apartment was taken away from us by some strangers. Our relatives were afraid to sue them, so they took us to live with them. This is how my sister and I were separated again. We had no place of our own. When I got married, I moved in with my mother-in-law. Where else could I go? My mother-in-law worked in a student canteen filling plates with food for a self-service line. This work was the only thing she could do to survive with three children. She could eat there and take home the leftovers for them. She used to sneak a little extra food onto my sister's plate, she knew her before I met her son, she felt sorry for us orphans. It was a small town, and people knew each other there.

My marriage was no good from the beginning; it was a one-way street. I loved him, and he... He had his own life, did what he wanted, never cared for us. He was violent, too. I remember when baby Margarita was sick, I made a mustard wrapping for her. He did not believe in it and got mad that I am torturing the child. If not for his mother, I would have had a concussion, but she stood between us and stopped him. She was always protective of me because she was an orphan herself, her parents died during the civil war in 1921. I could not take his abuse anymore, so I took little Margarita and left him. Then his mother came, "are you going to leave your child fatherless?" I listened to her and came back. She herself ran away from her husband, raised three children alone, but she used this pressure on me. This is how we, women, are: we forget about ourselves, we are afraid for our children, so we keep suffering for their sake. The financial situation is important, too. We never had a decent apartment or a decent salary to feed the children, so we stuck to our men even though they were so bad to us.

When we finally received our own space, the walls there were so wet that I did not know where to put the child's bed. He packed up and left us; went to live with his mother. Margarita and I stayed in that room in a hotel-style apartment for six families. We lived there, on 130 square feet, for seven years. There was no bathtub, only one shower, and a common kitchen with two stoves. I worked in a school, it was a madhouse there, then I would come home, and it was a madhouse number two. I was on a waiting list for a better apartment, but when my turn came, my husband's mother refused to remove his name from her apartment lease, so I obtained the living space only for my daughter and me. They gave me a room for a single mother, and then we exchanged it. We moved closer to his mother, this is how we ended up with two old apartments, close to each other.

We lived in these apartments until we left for America. There was no heating or plumbing in these apartments, so we had to take care of everything—obtaining fuel, chopping firewood and heating the stove. Every fall, we had to wait on line for two days and two nights to obtain some fuel. We lost all our health there, used it up just to survive. I damaged my spine carrying pails of coal, and my knee is bad. Here, of course, it is so different, more humane, all the amenities. Today the day was cold, so we had heating on in September, we did not ask for it, but they turned it on for half an hour in the morning—very good.

When we were leaving, we knew that we would live in better conditions, so we did not risk much. Many people left good apartments, even better than what they have here, but even these apartments were badly heated. My sister lived on the fifth floor; she used to freeze there. Things were getting worse after the fall of the Soviet Union. Margarita's position was cut and she could not find another one, so she was unemployed with a small child. Obtaining food has always been a horror there. We came here with huge amounts of cholesterol in our blood because of it. I was happy when I could buy a pig's head. I used to make head cheese, meat ravioli, I did tricks to feed the family, cut out better pieces for this or that, economized. I was trying to feed everybody, the whole family—my husband, Margarita, and Dosia. It was difficult financially, very difficult. Foodstuffs became even more scarce and hard to obtain after Ukraine separated from Russia.

Margarita wanted to leave, especially after her divorce, and I was afraid to let her go alone. I said, "I will not let you go with the child. We all should go together." My husband did not want to go even though his sister was willing to send us the papers. Of course, it was very stressful and hard, because whatever little we used to have, we were used to it, and we were advanced in age already, and we had to change it all. I did not feel bad leaving either of those apartments, especially we left one for my niece, and Margarita's friend managed somehow to move in the other one and even to pay us a little, this money helped us to leave.

Margarita has a job here, she has her own place, and she managed to furnish it according to her taste. She lives very close; we wanted it this way so that we can help her. We came here following Margarita and her daughter, for their sake, as it usually is among us. Dosia lived with us for a while, so that Margarita was able to work and to study. She does not depend on us as she did there. Naturally she did not feel this dependency because it was all done from the heart. We have to help our children, we love them; how else can it be? If not for our children, what are we living for in this world? Now I have to help my sister, too, she cannot survive without me. She is paralyzed now after her third stroke. I barely managed to pull her out of there. She lives with her children, daughter and son, he is 28, and she is 38. They left their spouses there, so their lives are not in order. Margarita is not married, either. Maybe such is her fate. She is 39 now, and my heart aches for her.

Maybe it is my parents' upbringing, but I feel that a person should do things for other people's good. This was my motto from my childhood, maybe I am romantically inclined, and this is why I am feeling this way, but I feel this need. If I haven't done anything useful for others, then why do I exist? I don't want to say that I am not selfish, I am selfish, too, I do love myself; I love doing things for myself. I am trying not to forget to take my medicine, to leave some time for myself to make my life interesting, to have contact with people. So I can't say that I am so particularly good. I am not an exception, all the mothers I know do for their children as much as I do.

When Margarita was growing up, I worked very far from home, so every day I was sitting on the bus and worrying if my child is hungry, I had no time to think of myself. Now I am filled with the sense of resentment, deep hurt, not personal, just pain about my whole miserable life. Maybe I said it the wrong way, but I don't know how to say it better—our life is pushing us into our own mess with our noses. I created so many of my own troubles, and I am paying too big a price for my mistakes. Why did I get married? I was better off without him. After he moved back to his mother, he lived there for 18 years, but he used to visit us from time to time, so I was half married. When Margarita got married, she and her husband lived with me until I moved back to my husband. I wanted to let them have the apartment to themselves. I returned to him for her sake, I had no other choice; no place to go.

My husband never wanted to do anything for the family. I had to claw things out of him, not for myself, for Margarita. I had no money to clothe her. I had some private music students, but it brought very little money—I did not have much time or energy for it. Maybe I wanted to love myself, but I didn't know how to. He is the person who loves himself, that's him. When I suffered heartache, he had no compassion for me, now he is ill, too, so I try to help him. He never asked me how I feel, and now when he is suffering, I try to take care of him. We live in the same apartment, but in separate rooms. We have our responsibilities, like he can fix things, so if I really need something, I ask him, but I try not to ask him anything. I cook and serve, he likes tasty food, but otherwise we live separate lives.

There is no love or kindness in my marriage. He is in charge of everything, so I am not free to do what I want and I have to accommodate him. We have one food stamp card, so he tells me what to buy, and I have no say in it. For example, I like homemade cottage cheese, so I wanted to make it here, too. He does not care; he likes the ready made kind, from the Russian store. I made a calculation and proved to him that homemade cottage cheese is not more expensive; it took me a lot of convincing until he finally let me do it my way. Margarita knows that he is a cheapskate, so she tries to help me in some ways. She bought me a TV set. He had a TV set in his room, and I did not. He watches sports and Russian TV, and I have my own interests. When he saw the new TV set, he was livid, furious. He yelled, "I allowed you to buy an air conditioner, and now you want the TV, too!" I don't even have a table in my room; I have to write letters on my lap because his table is always covered by stuff. It takes him a month to write a letter, and when I sit at his table, he would yell at me, "Don't touch my letter!" He takes a good care of himself, when we came, he immediately bought himself blue jeans, new shoes, but he was quarreling with me when I was sending medicine to my sister. He put it bluntly, "I don't need your relatives; I don't want them to come." He put his heavy paw on my whole life. He wants me to waste my entire life in the kitchen and serve him three times a day. This is the lordly manner of our Russian men, and I had my measure of it. The housekeeping was exhausting. I left all my strength there, came here sick and worn out. It is so good to live here, but I have no strength anymore. Of course, nobody wants to die, so I started paying a little more attention to my health, I want to see Dosia grow up, become a lawyer, have a good life.

My daughter took a lot after her father; I suffer because she lacks warmth. There is no heartfelt closeness between us. At times, she does not want to listen to me, she does not understand me at times; she should be kinder to me. Sometimes I feel hurt by the tone of her voice or by her choice of the conversation topic or she would not listen to me. I cannot open my heart to her, cannot confide in her. Probably a mother should not confide in her daughter, it is not right. Dosia listens to me more, I can give her advice, but her mother is closer to her. I am closer to my sister, but she is a very sick person, so I cannot burden her with my pain.

I always feel guilty that I was not like my mother-in-law who saved the father for Margarita. I triggered their divorce, and I blame myself for it all the time. I was unhappy with her marriage, and I did not hide my dislike for her husband. I don't know if they were together if I did, but I feel so guilty. We are guilty of not being good parents, always guilty. Dosia is fatherless because of me, I don't want to talk about Margarita's husband, but I should have done it differently. Only now I started understanding things, I lived without thinking before, and it hurts so much now, but it is too late to change anything. If Margarita had a loving father, everything would have been different, but I have created my fate with my own hands, and this is my punishment. I am very lonely in spite of having a family.

I can survive on my own. I am a strong person—I have my music, my books, they keep me alive. I have a complete set of Feuhtwanger's novels, so I am re-reading them. This is my sustenance—I love classical music, I always listen to the classical station on the radio and watch the art channel on TV to get away from my thoughts and to get a shot of positive energy. When I have the strength, I go to the day care center, I play the piano there; accompany the singers. Probably this is my love for myself, and I want my granddaughter also to have some inner emotional, spiritual plank that will help her in times of hardship. She has musical talent, appreciation of classical music, so I feel very sorry that she is not getting formal training in music. She sings in the school choir, brings the notes to me, participates in concerts. This is our point of contact, and I am happy for it.

When we came to America, we started living together in this apartment—my husband and I in the living room, and Margarita with her daughter in the bedroom. We rented this apartment together. We took care of Dosia, I used to give her all my time, who else would I take care of? I did not attend English classes; I did not have the time. "Mama, you are a teacher, so help Dosia with homework." How can I do it if I don't know a single English word? I used the international transcription system I learned in college. This allowed me to help her in spelling and in understanding her books, and we used to study, study, study together. She moved ahead, and I got stuck somewhere. We used to solve mathematical problems, too. First, we would sweat a hundred times until we understood the verbal problem, and then it was easy to solve it. Poor Dosia was silent for almost a year; she did not speak English at all. Her teacher would despair, but then she started making progress toward the end of the year. Then she became one of her best students. I think part of it is my contribution. I think I gave Dosia a right start and direction in life

When Margarita decided to move out, she found a place next to us, so until my leg started hurting badly, I used to go there every day. Dosia used to go to this school across the street. I would meet her after school, walk her home and feed her dinner. Now, little by little, we are teaching her to be independent. She is 14, and she says, "Grandma, I'll do it myself, don't come, your leg hurts." She understands. I tell her, "But I want to see you." And she says, "Don't worry, I'll come to see you, I miss you, too." I bought a cake, the kind I like and she likes, so I tell her, "Dosia, come soon, because I will eat this cake all by myself, and I am not allowed to eat this much." So she says, "Just leave me a little piece." It is our game. She came yesterday, I treated her to the cake, but said, "You are going to eat dinner at home." "Yes, yes, grandma, don't you worry." She came to us right from school. She is in high school now.

I watch Dosia grow up. When I wake up, my first thought is about her, about her and Margarita. I think about them, naturally, all the time. I keep asking them about everything in their life. One day Margarita says to me, "Can you imagine, mama, she was so afraid to be late that she left before me, even though she has to be there later than I." This is how she is—responsible, serious girl, I am very glad that she is this way. Margarita was a very good student, but Dosia is especially good, she is disciplining herself. I consider it my responsibility to keep her in good health, too. I called Margarita today and said, "Margarita, Dosia told me how crowded her school is and that the elevators are filled to the brim. My love, please, buy a lemon, cut it into pieces, let it stand on the table. It will build up her immune system against any kind of infection, let vitamin C work." I mean I keep taking care of them on all fronts—how else can it be? I keep thinking about them most of the time. I am not always able to come see them, but there is a telephone. If I don't call one day, I do not feel right. I communicate with Dosia—she comes from school and calls her mother at work and then she calls us; sometimes she does not call us, then I call her. We talk once a day.

Margarita comes home from work and cooks. I do not cook in her place, because we are housekeepers of different styles. I may do something the way she dislikes, and I don't like being reprimanded by my daughter. So I said to her, "I will not cook in your place, I will rather cook at home and bring it to you." Dosia also likes all these American things on plastic plates. We go to the day care center, and I can't eat all they serve. I don't even open the containers, just look around and see what others have. "Uh-huh, pea soup; Dosia will eat it with pleasure." I put it in a plastic bag and give it to her. I used to go there often when I could. I buy food for them in a Russian store, too. Feeding the family is no problem here, but I necessarily have to know what is going on. I ask Dosia, "What did mom cook today?" If Margarita has stuffed peppers for 3 days, I know that Dosia would eat them on the first day, the second day—maybe, and on the third day she would not touch them. So I know that I have to make something myself. Then Margarita comes home from work and asks me, "Mama, why isn't she eating peppers?" I say, "She won't eat them on the third day. You cook, I bring things for her, so she will eat what she wants." We make a variety of things.

Back in the Soviet Union, my responsibility was to make sure everybody had breakfast, dinner, and supper. We had no snacks to spoil one's appetite. We liked to eat heartily, especially men. A man wants some first course, like borscht, then cutlets or fish with garnish, like hot cereal, for sure. By the way, I invited my American neighbors once and served some Ukrainian borscht, they ate with pleasure. I had to cook for the family. At times, I did not have enough time or energy, so the dinner was incomplete, like borscht with boiled meat, and this was filling enough.

I remember one day we had a delivery of coal, and it had to be carried into the shed. I called my husband at work. He said, "Two guys will come, but you got to feed them." I fried fresh flounder and made a large bowl of potato salad vinaigrette; this was my payment. I gave them an opportunity to sit down and eat in the house, not in some dirty canteen with flies and sticky oilcloth on large tables. They were young guys, without families. They had nobody to cook for them, so they valued real food, not that stinky cabbage soup and those terrible hamburgers made out of bread. They loved to come to our place.

We used to cook a lot for birthdays, so that there was everything— meat and fish dishes, and appetizers, and dessert, and something to drink, and this and that... We used to cook it all ourselves one or two days in advance, we did not buy ready made stuff. It would be too expensive, and there was no place to go and buy. We drank very little; there were no alcoholics in our family, except for my sister's husband. He drank himself into nothing. When her family left for America, they left him there in an asylum for hopeless alcoholics.

It is so much better for us here, of course. I cannot even imagine what I would be doing there now. They don't pay pensions on time, so people starve there. My sister used to go hungry. Of course, we kept sending them food packages and a little money, so that they made it to here, but they were emaciated and looked horrible. When we came, we were not such beauties, either, but by now we filled up into shape a little.

When Dosia was 7, she got gravely ill, had acetone in her urine. She lost a lot of liquid, and Margarita did not know what to do. I ran to my cousin, a pediatrician. She said, "Don't even try to treat her yourselves, you may lose the child." We had to carry her to the hospital; she could not walk. To make a long story short, we saved her, but we were scared stiff. We decided against keeping the weakened child in kindergarten. I taught her at home, to count, to write, to read.

When we came here, Dosia was 8, so she was accepted into the third grade. Without attending school for a single day in Russia, she had to go to the third grade in America and learn everything in the foreign language. It is clear that Dosia stopped learning the Russian language. When she lived with us, we used to read with her. We took a lot of Russian books with us. Now Dosia reads Russian the way I read English, with mistakes, of course, but at least we can help her in mathematics. It is so strange for me; she started geometry only now, in the ninth grade. I am interested in her classes; I cannot let my granddaughter's education pass by me. I have to stick my nose, "Dosia, what are you learning now?" I worked in schools for seventeen years, so I remember the programs for every subject. When my students were graduating from the tenth grade, it was such an emotional goodbye for the whole group. They were like family to me and to each other, and we kept the ties after the graduation, ten years together is not a trifle.

Margarita looks very well now, she stopped smoking and gained some weight, and she looks better this way. She is healthier now, too. She was pale, very thin, so my heart used to ache for her. And Dosia is also too thin. But she is growing, so I take this factor into consideration, and she likes sports. I have never been athletic. Margarita did what was required in school, but she was not that good in sports, either. My husband used to lead tourist groups up the mountains, it was his second job. When Margarita turned 14, I said that we would go, too, "You will have to suffer having us around." He did not want us to go. We were an extra burden for him. Briefly speaking, he climbed with the group; Margarita and I were struggling at the bottom. That was the first and the last time we went.

Margarita was plump at that time. She was so beautiful in her youth. My heart used to ache for her, always for her health, that's the main thing. It never occurred to me to think about her in terms of her looks or her body shape. Nobody needs extra flesh. I remember Bystritskaya, my favorite actress. She was very plump; I think she had to gain weight on purpose to star in the "Quietly Flows the River Don." Even before that she was a corpulent woman, she did not have an ideal figure, but I liked her face. I like Gurchenko, too. I think she is a tough cookie; she doesn't have an ideal body, either, she is too thin, but she is youthful and dances well. Probably it is better to be thin than heavy; it is healthier.

I remember my grandmother well, my mother's mother. She was a good woman, smart, literate; she used to teach me Hebrew. She and Fira, her other daughter, lived in their old house in a tiny room. When the war started, my father's mother was evacuated with us, and my mother's mother returned to our city. She came to the railway station with us and said, "I have no strength, I will stay." Fira went back home with her. My father's brother was in the motorized division, so he left the city with the last trucks. He was passing their house, so he stopped for a moment and begged them to come with him, he told them that everybody who stayed would be killed. My grandma had no strength to get up, and Fira said, "I will not leave my mother." They were close, in life and death. All the Jews in our town were rounded by the Germans, shot on the 11th kilometer from our city and buried in the common grave.

Dosia and I are very close, too. She tells me everything, yes. Yesterday I asked her, "Tell me in detail what is your school like? What are your difficulties in?" She told me everything with pleasure. She used to carry tons of books, such thick volumes. And now they have lockers, so they take home only what they need for tomorrow. She told me all the details, she doesn't hide anything from me, I think so, and she doesn't have anything to hide yet. Maybe later she will. She always tells me, "Grandma, I love you. Don't worry, I love you." She is such a good girl.

Margarita

Margarita chose to be interviewed in the evening, after a full day's work. Her sultry Mediterranean beauty was toned down by fatigue. Bluish-black locks surrounded Margarita's elongated face with enormous almond eyes and long lashes; slightly sallow skin was tight on high cheekbones. Narrow shoulders, small hands and feet, and small stature gave Margarita a frail, vulnerable look.

Margarita lives in a small one-bedroom apartment in an older walk-up tenement. The outside and common areas of the building are in various states of disrepair. Margarita's apartment is a pleasant contrast to its surrounding. During the interview, she told me about her enjoyment of "playing house," fixing and decorating as much as she could afford. Margarita showed me her elongated living room, crowded by dark oversized furniture and led me to the narrow cluttered kitchen. She pushed aside several cereal boxes, wiped the vinyl tablecloth, and invited me to sit down at the kitchen table. She interrupted the interview several times to attend to the simmering pots and to talk to her daughter.

Margarita's Story

I am a child of the 60s. We do not remember the times of starvation, but nobody enjoyed a wild abundance, either. I grew up in absolutely disgusting living conditions. Our apartment was, in reality, a shack with wet walls and a coal stove. Running water and an outhouse were in the backyard. It is hard to imagine it here, but I was heating the coal stove until the day before we left for America. Housekeeping was physically strenuous. Emotionally it was easier there, because it was your own language. Here, the language is the major stumbling block for all of us. Then, you are a child of the society in which you have grown up, so you feel more comfortable in it. And here, you come to a strange society that maybe is more perfect and better, but you are a stranger in it.

The friends I had in my childhood, were the only true friends I ever had in my life. We still keep in touch, unfortunately, less and less often. It was a very strong friendship; I don't have it here. As it became clear to me, here it is very difficult to find friends. The people I grew up with understood me before I finished the sentence or on a subtle emotional tone, we sensed each other's inner condition. We talked about boys, about clothes, about love, about our inner lives. I had a friend, we could talk for hours on end, and we were never bored with each other. She was a real friend. And here women from the Soviet Union are like that Russian fairy tale character—it was not enough for her to be a princess, she wanted to be a queen. I mean she has to prove to you that she is better than you. It looks ridiculous and ugly. I have a friend from my town; we are almost the same age. There, we barely knew each other, but here we have so few connections, and decent people are hard to come by, so we became close friends. I know that if something happens, I can lean on him.

I almost don't remember my puberty. It happened so that I never had this adolescent gawky look. I have always been small and plump, and my breasts grew somehow slowly and naturally, so I never had terrible outward changes. At the age of 12, I was well developed already, but it did not bother me, I still played with dolls. I was still a child and stayed one for a long time. At 16, I was a plump girl with appetizing curves. I wore a bra size C, had a thin waistline, wide hips, a feminine silhouette. After graduating high school, I gained a lot of weight.

I worked at a dressmaking shop, and there was a bakery next door. They had great pastry, especially small mince pies and flaky dough cigars filled with whipped cream and dusted with confectioner's sugar. The aroma was so great that I could hardly wait for the lunch break to run there and buy a pie and a cigar. I did it every day until I realized how much weight I gained, and then I got scared. I noticed it because of a tragic love story. Probably I would not be happy with that guy anyway, but since it did not happen for us, I started looking for the reason of my sorrow. I was blaming myself; I always do it—look for reasons of anything that happened in myself. People who blame others have it easier in life. I started examining myself skeptically. I had a short haircut then, so it was visible that I accumulated a lot of fat on the nape of my neck and became plump all around. I set a goal for myself to lose weight. During that whole year I did not touch a single piece of cake, candy, or pastry. I drank tea without sugar and ate very little bread. I exercised every morning, which I cannot say about myself now. I got up early in the morning and exercised before work. I lost weight and my stomach became as tight as a wood board. My hair grew long, I had a thick mane of gorgeous long curls. After this, I relaxed a bit about dieting.

When I was in college, I did not watch what I ate, but I was in perpetual motion, always rushing; I had many friends. I worked full-time and studied by correspondence, this was time-consuming and stressful, so I looked like a skeleton after every semester's end. My college was in Odessa, food there was very good, so my roommates and I ate well—we used to buy hot dogs, boiled some potatoes, what could we cook there when we were renting a room in somebody's apartment? It never occurred to me that one should not eat hot dogs with potatoes or that one should eat salads. We used to make salads, just because we liked them, but I never gave it a thought, I was not gaining weight, and then other problems occupied my mind so completely, that I did not concentrate on food.

When I got married and gave birth to my daughter, I gained a little weight, but I did not become fat. I weighed 138 pounds while I was breast-feeding; when I stopped, I lost weight very quickly. Not that I tried to, I had to finish college, to take care of my little daughter, and I was going through the divorce—all together. I lost so much weight that my classmates did not recognize me. I became like a teenager from stress; my life was full of it. I lost my appetite completely, like I was unable to push a piece down my throat. And I used to smoke then—if you smoke instead of eating dinner, you don't gain weight.

When I was overweight, my mother liked it, she used to tell me later, "You were exactly right—very good." When I lost weight, she said, "What do you look like? You have only your nose left." At that time, some new kind of ideal formed—one had to be thin, and all of us were diligently trying to lose weight. Probably it happened because of blue jeans. Here everybody wears jeans, and there they were a rare imported luxury. A heavy girl could not wear jeans—everybody would laugh at her. Everybody wanted to look fashionable, contemporary, and you wanted to be liked, too. Besides, wearing blue jeans would put you on an equal footing with a boy. I was born in 1960, and my mother was formed by the prewar years. All the actresses of that time were rather robust; not one of them was thin. Now my daughter goes through magazines and says, "This is how one should apply makeup now." We form stereotypes based on what we see around us.

I like a normal body—thin waist, beautiful breasts necessarily, not small, it is very beautiful with a thin waist. The shoulders should not be very sloped, I have very sloped shoulders and I don't like it, I always wear shoulder pads. Not skinny, I do not like such women, and I don't like fat women, either, in the middle, with no stomach. An ideal woman should be a little taller than I, but not too tall, either; 5'6", size 6 is probably ideal. Thank G-d, there is makeup and clothes that can make one look better, because there is no ideal body.

My mother was always normal, not too thin, and not too fat, probably size eight. She was shapely, with a nice light gait. She was shorter than me, but everybody thought she was taller because she had better body proportions. She always had all the makings for beauty, but never realized them. She never used makeup, if I put some on her, she would come home all smeared, because she would forget about it and rub her eyes. She is a child of the WWII. Her miserable childhood during the war and, later, in the orphanages, with fighting for a dry crust of bread, formed her personality, tastes, and perspective on life. She always lived by her inner, spiritual world, not by the surface matters, so we never discussed looks or beauty. She never had the luxury of taking care of herself. She had a very good figure, so when she did buy something that fitted her well, she looked very good, but she never paid much attention to clothes or to her appearance, she could do without and did not mind it. I disliked this part of my mother's attitude, even was irritated by it. I thought that she had to take care of herself; I was paying attention to other women in the movies and to real people around me. I realized that we could not afford to buy good clothes, so I had to learn how to make them by myself. I did it out of necessity. Now, I don't want to spend my time sewing, and there is no need for it. Besides, clothing is not that important here. Our town was small, you might meet somebody you knew every ten minutes; so I always wanted to dress up. Here you can cross the whole New York City and meet nobody you know. I have so few acquaintances. It is not the same as the town where you have grown up.

My mother taught me to love music, Russian classical literature, she tried to develop my mind to the limit of her possibilities, she gave me everything she could—I was taking dance lessons from the early childhood, learned how to sew, played the piano. She also used to help me in elementary school. She taught me that learning is my responsibility; so after the 5th grade I was a very good student all the time, I would study to exhaustion. Thanks to her, I used to read a lot in my childhood. Actually, all my friends did. Our children don't read this much, honestly speaking, they don't read at all. I think that TV should not be transmitted 24 hours a day as it is here. I remember when I was growing up, TV programs were available a few hours during the day and a few hours during the evening, not that my mother forbade me to watch TV or turned it off. One could watch a cartoon, a movie, and, in general, if a family owned a TV set when I was five, it was a luxury.

My mother played the piano, I loved listening to her playing, especially Chopin. She was not forcing music on me; she was just studying in a musical college when I was growing up. I did my homework listening to her practice. I used to spend a lot of time alone when I was growing up; she had nobody to watch me. I had no maternal grandmother; she died when my mother was 12. My other grandmother lived too far from us. She had pity on my mother for two reasons. First, she was an orphan herself, and also because my mother suffered from her son. My father has a very difficult personality, and my grandmother probably realized how it was for my mother.

I was struggling financially all my life, but it was the worst the year before we emigrated. I lost my job and did not work for a year. One has to eat, and at that time foodstuffs became wildly expensive. If I could buy something good, I would give it to my daughter. I almost lost my child due to acetone in her urine when she was seven. She was like a skeleton, unable to walk; I had to carry her to the hospital. After that, I had to feed her very carefully to prevent the relapse. Acetone was like epidemic in Russia; almost all the children had it. And then we left for America and forgot its name. Anyway, I had to eat something, and all I had at home was a huge bag of spaghetti, a can of sunflower oil, and a sack of onions. When I had nothing else to eat, I would cook spaghetti and eat them with sautéed onions. It was such a terrible year that I was only losing weight. The whole system started falling apart, and it was the hardest for those who lived in old houses. I had to buy tanks of cooking gas, and at times it was not delivered for two months. Every two or three hours we would lose electricity, because everybody was using electric heating devices in the absence of coal. Old electric cables could not bear the demand and burned out. We had electric fires all over the area because of the overload. So this was my life—no coal, no gas, and often no electricity. I had no job, and my daughter was little. It was like living during the war. I became so skinny that it was probably dangerous. If I stayed there, I would probably look like an old lady already.

After my graduation and divorce, I started working, and my mother was taking care of Dosia, and then she went to the kindergarten. My parents helped me during the emigration, too. My father loves Dosia with such passionate tenderness. If not for her, he would never come here. One day, I said, "We are leaving. We cannot live like this." I imagined what was in store for Dosia. I imagined my old age, even my middle age. My parents lived in the same area in the same conditions. I knew that I would have to take care of both homes, and I was barely managing with my own. My biceps were like a strong man's, because I carried endless buckets—two pails of water in, two pails out, coal in, cinders out, chop the wood, carry it in, and so on. You heat the room in the evening, and it is freezing when you get up. I was on a waiting list for a cooperative apartment. I was trying to save for the down payment, skimped on everything, and almost made the sum, and the building was almost ready. That very time, Tartars were allowed to return to Crimea, and all the living space was given to them. All the money I managed to put together turned into nothing. It was enough to pay for an English class before we emigrated. I felt totally isolated; my former husband could not care less about my problems or our child's illness. He lived without seeing us for years in a row. I realized that I had to change something radically; otherwise my life would be completely over at 31. My life was senseless; my future was hopeless.

I wrote a letter to my aunt and asked her to make the necessary papers. When we were leaving, I invited all my friends and former classmates for a farewell party. They left their husbands at home with children with such pleasure, and I took Dosia to my mother. In my class, I was among the heavier girls. And before the departure, I noticed that I was the thinnest. It was really funny that all the girls that were so thin in their youth became very fat after giving birth. They had a more or less stable life, so they kind of lost the drive to look good, turned into mother hens. This is the disease of all Russian women—as soon as they get married, they stop taking care of themselves, and if the man leaves, they start taking care of themselves right away. I spent most of my adult life as a single woman; so I was always kind of on my toes.

After that farewell party I cried alone, all night long. Of course, I do not miss the country, just my friends. This is what motherland is, not that damned stove. The worst basement in New York does not compare with the hut I lived in, and here I have a very nice apartment. I told my friends not to come to the station to see me off; it was dangerous during these times. One man in my town was killed on the night before his departure. The racketeers knew that he sold everything he had, so they robbed him and cut his throat. My friends came anyway, all of them. I did not know if we would ever see each other again, so I wanted my friends to remember me as a young, happy, good looking person. I dressed well on purpose, applied some makeup; had my hair set.

When we just arrived in New York, I had to make a living somehow, so I washed floors and took care of elderly ladies. One of them died in my care. She had diarrhea for two days, and then she died. I realized that if I didn't improve my situation, I was not worth a good word. I found a job in a store and evening classes in computer-assisted design. Now I work in a large company. I am not totally happy there; hopefully a better job will come, too.

When I came here, I weighed 106 lbs. and now I am afraid to step on the scale because I know that I weigh much more. I gained at least 15 lbs. or even more. Of course, I would like to be thinner. I'd feel lighter, more mobile. It is easier to climb to the fifth floor carrying grocery bags. Besides, people with extra weight look older, and the age is the very thing we are trying to fight off. After 35 a woman is middle-aged, life is life. I consider myself middle-aged, of course.

I don't think I eat more here than I did there. I would say I eat less now—I am limiting my cookies and pastries. I used to bake all the time, and here I don't bake at all. I have neither energy, nor desire, nor time for it. In the Soviet Union, I used to work so close to home; it took me 5 minutes to walk there. When I come home now, I want to cook something quickly to feed Dosia or to have something for tomorrow, and to lie down. I have no energy left. It is so good here, if you want to, you can buy ready-made food or oven-ready stuff. In America, cooking is not a dire necessity as it was there.

I gained weight in America because food here contains something, I don't know what. I think I gain weight here even by eating salads because they contain some kind of chemicals. I was warned to be careful here. Calories too, of course, but I know that chickens are stuffed with hormones, so you ingest them with the meat. When I take a container off a supermarket shelf, I read the contents, and usually there are all kinds of chemicals there. I don't know what "flavorings" are, they are not for the aroma only; I think people gain weight from eating these. The only way to fight extra weight is to starve a day or two every week. I do it once in a while. It goes like this: I eat at 6 p.m. and then I don't eat the following day, only drink water. I eat at about noon the next day, so altogether it is a day and a half. This is not only for losing weight; it rejuvenates and purifies your whole body. Some famous American doctor wrote this book, *The Miracle of Hunger*. It was translated into Russian; I read it there. I remember everybody was doing it.

At times, I think, "I look OK, I am not fat yet," and at other times, I dislike myself very much for gaining weight, so I start my hunger regimen, and my weight goes down. I used to do it every week, but lately I stopped because I started driving. I did not want the risk; I may get dizzy in the evening. I also listen to my cousin's advice. She gave me all kinds of information about separate eating, like what foods should not be eaten together. She is a professor of separate eating, like meat is not to be eaten with starches, I mean meat and bread. Red vegetables should be eaten separately from green ones. This is her hobby. She used to fast for the whole week at a time. When I came to America, she looked like a barrel, and now she is slim. I admire her;

she takes great care of herself. Of course, I would like to take better care of myself, too.

Of course, I think one should exercise to keep herself in shape, at least once in a while, to swim in the summer, to play tennis, whatever one can do to be active. My work starts at eight, so I get up at six, I have no energy to get up at five to exercise. There, my town was small; I used to work in a walking distance from work, about five minutes. This is a big difference in my lifestyle. I spend about two hours a day on the road. Probably I am looking for excuses—I am tired, I want to hug the pillow. When I come home after sitting ten hours behind the computer, I don't want to move a finger.

It is very important for a woman to have a stimulus. If I were involved with somebody, I would be taking a much better care of myself. I became lazy because I don't like anybody and I don't care, with the passage of years one becomes more apathetic. I do have a man, but I am not so interested in him as I would like to be. Love changes a person, at any age a woman starts looking younger, becomes more attractive; her eyes shine differently, she acts differently. The tone of her voice changes, her gait; she starts taking much better care of herself, her skin and her body. And when a woman does not have this stimulus, life becomes colorless; a person must love somebody. Probably I lost weight at eighteen because in my subconscious mind I was hoping to make that man return to me and see me looking absolutely different.

I go to the gym, but not so often, once in two weeks. During the summer, I don't feel like going to the crowded, stuffy gym and swimming in the pool, reeking of chlorine. I adore the sea; I go to the beach every weekend, all summer long. Dosia and I went to the Dominican Republic last summer. This was my first vacation in America. Every morning I used to get up at six, when the beach was deserted; I exercised on the sand and swam. I was the first person to go swimming and the last one to leave in the evening. This vacation was like a fairy tale.

In Russia, I used to take Dosia to a gymnastic class for three years. Her body is perfect for this kind of sports. She is not too tall, but very thin and flexible, with long legs. She did splits easily, other things. She just started showing promise when we left the country. When we came here, we had so many problems and our financial situation was bad. We could not afford gymnastics classes and we had no car to take her there. I was happy that my parents were able to pick her up after school and to feed her. But to drag them somewhere for gymnastics was too much. Everything stems from financial difficulties. Besides, she had school and the new language—tears every day for several months. Now, she is involved in only one sport—sitting on the couch and watching these taped ha-has, these TV shows. Honestly speaking, it is my pain. I don't think I have the right to force her, like other parents who turn the TV off, but I wish she could spend her time better.

Dosia is thin, and I like it very much. She is well-built—narrow hips and a pretty, round butt. The only thing I would like to change about her is her posture; she slouches. She is short and thin, but she looks like a little woman already. We like to go shopping together, like two friends. We look at catalogues, like Victoria's Secret; discuss every model. There is one there, so beautiful, face and body. She would have been perfect if her legs were just a little fuller. She is tall, size 4 or 6, probably 6. If she were size 4, she would look like a skeleton. I think that people with different body shapes should be models, because they model clothes for different people. And when you look at a magazine, they all look skinny.

Dosia is a combination of Russian and American ways. She was brought up by her grandmother and grandfather; they don't speak English, they will never be Americans. She also picks up a lot of things from American kids in school. Two cultures live in her; at times, they are at peace, and other times, they contradict each other. She likes Russian songs, movies; she even has favorite ones. My mother used to spend a lot of time with her. It is natural that she had a big influence on her. Dosia has musical abilities, she can sing well, too. My mother tried to stimulate her interest in music; she cannot forgive me that I did not make Dosia take music lessons. But Dosia refused to, and I did not want to force her. In America, it might not become her future. Life here is hard, and she should not spread out too thin doing this and that, like I did. She has to choose a path for herself and to follow it.

Our children are more motivated than their peers who were born here. They survived the emigration together with us, and they had language problems, too. They know the meaning of "there is no money." A family from my town came here when their daughter was five; now she is thirty. She has not achieved anything in life, and she is not going to, because her parents have achieved a lot financially and otherwise. When parents are in a difficult financial situation, their children are ambitious and motivated to work hard and to succeed. We had a similar situation in the Soviet Union. Young people from distant provinces and remote villages, who wanted to live in Moscow or Leningrad, had to obtain so called "limited permits." They would take any job to be allowed to stay in the city and to get a dormitory bed. They clawed their way up, because they lived in hard conditions. And kids who were born in Moscow and Leningrad hardly ever reached the same levels of achievement. Emigration makes us work ten times harder. Our children do not have everything ready for them, like American children, so they are more motivated. They have different moral values, too.

I hope that my daughter will give me more of her time and attention in my old age than American children do for their parents. Here it is an absurdity, and it comes from their childhood. American grandmothers do not spend much time with their children, and it was a norm in Russia. Instead, American mothers have babysitters. As a result, there is general lack of good upbringing. A babysitter is a stranger, she does not care what the child is doing; she just watches the child. Since parents spend little time with their children, the children spend little time with them when they grow old. They have nice and pleasant relationships, but they may live for years without seeing each other, just talking on the phone. They do not have such strong ties like we do. Yes, we were squeezed into a bunch in one apartment, it was like a noose on one's neck, but we were so much closer to each other, everything was passed from one generation to the next. In most families, several generations lived in one apartment. At times, families used to break because of this, but family members were closer. Since grandmothers took care of grandchildren, it happened that children had a better upbringing. Grandparents always have more time than parents, and this is where manners, culture, general orientation were coming from. One could see what the grandmother is all about by looking at the granddaughter, not the mother, and here generations are very much separated. I cleaned one elderly American woman's apartment, she had several children, dozens of grandchildren, so they used to take her home once a year for holidays. I hope my daughter will keep her Russian attitude in this respect, I am afraid that it can be otherwise. Honestly speaking, she is the only soul I have in this world, she and my parents, and they, unfortunately, are very elderly. I have no hope to get settled some other way, so I don't plan things I cannot realistically expect. For me it will be a disaster if my child forgets me, I am scared even to think about it. I am very devoted to her and give her everything I have. Everything I have and everything I do is for her. If I am trying to achieve something, it is not for me, but for her. I want to help her have a better life, to have a good future and possibilities for this future. I want her to have an opportunity to study in a good college and to have a good job later on. I want her to marry better than I did, it is very important. I want her to be happy.

Dosia

Dosia, a thin fourteen-year old girl of short stature, looked younger than her chronological age. Her raven-black wavy hair was cut short and brushed back. Large dark eyes had a somewhat distant, even glassy look. Dosia's bright yellow terry bathrobe was way too large for her; she wrapped it around her waist and tied the belt before sitting down. Her thin wrists looked even thinner in the wide sleeve openings. Her short nails were unevenly covered with bright polish. Dosia agreed to participate in the study, although reluctantly, and tended to be brief in her answers. During the interview, she looked at her watch several times and made impatient gestures while asking me, "Is this all?" Dosia ran to the living room as soon as the interview was finished and turned on the TV.

Dosia's Story

I want to be smart and rich. I want to be a lawyer. I like talking; I can study things that lawyers need. I like fighting, I mean arguing. In school I am a member of a debate club, and I do well there. It is a little too long to study for it, so what? And about my looks—I don't even know, I have never thought about it and I am not very interested in it, true.

I like thin actresses and models. I think I am thin, but I don't know how much I weigh. I wear size 1; I don't want to weigh more. I feel the same way now I felt before my body change, no difference. I know that I am older and everything, but it is not that important. I think about different things, of course, about college, what career I want to choose, and what I want to do with my life. My friends are the same way, we talk how to study better and so on, how to save time. I have Russian friends and Chinese friends. In my class most of the kids are Chinese. We talk about how much we hate school, how much homework we have and how much we are sick and tired of it even though only one week of school has passed. Not that we hate it, we just don't like to get up early, the summer just ended, so it is a pity, we want to have more of the summer. Sometimes we talk about clothes, like when it is important to dress up to go somewhere; then we ask each other, "What are you going to wear?" We talk about what is in style now, how it looks, about color, how to put on things to match, like what kind of top goes with these pants.

At times I am not too nice to my grandmother—like if I am busy and she would call, I would yell at her, and then I apologize. We used to spend a lot of time together, and now I don't have the time. I come home at four, relax for half an hour, and then I do my homework till 7:30, then I want to watch TV a little. She used to play the piano and I tried to sing, but now I do not like it too much. We used to watch Russian movies together, the old ones, but I like American movies more. Some Russian actresses look like American ones, and some don't. Some are very different. In America such a girl would not be an actress. American actresses are all thin, and Russian ones are fat. To be an actress in America a girl has to be beautiful.

After school, I don't feel like doing any sports. In school I have gym, of course, so it is my only 40 minutes of sports a day, but I do more sports than I even know. Our school is huge—nine floors; we run from the first floor to the eighth, so I have a lot of running to do with a bag full of books. I noticed that every year my bag gets lighter—the older I get, the fewer books I have to carry around. When I was in lower grades, I had to carry a huge bag full of books. I did not know what books to carry. And older kids have already empty bags, only one thin notebook. In gym, we have weight training, so we do exercises with heavy weights and we have training machines. Every semester we have a different kind of gym class. I don't like gym. Actually, I don't like changing for gym. I am uncomfortable undressing in a large locker room. After gym you are sweaty, and you have to put on your regular clothes, it feels so bad. I don't like going to the gym after school. We have a lot of homework. Sometimes I go with my friend or play basketball, but rarely. I plan to attend Bally's gym this winter, not that I really want to. I like running, we run for fun sometimes. I am satisfied with my body, so I don't do it for other reasons.

I like different foods, but I like food that is not cooked by my mom. I mean she cooks tasty food, but she repeats herself too often. And my taste changes, too. One time I used to eat pizza very often, then Chinese food—my mom used to order in, but now we eat more homemade stuff. I like sushi. It is small, but fills you. Sometimes I eat potato chips, sweets. I like cheesecake. I know that I shouldn't eat it, but I eat it anyway. I know one shouldn't eat much candy or to chew gum—I have braces, but I eat it anyway, I like dark chocolate, too. My friends eat more of this stuff than I do. In school, I have orange juice, salad, some vegetables, every day they serve something different. I don't like school food. Sometimes I check how many calories I eat, but it is only for fun, not that I care, not at all.

THE GOLDERS

The Golder family consists of Maya, age 40, her husband, and their daughter Daniela, age 16. Maya's mother, Greta, age 70, lives in the same apartment in the Riverdale section of the Bronx, N.Y. Maya came to the United States 7 years ago from one of the former Soviet Republics, deep in Islamic Asia. Greta came one year later. Maya worked as a social worker in the Soviet Union and now works in the same professional area in the U.S.

The Golder family lives in a spacious three-bedroom apartment on the second floor of a private house. A combined living/dining room is furnished with a modern lacquered dining set. A large matching breakfront, filled with crystal, dishes, and colorful arrangements of silk flowers dominates the room. Daniela has her own room. Maya and Daniela were interviewed in Maya's study—a narrow room lined with bookshelves.

Greta

Greta is a plump, pleasant looking woman with small facial features and sad eyes. She chose to be interviewed in her friend's apartment and seemed more relaxed and cheerful there, than at home. She agreed to be interviewed on a condition that she would not sign the consent form with her last name. Her interest in participation seemed to be influenced by her desire to share her experience and to seek advice from a professional with the same cultural background, as she reported being stressed out by significant family issues.

Greta spoke with elegant fluency of a person accustomed to teaching and lecturing. Her manner suggested deep emotional involvement in her children's life and revealed deep inner struggles. When she turned the conversation to the major family problem—conflict between her son-in-law and her granddaughter, her weary eyes welled with tears. Grateful for attention, Greta brought up and elaborated several issues that were significant for her and other women, even though I did not ask about them during the interview.

Greta's Story

Of course, my life here differs significantly, in principle. While living at home, in our country, we all worked. I worked as a teacher of Russian language for forty years. My career spans from the first to the tenth grade. I also taught in a college for elementary school teachers and at the university level, training high school teachers of Russian language. This is my list of accomplishments.

I had to retire early when my mother became very ill. I could not leave her alone; she was blind the last twenty years of her life. After thirty years of married life I became a free lady, my husband and I divorced, and I returned to my childhood home. Starting from 1983, I had to be by my mother's sick bed, I had to dedicate a lot of time and attention to her. Then my granddaughter Daniela started school, and I had to help my children to take care of her. My daughter or son-in-law used to take her to school, and I would pick her up from school. She stayed with me until her parents came home from work. It was the same way when my children were growing up. My mother was also a teacher, so we arranged our schedules in such a way, that I could bunch up my kids and take them to her place. My mother worked for forty-five years. She was an Honored Teacher of the Republic. She was one of the people who founded schools for girls when they just started getting rid of veils. Our family consisted mainly of teachers of various profiles, of people who believed that they were working to create a better life for future generations and devoted a lot of energy to it.

I read a lot about emigration, so I realized how hard it is to adjust to life in a new country. I read about nostalgia and could imagine how it would be. I knew it would be especially hard for me because I have a catlike personality—I get very attached to the house and to the people. This is why every break is a painful event for me. During my entire life I lived in two places—in my parents' house and in my husband's house. But the situation in our republic was getting such that there was nothing for us to do—Islam was returning. I had a non-Jewish friend who would ask me, "I don't understand, why aren't you leaving? You have a chance to leave, we don't have it." I was not able to return to work, and I love my profession very much. Here I suffer a lot because I can't find any use for my teaching abilities. It may sound ridiculous, but I took with me several textbooks and some of my own works in phonetics… I hoped that something may happen and I would get lucky, even though I realized that I would need to learn English for it. The second reason for my decision to leave was that I had my daughter here. I came here to help her as much as I can, to support them in their hard life. I think that the middle generation is having the hardest time here. It is so difficult to establish themselves professionally, to prove themselves again.

I cook, serve and clean up the table, trying to help them at least this way. This is how I see my mission—to support my family as much as possible. I took upon myself all the housekeeping for my daughter's family. I live with my daughter, even though I have a separate room and theoretically I live separately. In reality, I must do the cleaning, and the laundry, and this and that. This *must* is defined by me; so I must cook dinner. There, meat-based borscht and soups were prevalent, necessary, and here I make them rarely, only for my son-in-law. My cholesterol level is high, my daughter's cholesterol is climbing; so we are trying to eat more vegetables and less meat. I think it is good for us.

My family loves tasty food, traditional dishes, basically made of meat and dough, pies and steamed lamb dumplings. I used to make them often, but now we stopped eating them, upon urgings of my gym teacher and of Daniela. She loved lamb dumplings, but now she does not allow herself to eat many of them. She is a bad eater from her childhood. Feeding her was always a problem for us, so I have to cook what she wants. Now I have a restaurant at home—what is this one going to eat, what is the other one going to eat? I cook practically every day. If I cooked a pot roast yesterday and I have enough for two days, today I have to make some kind of stewed vegetable dish. Daniela used to eat a lot of sweets, now she eats no sweets at all, she does not want to gain weight. In general, she eats little, she watches herself. She is a real top model—tall, trim, with a good figure.

Maya is full-bodied; she suffers a lot because of it. Unfortunately, pregnancy had screwed up her entire hormonal system, so diets won't help her. Her weight comes from hormonal imbalance. Daniela watches what Maya eats; at dinner, she would yell to me, "Grandma, look, you see what she is eating, she gained weight again!" She is unhappy that her mother is overweight. I don't like it, either. Even now being so rounded irritates me, too. But I am at the age when it is not so easy to shed kilograms. I weigh as much as I weighed before the emigration, but prior to this I used to be thinner and in general I was always slim. I started gaining weight after fifty-five, it had nothing to do with the emigration. I know that if I want to lose weight, I have to force myself to stop eating sweets and dough. I like to bake. My simplest recipe is banana bread. You take three bananas, mash them, add a cup of sugar, three eggs, then a cup of butter, and mix it all well, and add two cups of flour. That is it, the whole recipe. Bake it in the oven, and when it is ready, sprinkle it with powdered sugar. Your banana bread is ready for the evening tea. Lately I started baking less because we buy ready-made cakes, especially when the weather is hot. Besides, I have no time for it and we are trying to limit ourselves. Maya shouldn't eat it, Daniela shouldn't, and I shouldn't. So I don't make it at all.

I used to bake a lot for parties, but here everything is changing. In the beginning we had big gatherings at home, and now at times, on birthdays, we get together at home or friends visit on weekends. But now they are trying more, even I, we are trying not to do it at home, but to go to some restaurant because it is easier than to cook at home.

What really makes me suffer is that both my daughter and my granddaughter have changed very significantly. I understand that it is the surrounding, the situation they found themselves in. They lack the time and understanding, even though my daughter is a social worker, that buying me an extra piece of clothing does not make me happy. I know worse situations—the elders get no attention from their children or all juices are squeezed out of them and they are thrown away as unnecessary garbage. I cannot say that I get no attention from my children, but I suffer very much. I don't get enough of their warmth, especially from my granddaughter. She even told me very straight, "You know, grandma, it is not your fault, it is my fault, but it is my business." She is right in her own way. She was on the phone one day; she speaks mostly in English. I asked her, "What were you talking about with Vickie?" She answered, "I don't want you to discuss my problems and relationships with your friends. I know you report everything to each other."

I would like it to be the way it used to be in our family before. I don't think that my daughter should tell me absolutely everything, like what is going on in her life, but at least something. I think that many things are not absolutely secret. I understand that they have their own problems, issues they want to discuss only with each other, without my participation. I strongly agree with the old saying that in order to live together with one's children, one has to be a little blind, a little deaf, and a little stupid. I am trying not to meddle in their affairs, but nevertheless, I would like to be more informed. Let's say, they are invited somewhere. This is not a secret, but I found it out from a conversation I happened to overhear. My daughter was talking on the phone with her friend and said that they were planning to go. Could she say, "Mama, we are going to this place on Sunday." Or another example—in our family it is a usual thing—when they go somewhere they call or tell me that they are going to this place or that, "We are over there, will be back at such and such time, don't worry." But at times I worry myself sick. One day they left... my son-in-law has a younger brother, so they went shopping, and on the way back they stopped over at his place. They told me that they would be back soon. They left at noon and returned at six. Starting from three o'clock and until six I was dead from worry, and my idiotic personality is such that my mind immediately gets flooded by a million of "pleasant" pictures like a car crash or something of the same kind.

I also get very upset that my children, obsessed by their own cares and concerns, move away from cultural pursuits, not that they are not interested, but they have no time for it. I think that the main reason for it is that my daughter's spouse is pulling her into his philistine mire. I believe that my daughter and granddaughter are losing so much, limiting their inner, spiritual life. My granddaughter has practically lost her Russian, which makes me very unhappy. Of course, she speaks and understands, but it is not fluent, and she has no desire to go see a drama production, to read a book, I believe it is very sad.

I love the way Daniela looks, no doubt about it, but my heart aches all the time. She is beautiful, with a great slender body, and smart, too.

But I know from the experience that it is better to be born lucky than beautiful, so I am very tense and fearful inside. The morals are so lax here. For example, she bought herself a shirt with a very low neck, and she wears it to school. How can one wear such a thing to school? On the other hand, yesterday I saw three kids her age; one was wearing a tiny skirt barely covering her underwear, the other one had skimpy shorts on, and the third one wore such super tight pants that one could see every line and contour of her body. I am not a prude, but I don't think that this kind of clothes is for school. Looking at these girls, I think that she is doing the same things that her peers are doing, so how can one say no to her? And saying yes is no good, either. One can say that Daniela has a difficult personality and is very spoiled. She is the only child; of course, they overprotect her to an extreme. As a result, she does whatever she wants, like goes to school with a bare navel. I cannot accept it, but her peers do the same, so I have to keep silence. And she does not tolerate a negative comment about her. I cannot even say a word, she gets offended right away, explodes, and a fragile peace is immediately broken.

Now Maya functions as a barrier between her husband and Daniela, because he, with his mentality peculiar to the natives of our republic, does not understand the new ways of life and new circumstances here. Daniela behaves exactly the way other kids her age do here, and he goes ballistic on a drop of a hat. Would anybody approve if his sixteen-year-old daughter came home after one o'clock in the morning? Can he lock her up? He is a choleric by nature, so he explodes immediately, and he loves his baby madly. I don't know if there is anything in the world he would not do for her, whatever he can do, he would. He is destroying her this way because the girl is not accustomed to overcoming hardships. When I talk to them about it, they do not change. She should be prepared for life; she should know that she will meet people who will not fulfill her slightest wishes. Who else will keep telling her that she is the most beautiful and the smartest? How many times did I tell her, "Darling, if your daddy says something you don't like, keep silent at that moment, and then tell him quietly," but she starts yelling back. Everything starts with an explosion, and every word breeds conflict, this is terrible. I keep begging her, "Darling, please, be calm. You know your father is like this." But she is the same way. Last week, she promised to come home at 12:30, and then she cannot make it, so she calls. "Why didn't you call at 12:30?" They were driving some girl home, and our daddy starts yelling. Daniela is in the car, and everybody in the car can hear her father yell at her. How should she react to it? Of course, she comes home all upset. The father starts yelling at her, and she yells back. Then she goes to her room, and the next morning she doesn't speak to him. My daughter starts explaining to him that he was not right, and he starts, "Why was I wrong? Why are you always supporting her?"

Daniela is a decent girl; she is smart and works a lot. She completed a very difficult two-year program in one year and then she went straight to the tenth grade. She decided that she wants to become a lawyer or a journalist and she would apply to the Hunter High School, it has a very good Liberal Arts program. It meant to spend about four hours a day in subways. So we had a dilemma—Hunter, or Stuyvesant, or The Bronx School of Science. The father was immediately yelling, "NO! That's it! NO!" Daniela said, "It is I who will study there, not you. Why are you deciding for me? I have to decide." Her position is already the result of the American influence, she is an individual; she plans her life herself. And her father is right, too. From our house to Hunter is two hours by train. She is so beautiful; she attracts attention, should she be allowed to go alone? Of course, I quietly talked to Maya; my friends gave me advice that he should drive her there. Let her take a look at the place she wants to go to, what kind of commute it is. That was it, the problem was solved; she is in a local high school now. She finished the tenth grade very well, with a 93 average. Besides, she attends Kaplan courses, does extra work. She knows what she is aiming for. But I am afraid that she has absolutely no flexibility, that she is blunt and at times rude. How can this be changed, how can I help my daughter? Maya is suffering terribly because of this; she is constantly between two fires. And I am afraid that she will not be able to continue this way. Now Daniela is talking about going away to college, but she is the only child. Without her they would be lost. She is the meaning of their life. They can't survive five minutes without her. I am sure she will leave for college. She said it many times that as soon as she graduates, she will run away from home. The question is how she will do it. She may do some wrong things. I worry terribly about her and about my daughter, and as a mother, I feel sorry for my son-in-law. He does it all with the best intentions, and I don't know why he does not understand the simplest things. How can one explain to him that in this case he has to retreat a bit, to give her some freedom? He cannot go on like this. No matter how my daughter tried to explain to him that he is pushing her away, losing her, it is impossible to change his nature. At times, I feel desperate because I am there and cannot help.

I badly miss so many members of my family. We were so close, and now my son is in Israel with his family, my nieces are in Germany, their mother is not Jewish. I hoped that my brother's family would come here, but a terrible tragedy happened—my brother died of lung cancer. He was fifty-five and had never been sick before. This was the price he paid for the new way of life. He adored his daughters, and when they were getting married, he needed money. He went to Turkey on business, and there he and his companions got into a terrible situation, they were locked in some kind of a cellar. They managed to get out of there two minutes before the ship's departure. When they returned, his companion got ill, and my brother developed a case of eczema. His friend, a physician, gave him some hormonal shots. Eczema disappeared, but my brother developed a galloping cancer, and in a month and a half he was gone.

My sister's younger daughter left for Israel in 1990. When she was expecting a baby, my sister hurried to get there for the time for her daughter to give birth. My sister has always been a very sickly person, but her physician told me that emigration hastened her death. On July 17th they left Moscow for Israel. Exactly in four months, on November 17, she died. The only letter I received from her from Israel was full of joyous descriptions of her tiny granddaughter, how happy she was to see her. She also wrote that she would never forgive herself for not being there for our mother's funeral. She survived our mother only by two and a half months. This is why I often feel rather lonely. Of course, with these losses it is very difficult for me to live. In the beginning, I started making good progress in English when I was taking classes at NYANA, but my brother's death ended all my efforts. I got stuck and can't move forward any longer. I am like that proverbial dog that understands everything but cannot speak. It is another source of my suffering. I was so depressed several times that I needed treatment.

I badly miss the motherland where I was born, where I lived all my life, and I miss the people I lost. I miss my son who lives across the Atlantic Ocean; I miss my relatives who are no longer living. I miss my nieces who are like my own children, because they grew up so close to me. My brother was so precious for me; we were very close. When I hear a melody that we used to play together with him, or *Freilechs_*(a merry Jewish folk tune), I see myself dancing with him; all these pictures present themselves so clearly and painfully. Even a smell, a book, everything brings the memories back. The nostalgic feelings crowd in my heart, so I have to pull myself out of this by my bootstraps.

I get help from my new circle of friends. In our Jewish center there is a book club. An energetic and dedicated person is in charge, so we have very interesting meetings. We had a meeting on Sholem Alechem; his granddaughter, Bel Kaufman, came and spoke to us. Other writers and poets come to our club, and this is healing for me. I read a book for every meeting, express my opinion about it; participate in a discussion, this is my emotional nourishment.

I have to say that I live a life I would have never had there, no doubt. I go to theaters, concerts, on sightseeing trips, and I have a possibility to read whatever I want. I live an interesting life. I found wonderful friends, we get together, have a good time, enjoy the activities. Now we are planning a trip to Washington, D.C. in November.

In my youth, I was a sportswoman; I had a high rating in gymnastics. Even after I had Maya, my coach met me and asked me to come back for training, but it was impossible to combine work, two children, two elderly parents, and sports. In the years before emigration I had almost no chance to do any sports. I exercised a little at home, on occasion. Here I am very happy that we have a group. It is a combination of gymnastics and elements of Tai Chi; it is good for my health. I attend these classes twice a week, two years already. I go to the swimming pool, too, thanks to Gita, our water-loving duck, she kind of pulled me there. My time is fully scheduled: twice a week we have English classes, twice a week—gym, twice a week—swimming pool.

Gita, my best, closest friend, my soul mate, is such a special person. We go to the center for gymnastics classes, so one day I told her, "No matter how I am trying to run away from being old, it catches up with me. Now, my leg hurts." She stopped, looked at me, and answered, "Madam, you are not sixteen. Are you walking on your own? Can you see the sun? Be grateful for this. What else do you need?" She is an optimist and such a wise human being. She has the unique ability to convince you that every little thing in life is valuable, to teach you to enjoy it and stop thinking about your losses and your past. Of course, this helps, too. She stimulates my energy, helps me go on living.

Maya

Maya is a full-bodied, warm woman with large expressive eyes and short curly hair. She grew up with her mother, father, and brother in one of the former Soviet Republics, deep in Islamic Asia. She emigrated with her husband and daughter Daniela 7 years ago. At the present time, Maya works as a social worker in a large hospital.

When I arrived for the interview, Maya was pleasant and interested, willingly sharing personal information and her own conclusions about life in America. Bright and well read, she used sophisticated language and stressed her preference for intellectual pursuits over appearances, which she considered shallow and not worthy of a more detailed discussion. Even though she was informed about the interview topics in advance, she preferred discussing the issues she considered more important—her professional, social, and cultural life in the United States and in the former Soviet Union. While discussing body image or other body-related issues, she tended to steer the conversation to health or sports. At one point, she even made a surprised remark about my subtle ways of turning the conversation to the main topic of the interview.

Maya's Story

In America, I work the same hours—from 9 to 5, but work here is more demanding, plus you speak the foreign language. There I was able to fill out some papers while talking on the phone, I am not saying I am Julius Cesar, but the process was parallel. Speaking my native language I didn't have to search for words or to control every phrase, here it is absolutely impossible. I would also say that there is much more responsibility in your work here. The separation of work from personal life is much clearer. We used to know each other very intimately, all 20 of us. We knew each other's families, parents, children, closest friends, but here it is not so. I know my colleagues, every one of them, but there is no such closeness as we had in the [Soviet] Union, and people are not striving for it. There are a few colleagues with whom I am a little closer, but to openly tell them everything that worries me—of course, not.

My home life changed a lot—the problems are absolutely different. The need to stand in lines, to obtain foodstuffs or, let's say, furniture, has disappeared completely. Here we, rather, have an opposite problem—if you need something, you go to a store, and your head starts spinning from trying to make a choice. Every aspect of housekeeping is easier here, requires less time. But at the same time, this being spoiled creates problems, too. My mother worries all the time—nobody wants to eat whatever she cooks. I come to a store and start, "I don't want this, I don't want that. Maybe I should try this." We did not have it there. One was happy that food was obtained and cooked. We are very spoiled by the possibility to obtain practically anything and by this wide variety of choice. My colleagues, immigrants from different, not necessarily communist countries, know how it is to have a limited choice of goods or not to have something. Americans can't even imagine how it is to have shortages. People quickly get used to having it good, but probably a person should appreciate it. I know that our parents' generation appreciates it a lot, my generation—too, because we remember how it was there. Our children take it for granted, and probably it is a natural process.

My husband and I do the food shopping, and my mother does most of the cooking. She cooks to order, as she says, trying to make things we would eat. I cook on weekends to give her a break. We always cooked a lot; there were many people in the house. I used to bake great things from a thick book with hand-written recipes. Now it is collecting dust somewhere. We made preserves, all kinds of jams, pickles; it gave you pleasure to treat your guests to something of your own making, the family special. Now it lost its necessity. Of course, we cook now, too; we don't go out that often, mostly on special occasions, but not regularly. We still don't do it the American way. When I just started working, it was a standard joke—on Mondays my colleagues asked each other, "How did you spend your weekend?" Every time they asked me, I answered that I was cooking. One of my co-workers said, "It does not make sense to spend so much time on cooking." I said, "But going out is expensive." She answered, "Just do some calculations. You spend three hours to make soup, main course, and a dessert. Multiply it by your hourly rate." She used herself as an example, for her it meant spending $300 on cooking, she considered it wrong. It did not even occur to me at that time to think this way. I was not making $100 an hour then, by the way, I am not making it now, either, but from this point of view, it makes sense to order food in or to eat out. On the other hand, we are used to home cooking; when we have guests, we also cook. Besides, the generation of my mother practically does not eat out. They do not eat Chinese food, Japanese or Italian food; as a result, it is better to cook what people are used to rather than to disappoint them. However, the desire and the need for food the way it was in the [Soviet] Union is gradually declining. I see it clearly in my family. We cook much less than we used to there, and the desire for it wanes. Cooking gets moved to the back burner, probably due to the availability of all the foodstuffs. Home cooking became less important and lost its primacy.

We had a very large family, lots of friends and relatives; on celebrations we used to spread the table for 50-60 people. To cook for such numbers, to serve and to clean afterwards is very difficult. But it gave us pleasure, because everybody you loved and wanted to see and talk to would come. And here I don't have such a number of friends and relatives, our circle has shrunk drastically, this is another dramatic change—in social contact. We were very close with seven other families of approximately the same age; they all lived nearby. Everybody cooked very well, and everybody had his own special dishes. So when we were getting together, it was not at all difficult to cook one or two things. We used to call each other, "What can I do to help?" "Make this and this, I'll deliver the groceries." Every couple would bring their special dish known and loved by everybody, it was so satisfying, and the exchange of recipes, how funny it sounds now. The food itself was not the purpose of this dinner; the real point was personal contact, but in addition to it, hedonistic elements. There were gourmands among us, and others did not care for what we were eating, just to get together and to have fun, but it was more interesting.

One can clearly see the difference in attitudes toward food; our tastes have changed, too. Who had ever heard there about cholesterol, saturated fats, or free radicals? These problems did not occur to us. People here pay much more attention to their health and nutrition, and this information is in the air. It is in the press, on TV, everywhere. I can see how other people pay attention to it and how significant it is. So in theory, I am informed, but practically I do not pay enough attention to my health. Because of my occupation, I sit all day long. I know for sure that I should be more physically active and limit my food consumption. Changes in our lifestyle are manifested in more caloric, more flavorful, and more readily available nutrition. We are trying to eat healthier food; for example, we don't fry things as much as we used before. Still, all these extra pounds that we gained are visible on us. With time, metabolism slows down, and all extra calories get stored in the body. I gained about 25-30 pounds since our arrival seven years ago. I have hormonal imbalance and a very slow metabolism, and it gets worse with age. In order to keep myself in my former shape or at least not to gain weight now, I have to take better care of myself. Luckily, there are several people in my office who take very good care of their health, attend special programs, and thanks to them I am well informed about the types of human body structure, hormonal system, what one should and shouldn't eat. Most of these people are Americans. I cannot follow their system completely. First of all, it is very expensive; then one has to attend the program regularly, every week, and spend half a day there. They have leaders, discussion groups, support groups, so financially and time-wise it is rather difficult to follow.

I have some back problem, so once a week I attend an exercise group. I know that I have to do it at least three times a week. From time to time, I go to the gym. I am a member. It happens so rarely that it makes no sense even mentioning it. I used to go rather often, once in two weeks, not more, but during the summer this schedule somehow was neglected. I used to spend an hour working out on the machines, with very easy programs because I am not that fit, and then the pool, sauna, changing, altogether it takes more than two hours.

In my student years, I was in track and field and basketball teams. Later, my close friends and I used to train and play twice a week. It was good for our health and a way to socialize. I miss these games now, but my own laziness and lack of organization skills prevent me from doing it here. I cannot even say that the distance is the reason; there it was rather far, too. We were more mobile, even though we can drive here. Maybe it is because of a bigger intensity of our lifestyle, not physical, mental. When I come home from work, I don't feel like moving a finger or saying a word.

Of course, it is very unpleasant to have gained so much weight. First of all, I feel physically heavy. My physician was half-joking when he said, "Don't come for the next checkup until you lose some weight."

He was right, I see that purely medical problems started appearing—my veins are bulging, I gasp for breath. I am not even talking about such aspects as satisfaction with my looks. Here a lot of attention is paid to the person's appearance; the ideal of beauty is a slim body. I have never been especially thin, even in my student years, just a normal body. I was always more oriented toward being interesting for other people or if these people are interesting for me, how much this person fulfills my intellectual needs. Yes, of course, it is pleasant when you see beautiful people close by and when you look beautiful, but for me the inner content of a person is more important than the looks.

Here the attitude toward age categories is absolutely different. When I came here, I was 34. I had worked already for a sufficient number of years after the university; I was a professional of a certain level. I considered myself a middle-aged woman, absolutely honestly. When I sad so in my English class; everybody was shocked. I still remember these astonished looks, because for Americans middle age starts after fifty. The time frames are so disparate between two cultures. Here people try, as much as possible, to prevent illnesses, and weight gain is also considered a health hazard. And the older American women get, the more attention they pay to their appearance. In the [Soviet] Union, a woman after certain age would not take much care of herself. And not only because housekeeping responsibilities left no free time, it was not a custom.

From a very young age, I liked athletic women, and since we ourselves were involved in sports, we liked and kept company with those people who were athletic, and it was what we were used to seeing. I think that subconsciously we are attracted to those aspects that are connected with health, as I understand it now. We find features that symbolize health to be the most attractive. An athletic body probably corresponds to these rules. I did not have an ideal I wanted to follow in appearance. If there was one, I don't remember it; probably I was not focused on it. Of course, I wanted to be generally beautiful, attractive, interesting, and so on, but because of my personality, I am analytically inclined, as a rule people feel attraction for the opposing qualities. I can't say that I always wanted to be a blue-eyed blonde, but I wanted to look better groomed, more elegant. I was afraid to be like a little gray mouse—unnoticed. Actually I never was in danger—I am a sufficiently large and colorful lady, but I remember it well, in my school days, we had several girls in our class who were not noticeable, even though they had good personalities. Maybe their unappealing looks influenced their behavior, or their self-esteem.

In the American school system, low self-esteem is considered emotionally bad. I was so shocked when we just arrived—every year children, starting from a very young school age, are moved from one class to another. We used to graduate practically with the same group of students we started with in the first grade. This system fosters close contacts. I remember I discussed this, as my English allowed it, with my daughter's school principal. He explained that this is done on purpose—to help students develop their own system of self-adaptation and to boost their self-esteem. American society is focused on individuality, not *we*, but *I*, as it differs from the former [Soviet] Union. I remember, "We, the collective of the 9-B class decided to collect and deliver this much scrap paper for the national economy..." Here, nobody needs this, and personal opinion is to be developed on any issue. They don't need to fit in like we did, even though Americans value the ability to be a team player very highly. Nevertheless, individual differences are valued and cherished.

I was growing very fast, maybe because I played basketball. By the fourth grade I was the same height as I am now. I felt a little uncomfortable, but, luckily, I was not the tallest in my class. My weight was normal; I was not very plump, not skinny, nor fat. We had fat girls in class, some were very fat; luckily for them, we had a very united class, so there was no teasing among us. I had practical problems when my breasts started growing. My friend and I were unable to find fitting bras. Only this, I never had feelings of shame or discomfort. I was developing in accordance with age norms; so problems of puberty and sexual maturation did not especially concern me. Not that they did not attract my attention, but I passed this period very calmly. I had a friend who kept worrying when she would get her menstrual period. I did not have such worries. We had a great anatomy teacher—she managed to create such a good relationship with the class and to explain things to us in such a way that we had none of half-dirty, half-scientific discussions.

My cousin of the same age was in a different school, and they had swimming classes. She always worried that she had to wear a bathing suit in front of the whole class. We had regular gym classes, and this was much easier for us. They paid more attention to appearances in my cousin's class. Neither in her family, nor in mine it was customary to pay much attention to one's looks; our intellectual development was much more stressed. My classmate's mother wanted to dress her better than others and to make her stick out. The girl would tell her mom, "Stop it, everybody is like this, and I want to be the same way." This is dramatically different from how it is here—brand names, makeup and clothes. Commercials, everything is based exclusively on attractiveness, and teenagers are focused on appearances. In the [Soviet] Union, we had it, too, maybe the choice was not so wide, but we had Chanel, Yves de Saint Laurent. There was no such need to assert myself exclusively on my appearance. Probably we asserted ourselves by other means—we had other interests, purely intellectual needs were more stressed. Maybe it was a compensation for the lack of material goods, but our generation had less pressure about looking good than our children have now. I was lucky in this way in my development—I never had any special complexes about my body, my looks, now I do have them, but not in my youth.

Now I am so overweight that I feel it too well, not only by the looks, but I pay more attention to it as a health issue. On the outside, I would like to be slimmer, younger, more attractive. But I understand that I do too little for it. From the medical point of view, I understand that I have to do something to avoid getting more problems.

My mother takes my weight gain to heart; it saddens her. We have open discussions about it. My mother attends the pool, she was a sportswoman in her youth, and she returned to sports here. I am very glad that she found her circle of social contact. She goes swimming, takes gym classes, so since she has more free time, she leads a more open lifestyle, and I am very happy about it because she is a very sociable person, and it would have been very hard for her to stay alone at home. She is more careful in her food choices than she was time ago. It came with age, with doctors' advice; also there are things on our tables that we never had before, like broccoli.

My mother's mother was a very energetic and sociable woman. She was a Distinguished Teacher of our Republic. Her students loved her, her colleagues respected her; a lot of people came to her for advice. She always had good relationships with people and maintained them for dozens of years. I was an adult already when I used to go to Moscow and Leningrad during my student years, and then on business, and I would often meet my grandmother's friends who remembered me from the age of two or three. She had a very big influence on me. My grandparents loved to travel and did it rather often. I remember going with them to visit some relatives in Odessa, to the Baltic republics, to Moscow. They had the means and the desire to do it. Not just to stuff grandchildren with food and to wipe their noses, but to take them along on trips and to show them interesting places.

As I realize it now, my grandmother was a real woman. She always managed to look good, very unnoticeably she took care of her appearance. She always chose her clothes carefully, and she looked good with very modest expenditures. There was the revolution, then the 30s, Stalin's dark years, then the War, three little kids, so with minimal financial resources she always managed to look good because she always was in the spotlight, making speeches, so she considered it important how she looked. She was small, very trim, until her last days she used to joke that she had a front of a retired person and a back of a girl scout. She always stressed that she never did anything special for weight control; she never followed a diet or limited herself in any way. Until a rather advanced age she used to attend a health group at the city stadium. Now it is cute to recall, old ladies exercised in the fresh air. In the Soviet Union, the retirement age was 55. She retired much later, but at 55 a woman was considered old.

My grandmother suffered from glaucoma, and when Daniela was born, she was practically blind. Daniela remembers that she knew an absolutely unbelievable number of poems by heart and she used to recite them to her since she was unable to read to her. When Daniela was a baby, my grandmother used to sit at her crib in case the baby would start squirming, so she would call somebody, and so on. My mother was still working, but she used to help me very much. I stayed at home with Daniela until she turned two. She had a lot of medical problems when she was born, so I could not send her to a pre-kindergarten when she was three or four month old. By the age of two she could speak, dress herself, so there was no problem sending her to the kindergarten. If she got sick, my mother would always come. If I needed to leave her to go somewhere or to lecture after work, she would babysit. When my mother went to other cities to visit friends, she took Daniela along. I remember she used to take her to the theater many times. In general, she took a rather active role in her upbringing. It is different now. My mother came to this country two years after us, and Daniela has grown out of the habit of contact with her. Sometimes in emigrant families the grandmother would arrive later, and she and her grandchildren don't understand each other anymore. To some degree it did happen to us, there is a cultural and language discrepancy between them. Daniela was nine when we came, since then her language development continued in English. She speaks a rather acceptable Russian, but she has formed most abstract concepts in English. Maybe her Russian is developing, but it is lower than her biological age. Very often it happens that if Daniela is in a hurry or talks about something emotionally involving or stressful, she would quickly turn to English. Her English will be going its course, and at home we are trying to speak Russian because I don't want her to lose the language and culture. I have a co-worker whose grandparents came from Russia as young people. She does not know a single Russian word.

I never had special expectations about how Daniela would look, and as it often happens with parents of teenage girls, she has grown up so unexpectedly quickly. When the child is little, there are sicknesses, problems every day. Then, all of a sudden I look at her and theoretically I understand that she is my child, but it is an absolutely independent grown up person with her own point of view on probably 99.9% of issues. She has her own ideas and it often happens that she knows and understands things here much better than we do, which probably is a foundation of human progress. The next generation should know more than the previous one. I think that she could have a better use for all the time she spends in front of the mirror, like she could have read something, but, probably, it is a sin to complain. The kid worked very hard and achieved a lot in school. I do not have any special concerns about her looks, but I know she does. I think that she looks rather normal for her age. She knows her weight, the ratio of height and weight, she watches all the medical variables, not only because of her looks—she took Health Science last year. It will be useful in her life. I had good use of my theoretical knowledge of physiology, anatomy, and child development. I believe that no knowledge is unnecessary, and natural sciences are useful in everyday life. They give you a clearer picture of what, how, and why things happen to you.

Daniela

Daniela, a tall, very attractive girl of 16 with chiseled features of an elongated face and marble-white skin, was a charming and pleasant participant. Her curly knee-long fair hair was part loose and part braided and set in an elaborate arrangement above her high forehead. Tall and slim, she wore well-fitting fashionable clothes, tasteful makeup and a few pieces of gold jewelry. Daniela seemed open to my questions and willing to share her experience, but her manner suggested agitation and tension. Daniela's voice was high-pitched and her speech production was so rapid that I had difficulty understanding her. When I asked her to speak slowly, she apologized and mentioned "tons of homework," but returned to the same pattern the next moment.

Daniela's Story

My eating habits are pretty bad. Now I am trying to improve them, but I get, like, cravings for sweets, so I go and eat, like, a doughnut at night, but I don't really gain weight. I guess my metabolism pretty much works with it, but I could eat better. I don't eat much healthy food or anything. In the morning, I have tea with doughnuts; it is really a fast breakfast. I am not used to this schedule. I have to get up at 5 a.m. to get to school on time at 7 a.m. The last term I had to be at school by 10:50 and in the summer, I used to get up at 11 a.m. every day. Most of the time, I just eat a sandwich and tea or juice. I eat school lunch, like deli sandwiches, and juice and salad, and when I get home, we eat dinner, like a pretty big dinner. Today we had chicken and fish and salad, and that's it. I try not to eat after 8 p.m. When we go out, me and my friends, at night, like to a diner, I just get a fruit salad or something. Oh, and I love steamed lamb dumplings and shish-kebab. I like barbecue a lot; pizza is OK. I'd eat pretty much everything, but I am not big on food.

I am big on shopping. I can spend a day shopping for clothes and stuff. My mom says it's not so good. My mom is overweight; she could definitely improve her body. Two years ago she lost a lot of weight. When she comes home, she mostly sits at the computer and plays games when she can go to the gym. I understand that she is tired after work and stuff, but she can stand to do something for herself. I don't go to the gym myself, so I have no right to complain about her. We are pretty close, we talk a lot with her, about clothes, boys, other things. I don't like it when she gives me compliments, like, "Shut up, Daniela, you have a good body." If we are trying clothes and I don't like how something looks, I am not going to buy it, but she keeps telling me to take it because she likes it. Not everything looks right on me.

My mom thinks I have a pretty good body. And my father thinks I am the best, probably because I am the only girl and the only child, period. But he gets very annoying sometimes. He comes home, "Daniela, go to eat," as if I cannot figure it out myself. I guess he is pretty worried about me, very attached. I understand it when I sit down and think about it, but on the spur of the moment he gets me *so* annoyed. I yell at him sometimes. Then I get over it. My mom says this is because we have very similar tempers, so we don't get along. I see it, too, and it scares me. I don't like how he is—always, like, thinking about what I am doing. I don't want to be this way when I grow up. My grandma always gets upset when we fight.

My grandma, she likes to talk, but when I come home from school, I am very tired. When I am tired, I don't want to be bothered, so I go to my room and finish my homework, and then I can talk. But she is always, like, "How are you, how was your day?" So sometimes when I had a bad day, I take it out on her, and then I feel bad when I think about it, but I cannot do much about it when she wants to talk. We have a lot of good times, too, she is very easy to talk to, she understands more than my parents, maybe because she is a grandmother and she is used to raising families. She asks me about boys a lot. Me and my mom go shopping with her, we help her buy clothes when she needs something. She takes my opinion as a rule a lot of times. If I like something, she'll buy it. She appreciates me, I guess. And I am sure she has a lot of influence on me. She was a Russian teacher, so she taught me a lot of Russian grammar. When I was younger, I did not want to learn anything Russian, but now, sometimes I take a Russian book and read on my own, because I know that I am losing this language. At times, she calms me down because I have a very hot temper. She has an influence on the whole family. She cooks, and I learn from her sometimes. She teaches me little things, like to put salt in the water so macaroni won't stick together. You don't even notice them, but she does. She taught me how to cook, to sew, things like this. I don't think you appreciate it until you put it to use. Like, I don't cook, probably because she cooks for us, so I don't have to. I am sure if I was alone, I would. When I am home alone or with my father and there is nothing to eat, I make myself macaroni or something. Not many men I know can cook. Most of them make sandwiches, like my father. I don't mind; I like cold cuts.

I was kind of expecting my body change because my closest friend, she got her period earlier than me, not a lot, like a year, maybe, so I was kind of expecting it. I knew what to expect because my mother talked to me, and we had Health classes. I think I started developing even before I got my period. I was kind of anxious because I saw all the older girls and stuff, and you want to look like them. I guess I am open to gaining weight because my mother is not the skinniest person. I guess I accept myself for what I am, like if I will gain weight, I gain weight, there is nothing I can do about it, but trying to work out more, eat healthier. Honestly speaking, I am not really doing anything for it, not yet. Last year I had a very late schedule in school, plus my bad organization skills. I did not have the time to do my homework and to exercise. This year, I will try to go to the gym. Right now I am on a volleyball team; it is the season now. I like sports; I am pretty athletic. I took karate when I was younger, like three years ago. I swim a lot, that's about it. Since I am not doing much to improve it, I can say that I am satisfied with my body, but it could be better when you look, like, at models and stuff. I can stand to tighten up in some places, lose a few pounds. Compared to magazine pictures, I look fat, but among other girls I am fine.

I think that media shouldn't be so focused on this one stereotype of the body, because people have all kinds of genes. The media, like, drill into children's heads, "This is the way one should be," this kind of pressure. Maybe it is just not in your bone structure. Like my best friend Vickie, she is Russian. She is not fat, but she got big bones. She is short and very wide, and it makes her upset. We go shopping a lot together, it's like our quality time, we talk about clothes, guys, I guess, too. We don't really go to museums or anything. In the summer, we went even to the city, to, like, some museum, art collection, and that's about it. Vickie is constantly on a diet; she has very high self-control. I can't be like this. If I am hungry, I can't just sit there and not eat. But Vickie can eat an apple for the whole day. If she wants to lose weight, she really does, and she always complains. Everyone complains about their bodies. Not everyone, but most people. When they see girls with better bodies, maybe this is why they complain. I know Vickie likes support and sympathy, like when she says, "I am fat," I am like, "Yeah,

Vickie, do not worry, Vickie, you are not fat, you are skinny." She likes that. It boosts her self-esteem.

In junior high school, I had mostly American friends, and in high school, two years ago I started mingling with the Russians; and most of my friends are Russians. I still have a lot of mixed racial people, different nationalities, but most friends outside the school, if I am hanging out, are mostly Russian. I have more preference toward Russian boys, too, because I know my parents would approve of them more. I have a lot of guy friends and they always come over, one of my best friends is a guy, and he is Russian. We speak English all the time, sticking a Russian word in once in a while. My parents can talk to him, my mom loves him, he is a very nice boy, and his mom likes me, we are both Russian. For me it is all the same, but it is family stuff, I mean it is much better for the family.

THE KAPLANS

The Kaplan family consists of Marlena, age 40, her husband, and her daughter Dina, age 16. They live in their own house in Westchester County, New York. Marlena's mother, Gita, age 72, lives in the Bronx, N.Y. Marlena came to the USA 7 years ago, from a middle-sized town in Byelorus. Gita came 2 years later with Marlena's brother.

Marlena's family lives in an elegant spacious suburban home with a large swimming pool. Sparse modern furniture and profusion of exotic plants give the house an attractive, airy look. Dina has her own room with a TV set and a computer.

Gita was interviewed in her small one-bedroom apartment in an older walk-up building. She shares this apartment with her bachelor son. Marlena and Dina were interviewed in Marlena's house, in the guestroom.

Gita

Gita is a somewhat round, energetic, and warm woman of 72 with short gray hair and a ready smile on deeply wrinkled face. For the interview, she wore an inexpensive, well-fitting cotton dress and had no makeup on. Gita was glad to accommodate Greta's request to be interviewed in her apartment and used the occasion to create a pleasant social event. When Gita's friends Greta and Julia led me to Gita's apartment, a delectable aroma accompanied her warm welcome. A large tray of fragrant just-baked cabbage and potato *pirozhki* (small pies), orange juice, and Manishewitz wine in crystal goblets were ready on the table. When Greta saw the spread, she admiringly praised Gita's generous heart and her desire to greet people with food of her own making. Gita made an attempt of downplaying this compliment, insisting that cooking is a quick, pleasurable activity for her. Her green eyes were beaming with joy and pride behind plain horn-rimmed glasses. Then she described the delicacies she prepared for the lunch she planned to serve after the interviews. Gita's friend Julia, a strikingly attractive woman and a highly accomplished professional in the former Soviet Union, looked uncomfortable. With no apparent reason, she started explaining her own minimal cooking and baking by the summer heat and by the limited space in her studio apartment. After the interviews, Gita ran to the kitchen, opened the refrigerator and took out several pots and containers. I reminded her that the original plan was that I take her and her friends out for lunch. Gita gave me an uncertain look and said, "But it is so expensive, and I have food at home." It took me some convincing to get them going, but when we finally made it to the open-air café, they visibly enjoyed the treat.

During the interview, Gita was cooperative, but brief. She spoke with a concise manner of a person, not used to talking about herself. She looked more comfortable showing me pictures of her children and grandchildren and talking about them or sharing her recipes. Her tone was matter-of-fact when she was describing hardships and struggles of her life. I learned about Gita's sense of humor and other admirable characteristics from Greta who was more descriptive and verbal in general and appreciative of Gita's friendship.

Gita's Story

My husband and I got divorced in the Soviet Union; I was forty-seven then. Children, of course, were supportive of me. My daughter went to America with her husband. My son and I came three years later. My other son is still there; his family did not want to go. I also have a granddaughter there; she is eighteen already.

Here we came to my daughter, and my granddaughter said, "Grandma, you know, here in America people don't live with their parents. So when we move to a new apartment or buy a house we will live separately from you." In the beginning, I got upset and said, "How can it be, I came here and I thought that I would live with my daughter." My daughter is my special child. We lived together with Marlena for two months. Then they moved to another apartment, and then, when they got a bit richer, they bought a house. I was very upset that they moved to a different city in Westchester County. Then I got used to it. Now, I visit her whenever I want. If I cannot take a train on my own, I meet my daughter in the city, and we take the train together. My son-in-law meets us with the car at the station. When it is very hot here, I stay with them; they have a pool in the backyard, and I stay in the pool all day long, I go swimming five to six times a day. My son-in-law jokes, "My mother-in-law has probably grown gills." I have a very good daughter. She calls me every day. She always says, "Mama, don't worry, G-d forbid, if the need comes, there is always room for you in my house." So far, I don't need it. It is better to live separately.

My granddaughter is such a lovely child. I ask her, "My love, may I bring you something to eat?" And she says, "Grandma, I am a big girl already, have you forgotten? I am sixteen." When she came, she had long curly hair, and she was very upset by it, and then when she was fourteen she had her hair straightened, and now she does it herself. She is very slender. I am happy about it because I am not so thin, and my daughter is of normal size. She is not plump and not slim, in the middle. I like it this way.

I did not gain weight in America. I am in the same shape as I came five years ago; I can wear the same dresses. I am not limiting myself—I eat whatever I want. I don't eat fried food, of course, because I have an ulcer, so I am careful and eat more stewed food and vegetables. I try to limit myself, but I still eat a lot of fatty food. I like coffee, but drink it once a day because I have high blood pressure. If I were allowed, I would drink more. I am better off here, and I like it. There is such a diversity of foods, and vegetables and everything else, and I can afford it all, and there we had nothing in the store except three or four basic staples, like potatoes, lard, and sugar. It was considered happiness if we could obtain something edible there, especially during the times before our emigration. There was no meat in stores at all.

It was painful in the beginning, but I am happy now. I found myself here. In the Jewish center I regularly go to the swimming pool, I love swimming. We attend a literary club, it is very interesting; we enjoy each other's company, meet interesting people who visit our center. The coordinator of the club is a very pleasant woman; she has a G-d sent talent.

I live with my son now; he is a bachelor. In Russia, he was kind of unfocused, but when I was getting ready for the emigration, I did not want to exert pressure on him, I kept telling him, "You have to decide on your own, you are an adult, I don't want you to blame me if things go wrong." He decided to go on his own, so he has no grudges against me. He keeps to himself. Now he kind of got used to things, he likes everything here, and he said it to me. He and his brother look so much alike, they have only a year difference in age. He works very hard, both of them work very hard, but this one can afford good things for himself, like better nutrition, an apartment. Of course, he did not become rich or buy a house, but he is OK now. If he finds his other half, then life would be easier for him.

Before I retired, I never participated in any organized sport. In the Soviet Union, with three kids, and housekeeping, and a vegetable garden, it was inconceivable. I had to work constantly, at work and at home. My family consisted of an elderly mother and three children, two boys and a girl, so there was plenty of washing to do. I had some ducks, some chickens, and a piglet. All my time was spent on this. Of course, I tried to read a little, to go to the movies, in the summer I used to go to a river nearby. I loved swimming from my childhood. When I retired, I started attending a health group twice a week. Here I also attend a gymnastics class in the center twice a week. I exercise constantly.

I had a large family, six people. We were not too comfortable financially, even though my husband had a good position at the Department of Health, so I had to cook. Nobody wanted to buy ready-made stuff there; it was so bad, so I had to cook all the time. My mother, too, cooked very tasty food, and, of course, while she was alive, I cooked less. It is in our genes. My sister lives in Israel, and she is also a great cook. I was watching my mother cook, and now I do it myself.

I cooked there, and I cook here, I love cooking very much. It is my hobby. Even here when I don't need to, because my son and I don't need that much, I still love it. I love guests. I love making all kinds of pies. Today, I got up a little earlier and made these pies with cabbage filling. I have meatballs and other stuff for lunch. When my daughter turned forty, we had a party, and I cooked a lot of Russian food. Everybody praised my cooking. I do it very quickly. It took me twenty-four hours to cook a full spread for thirty people, almost all by myself. I made a special dish out of thin dough. I rolled it out, spread the stuffing made of veal, beef, and chicken with all kinds of spices. I rolled it up, cut into pieces, fried them a little, then stewed them a little. It was very tasty. Blintzes, too; my son-in-law has a friend who loves my blintzes so much. My family loves them stuffed with minced chicken, or with apples, or with anything I make. I made great Georgian style chicken, too. I cooked a chicken, strained the stock to make sauce. I boiled it with breadcrumbs, lemon juice, and a little salt. Then, when it cooled down, I added a cup of ground walnuts and a chopped garlic bulb. I poured the sauce over the chicken and kept it in the refrigerator overnight; it was full of flavor. I also baked a lot of delicious rose-shaped pastries out of sweet dough. My granddaughter always helps me. She says, "Grandma, I don't like to cook, but I love making dessert." So to attract her I ask her to beat egg yolks, add egg whites, and make the dough. We roll out the dough, spread the filling evenly, and cut it into pieces. Then put we them the cut side up into a hot oven.

Dina lived mostly with me in Russia. She used to get sick often, so they used to drop her off at my house. Dina was a very quiet child. She lived with me for two years. She was a straight A student, the best in her class. And here she is getting a little lazy, but nevertheless she is a good girl. She was always very open with me, there and here, about who she likes, who she doesn't like, she tells me about the boy she is dating, shows me the photographs. She doesn't understand how it is not to tell her grandmother. We are so close. Not with my other granddaughter, because I was not taking care of her when she was growing up, the other grandmother did. When I call, she says, "Grandma, I miss you." I have not seen her for five years; of course I want to see her very much. Dina is always trying to do things the way I taught her. She always cleans her room and her bathroom. She is kind, bright, she knows how to use computers; she is a good girl in general. Dina is the only child. I wanted them to have more. Marlena was contemplating it for a long while, but then she said, "It is too late, she is sixteen already, and I am forty."

My other son, who lives in Russia, came to visit with his wife. He liked everything here, of course, but his wife's family, her mother, they don't want to come here. They have their roots there, everything. I don't want to push them, but they are brothers, they miss each other so much. When one calls, the other one is happy, both of them are happy. When he was here, the other one took time off work, went with them everywhere, showed them everything, he gave them so much attention. Just the fate is such that one is here and the other one is there.

When my mother died, she was ninety-two. She lived with me all the time. When I got married, my father died, I could not leave her to live alone. She was a very calm person, never meddled in our business. She helped me a lot when my children were little. She always stayed with my children, cooked. Later on, the boys took care of the coal stove, and my daughter cleaned the house. I did the laundry, and when my husband lived with us, he helped me on the plot, with vegetables. Here, my daughter cooks, but very little. She has no time for a lot of cooking. She comes home at 7:30, so she is tired and has no strength to do it. She usually fries something, makes something quickly, and that's it, all their meal. On weekends, naturally, she makes some soup, borscht, something else they like. She has a washing machine, not like we used to do it, by hand. They have a big house, a lot of cleaning for her. They constantly rake the leaves and clean the pool; in general, they have a lot of work.

They don't have the time for sports. Dina does some in school. She told me about her team, she even gave me the photograph. In Russia, she took ballroom dancing for a year; she liked it a lot and did very well in class. I used to take her to the town cultural club for classes. Marlena lived far away. When Dina's partner moved to another town, she switched to the modern dance group; one did not need a partner for it. She swims very well; I used to take her swimming very often. And here, she is in some kind of group; it is like dancing and gymnastics to the music. And now she is very much into drawing and painting, she says it is her hobby. She makes such beautiful pictures, like this one. I love it because she made it with her little hands.

Marlena

Marlena, age forty, grew up in a middle-size town in Belarus with her mother, father, grandmother, and two brothers. Her father, a mid-level party bureaucrat, named her after Marx and Lenin. She emigrated with her husband and daughter Dina 7 years ago. Marlena works full time as an accountant for a large company.

Marlena, a strikingly attractive woman with classical features, looked like a marble Greek sculpture enlivened by a radiant smile and sparkling cat-green eyes. Her soft blue jeans and powder blue knit sweater gave her a cozy, relaxed look. Generally warm and pleasant, she looked uncomfortable answering my questions about her appearance. Contemplating the reasons for these feelings, she concluded that Russian women, as a group, tend to undervalue themselves and have never learned to take care of their needs the way American women do. Even though I never asked Marlena about her move to Westchester, she initiated the conversation about it and sounded compelled to justify this decision. While musing on the subject, Marlena had an air of guilt and doubt about her.

Marlena's Story

Honestly speaking, we did not suffer from anti-Semitism. Of course, it existed, but we were used to it. We did not know anything else. Besides, my father was Russian, so I am a mixed breed. We did not plan to emigrate, but my husband's parents left for America several years ago, and then there was Chernobyl. We wanted to go to a safe place. From the letters we were getting, I knew that our life would not be easy. Like every emigration, mine was difficult, but everybody had his own bag. If anybody says about his emigration, "Everything was easy and wonderful," I will not believe this person. We had difficulties of all kinds—financial, psychological, in relationships between the children and the parents, between husband and wife. Of course, the most difficult part is the language; we still have language problems, and we will have them for the rest of our lives. Even now, after seven years, I feel unsure of myself, not comfortable. At times I catch myself thinking that I am kind of guest here, I am not at home. We will never be like Americans; we always sense the chasm we cannot cross because of the language. There you were sure that you expressed yourself correctly, that you were understood correctly, that you knew how to go about things. Here, one is fighting all the time, there is no relaxing, no full comfort; you are in constant tension.

I am luckier with my job here. There, I even developed a complex that something was wrong with my head that I had to change a lot of jobs for different reasons. Here I feel respected and appreciated, even though they had their measure of trouble with me, especially in the beginning. Now my husband and I have very good jobs, but we are still uncomfortable because of communication problems with Americans. If

Dina marries an American, I am afraid that we will have no communication with him and his parents. It will be, "Hello, good-bye, how are you doing? How is work?" but never a close relationship. This is why I hope that she finds some Russian immigrant and marries him. We have no American friends; at work I am on great terms with everybody, but there is no closeness, and the same with my neighbors. If Dina had some problems in school, I would go there for sure, but since she is fine, I don't feel like forcing myself to communicate there.

Financially, of course, it is much easier for us. We learned how to work like Americans, but we never learned how to relax. We don't know how to do it. Here people live differently—they think more about themselves, do what they want. Not in a bad way, but they live the way they want and think less about others and what they think about them. My daughter is not like this already, even though she has many complexes, I know. We brought such a load of them with us, and the strongest one is that we undervalue ourselves. No matter how many times people tell me, "You are smart, you are, let's say, beautiful, you are this, and this," anyway, at the bottom of my heart I don't believe them completely because I perceive myself totally differently. I believe them, but inside I hide a feeling of not valuing myself, and my husband is the same way.

I agree that I am attractive, let's say I am not ugly, but in my head, something tells me, "Look at others, there are women who are much better looking than you, both face and body." I know I brought it from Russia. Let's say people tell me, "You have a beautiful silhouette," and I want it to be different, I like a different one, thinner, slimmer, taller. Dina is even shorter than I, and I worry about it a lot, I want her to be taller than me. Besides, she has complexes about her hair. It is very curly and very thick. When we came here, she had it straightened in a salon. I feel bad to use chemicals on her hair, so now she does it herself. She looks very good with her beautiful curly hair, but she has this complex, she likes only straight hair, and she wanted to have straight hair so much. Maybe it is the desire to have what she does not have. And I want to be thinner, like I used to be.

When I gave birth to Dina, I gained a tremendous amount of weight, about 60 pounds, during my pregnancy. When I gave birth, my husband expected me to lose them all, right after leaving the hospital. He was surprised when I kept it on. A year later, I lost some weight, but I never returned to the shape I had before the pregnancy. Usually I lose weight when I am nervous, I cannot eat at all. Here I lost weight when I started working. I was a nervous wreck when I started my first job. When everything settled down, I gained more than 20 pounds. Now I want to lose weight, but I have lots of laziness and little time. My body is not managing, there I could lose weight by not eating one day a week, and now it is very difficult. There, everybody tried not to eat on Fridays or not to eat on Mondays, we only drank water, and here diets are not bad. My friends lost weight on a good American diet, but for that one you have to cook special dishes, it is more complicated than just not eating one day a week. She found it when her husband became ill. When you need to lose weight for medical reasons, it is a different thing. When it is connected with the desire to look better, it is a matter of priorities. I have no time to cook separately for my family and myself, because they would not eat the dishes from that diet. When I was pregnant and fat, it was terribly uncomfortable, I could not bend to tie my shoe or climb the stairs. If I were that fat, I would probably go on a diet or do a starvation routine again.

I stopped eating late at night like I used to. I know that I should exercise, but I don't. I take walks with Dina once in a while, but this is it. The only thing I do—I swim a lot in the summer. I love swimming and I naturally feel much better when I swim. In Russia I played volleyball, when I was Dina's age, I played soccer, ice hockey in the winter, skated, lots of things. And here I don't have the time for it. When we stopped participating in sports, we danced a lot. We had a lot of friends, lots of parties, once a week, twice a week, whatever we could arrange; we had parties. And here we dance less—the same parties, but no dancing. We eat, drink, sing songs to my husband's accompaniment, and that's it.

At parties, we serve homemade food; I make salads, grilled meat. I can cook well, but I don't like it. If I had a choice, I would like to do other things instead. I feel very good when my mother and my mother-in-law come to the kitchen, I readily give up the reigns and eat with pleasure whatever they cook. They make traditional dishes, especially out of dough—blintzes, filled rolls, cakes. Dina loves them, and my husband does, too. He loves everything, he is not picky; it is easy with him in this respect. Since I mentioned my mother's cooking, I have to say that she is overweight. She should lose some weight; she understands it, too. On the other hand, she is not that fat for her age and in comparison to some Americans. There are many grossly fat people here; it is a disaster. I used to think that in America everybody is thin, but now I see it differently. Probably it is not the food; it is some kind of chemicals in it. I have friends, who are thinner than I, and some are much heavier, but none of them is so huge that she has difficulty walking. I am in the middle—size 6-8, and I would like to be size 3-4.

I like thin women; I liked them in Russia, too. I have never been fat, but kind of curvy. I probably have small bones, so when I am dressed, I look thin, but when I undress, I see plump areas that should be removed. When I watch TV with all these actresses and models, I think about it. They have a wonderful show, I don't know if it is really wonderful for others, but I like it—*Sex and the City*. All the women in it are thin, and I like Sarah Jessica Parker. I would love to be like her, maybe a bit fuller, I think she is about my height. In magazines, too, all models are thin, at times maybe too much, but I think there is no such a thing as too thin. There are some, but these are sick people.

Dina is normal now, but she is short, and every ounce she gains will be visible on her. I know it because I had to go through the same thing and I am living with it now. We, shorties, have to be extra careful. I worry about it, because I want her to be happy, and she understands it, too. I don't think she needs to watch her diet so far, just to limit her eating French fries or chips, this kind of food. Now she does cheerleading, so she exercises, and she did a lot of swimming in the summer. One day, at dinner, she said, "I have to unbutton a little, I think I gained weight." I answered, "Let's walk together." We walked for half an hour last week, and that was the end of our walking. She was busy, I did not feel well and wanted to lie down, the same laziness. Excuses. I respect women who can force themselves to exercise, like brush their teeth—run, walk; go to a gym—whatever it takes. I cannot organize myself this way—I am lazy.

My grandmother was very thin; she did manual work all her life. I remember her constantly working on the vegetable plot; besides, she cooked dinners and everything else. This is why she and my mother did not need any sports. My grandmother lived with us all the time, so she took care of us, kids. Of course, she stuffed us with food like all grandmothers, how else could it be? She had this passion—to feed. She adored my husband because he liked to eat, she loved those who ate well, probably because she was a great cook, and like every cook, she wanted people to appreciate her creations. At times, Dina tells me that I do it, too, not to her, but to her friends. What kind of contact can I have with her American friends? We have nothing in common, and I have nothing to talk to them about, so the only thing I can ask them, is "Do you want to eat?" Dina tells me, "Mom, why do you keep asking them the same thing? They don't want to eat, leave them alone." This is my way to make contact. My mother is doing it, and my grandmother, and I do the same, even though I understand it is ridiculous. I did not like it when my friends were pulled to the table and almost forced to eat, and now I am doing the same thing. Maybe I will be the same kind of grandmother, but I hope I won't, I am changing. When we just arrived, I still had this idea that children have to be fed. G-d forbid if the child goes hungry or won't eat at the right time, or ate only once—I hovered over Dina all the time, but now I am absolutely cool.

I cook almost every day, after work. We come home at 7, 7:30 p.m. I need to have dinner ready in thirty minutes, so what can one cook in thirty minutes? Usually I make some pasta, chicken schnitzel, or fried fish. We eat a lot of fried food because it is quicker. Sometimes I make other things, like stewed cabbage, soup. I make it on weekends, and then we eat it as long as it lasts or gets thrown away. I think that eating together is communication; this is the reason I keep cooking, to get the family to stay together in the evening. We eat at home only one meal a day, so dinner means sitting around the table for at least 30 minutes and talking. Otherwise, we drift apart; go into separate rooms.

My husband is a homeboy; he does not like eating out in general. On weekends, he would say, "Let's have something quick at home, why do we need to go out?" I answer, "Quickly means that I have to stand and cook, and I feel lazy, I want to relax. I don't feel like cooking on weekends." He doesn't get it. If it were up to me, we would eat out much more often, five or six times more often, than once in two weeks, but the man is the head of the household. Sometimes we get invited to Russian restaurants for parties, but I don't consider it eating out, it is just entertainment. My husband likes house parties, probably because he does not cook. I do the cooking; this is why I like eating out.

In the [Soviet] Union we had more time, more desire, and more energy for cooking. Here, I have no energy left at the end of the day and I don't want to spend my time in the kitchen. There, we had no choice, eating in a restaurant was not an option. One would go to a restaurant to spend an evening, to drink, to eat a little, to dance, but not to have a meal. American restaurants are for eating. Dina also likes eating out, socializing with friends. I like Russian restaurants because they have dancing, but when I come there at 9 in the evening, I don't feel like eating any more. I feel sorry that such mountains of food go to waste.

Dina was my mother's favorite granddaughter, and she always took care of her. When we applied for emigration, my mother wanted to spend more time with her. She asked us to let Dina live with her. We agreed, we thought it would be easier for us to take care of all the paperwork, but it took longer than we planned—two years. My mother came three years later, we lived together in the Bronx, and they became close again. Then we moved to an apartment nearby, so my mother visited us regularly. Dina was still young, so my mother cooked, spent time with Dina, took her places, picked her up from school.

Of course, I wanted to live next to my mother, but we could not stay in the Bronx. We chose this area because it is close to the Bronx where our parents live. If we cannot pick them up or bring them back by car, they can get here by train. When we moved, my mother got very offended that we did not take her with us; she suffered terribly in the beginning. Now, she is satisfied that she did not make such a step. My mother has a life now, lots of friends; she is very active, she goes swimming, attends a book club. They go to theaters, restaurants; she is learning to like them. She is also experiencing a change in her attitude toward cooking. Her friends and she started celebrating their birthdays at some Chinese buffet, so she finally understood that she does not need to spend her time in the kitchen, and she does not have that much of it left. Let my mother be healthy until 100, but when she needs it, of course, I will take her here and she will live with me. Here she would be separated from the whole world. What can she do here? Dina does not need her already, she practically does not need us, the parents, honestly speaking, only if she has problems or needs money. When she goes to college, I don't know if I am going to see her as often as I want to see her. I will see her as often as she will want to see me.

When we moved, I needed my mother very much, because Dina was still young, she needed a babysitter. I was going crazy at work, not knowing what my child was doing. I used to call her every hour. Her friends would come when I was at work, at times I got scared, so I would tell her, "I will hire a babysitter for you. We don't have much money, but we will have to spend some to have somebody sit with you.

I cannot trust you." Of course, I did not hire anybody, but we had such conversations once in a while. I remember myself when I was her age; this is why I was so worried. Besides, Dina has a problem—she is not very open—she cannot come to me and say everything she needs to say, and if she does open up about something, it means she is hurting a lot. This is a dangerous age—the first love, and then the second love; children are curious, they want to know everything, to try everything, to be popular, to have many friends—this is what scared me. And once, my daughter said, "Mom, you have no choice, you only have to trust me," and I started feeling much better. She is right. We work very late, and she is totally in charge here. I don't know my daughter's every step and I have no control over her. I have no other choice, and torturing myself is not a good way to live, so I am trying to take it easier.

In Russia, all the children were stuffed with food the same way. My mother, my mother-in-law, and I used to tell fairy tales, stage shows, and dance for them just to make them eat. Everybody around me did it because we all believed that a child's health depends on her eating. My neighbor noticed that her sons ate better in a boat, so in the summer she would pack dinner in a crate and make her husband row while she was feeding the boys. My niece was stuffed exactly the same way, and when they came to America, she started eating more junk food and gained a terrible amount of weight. She is overweight, and she suffers because of it. She is a golden child, she has such a wonderful personality, she is funny; she does not get insulted if you say something about her weight. She should be more active, but she is clumsy and not athletic, this is why it is difficult for her to lose weight. Maybe she should do something at home, like a stationary bike, but it is boring even for me. At her age it is much more interesting to participate in team sports, to be with others, to be challenged. Nobody is stuffing her now, on the opposite, her mother constantly tells her, "Don't eat this, don't touch this." It is like a boomerang that came back—first, eat, eat, and now, don't eat. They see that the child is unhappy because of her weight.

Her mother is also trying to lose weight because everybody is doing it here. In Russia she was in good shape, the age did it. In Russia, if you are forty or forty-five, it is normal to be heavy. It was considered strange to be thin at that age, like you are sick or something is wrong with you. In Russia, 40-45 was considered a sunset for a woman, 50 is a grandmother, and that is it—all the life interest must be in grandchildren, she has to forget about her own life. Here a person is supposed to look good at forty, and at fifty you are still a woman. You have to work till I don't know what age here, and the retirement age there was 55. Attitude toward aging has changed here, of course, more than anything else did. I am forty, and my body does not feel much younger, but my brain tells me that I am still young. This attitude is probably working on my sister-in-law and her mother.

My mother-in-law is a great achiever. She lost weight; she changed her diet according to her doctor's advice. She is the only one in our family who leans more toward American food, fat-free, cholesterol-free. She read some literature about healthy eating, listened to her doctor, and she has willpower, so she takes better care of herself. She is right to do it; one can say she loves herself. And this is very good. In our country to say that she loves herself meant like an insult, how can a person love herself? And here it is the most important thing—to love oneself. She looks great at 65, she is very slim, probably size 10-12, and she was size 16. I think her daughter at 47 is heavier, not fat, but she could be thinner. They buy clothes in the same store, and when the daughter gains weight and cannot wear something anymore; she gives it to her mother. I admire my mother-in-law; she exercises and watches what she eats, even though her husband eats exactly the way he did in Russia. For him, she cooks fatty food, fried cutlets, dough, sweets, but she does not touch it, they eat separately.

My mother-in-law visits her daughter every day, she takes care of her granddaughter, but they don't have a good communication. She is a smart, strong-willed woman, but she is terribly pushy. I think this is the reason why the granddaughter does not listen to her. She understands that the grandmother is right, but when she is nagging, the girl gets spiteful to protect herself.

Dina

Dina, a petite, pretty girl of 16 with a pleasant round face and long curly hair, had little resemblance with her mother, except for her large cat-green eyes. Comfortably dressed in green overalls and a loose white shirt, she sat on her bed and invited me to sit in her armchair. Her large airy room was furnished with modern furniture and had a computer on a matching console. Film posters and photographs of movie stars and supermodels were adorning her walls, and her bedside table was strewn with magazines—Seventeen, YM, and others. During the interview, she looked comfortable and willingly answered my questions.

Dina's Story

I think I am an American now, I really don't have any Russian friends here in Westchester, in the neighborhood or in school, so I don't get to be around Russian people that much. I am always around American people. I have maybe a couple of Russian friends, but everybody else is American. My best friend is Chinese, and I hang out with a variety of people. I don't think I ever had a Russian boyfriend. When I was living in the Bronx, I had a stupid little boyfriend. He was Russian. I did not look for it, just because there were so many Russian people around. Now I have one guy friend who is Russian, he lives right here, and we are friends through our parents. In school, if I had a choice, I would go for Russian friends, it is easier to bring them home, to your family. We speak English to each other, but they can communicate with my parents. It would be easier, like my parents would feel more comfortable, but there are only maybe a couple of Russian people in my whole school, so the majority of my friends are Americans.

We usually hang out in somebody's house; go to the movies, to the mall. Every Friday night we go there just to walk around, see people, shop. I am into clothes. I buy a lot of stuff, I like material possessions, I guess. I go shopping with my friends when I have money, buy maybe a shirt, like, every two weeks or something else. I like two-piece bathing suits because I want to be tan all over. I have... not a big butt, but I have a butt, so I am trying to find bathing suits that will cover it up a little bit, not very revealing down there, but I feel OK if it covers it up. I like trying clothes on, I really have no problems with my body, like, I try to make myself confident about my body, I don't think anything is wrong with it. Everybody tells me, "Oh, you look perfect," that helps me out, too. Maybe they don't say *perfect,* but they tell me, "You have a nice body," that makes me feel assured. I guess; it matters what people think about me.

I started developing before everybody else in my grade. It did not make me feel weird, but kind of good, because nobody else had the breasts, and I did, so I felt really special. My mom explained to me everything, so I was not afraid of it. I think I am done growing; I am the same height for almost two years. I hope to stay like size one, or two, or three. Not for the rest of my life, until my twenties or so. When I am going to have a baby, I am going to get, like, more, not overweight, but gain more weight with the baby. It usually happens, unless you exercise, like extremely active, but I imagine, I don't really care.

I compare myself with other people around me, like people in the street, and on TV. I never compare myself with models; they are fake. Not really fake, but there are so many things that they have to, like, maintain, like you cannot be over certain mass, body weight, and you have to eat this and that, it's just too much work to keep a good figure. They look really skinny, like most of the time, they don't look, like, healthy, so when I look at them, I really don't care, like I have to look like them, nothing like that comes to my mind. My friend Michelle, she is kind of flat, and she always complains about that, so pictures like that bother her. I read a bunch of magazines, like *Teens*, I subscribe to *Seventeen*, so I get it every month. I usually look for fashion, I really don't read the major stories; they don't interest me.

I weigh myself once a month, just to do a little experiment, like before and after Thanksgiving. But I really did not eat that much, I wasn't in a good mood. The day before my friend got into a fight, and his face was all hurt. I did not gain that much, like, one or two pounds. Usually I eat more, but I felt, like, sick just thinking about him. This was really strange, because whenever I am upset, I always eat. I guess, it is not a good thing, but it makes me feel better.

Right now, I really don't watch what I eat; I just eat whatever I want. I should watch what I eat; well, I am going to. When you are a teenager, it comes easier, your metabolism is faster and as you grow, it slows down, so you have to watch what you eat. People in school tell me this, my teachers, my mom. She wants me to eat, but sometimes when I eat too much candy or sweets, she is, like, "Watch your butt." I love rice pudding; whenever I get it, I always end up eating the whole thing. I love chocolate. When I get bored and have nothing to do, I bake, like, brownies or something. I follow the directions on the box; I never do anything from scratch, not by myself. If my mom is making something or my grandmother, I help them out, but I really don't like cooking. I'd rather eat out or order food, like pizza or Chinese. Some of it is too sweet, but most of it is pretty good.

I eat lunch at school. Usually I eat French fries or a sandwich, like turkey and provolone cheese, lettuce and tomato, it is, like, a pretty healthy sandwich. In the morning I usually have tea with a muffin or something mom gives me every morning, or English muffin with butter. On weekdays, we eat dinner together, like every day. My mom usually makes salad and some kind of chicken or pasta, this is probably the easiest thing to make when she comes home. Sometimes she calls me after school and asks me to make pasta or something because she is going to come late or tired, so I do it.

We usually have a lot of Russian food in our house. It's funny, when my friends come over; they are always like, "What is this?" I explain it to them, like these are the cold cuts, or this or that, because there is Russian writing on the cans. They like it once they try it, but they are kind of reluctant to try it for the first time. They like Russian food my grandma makes, like rolled dough with meat, just anything she makes—like cakes she bakes, cookies, sweet stuff. When she makes it, I eat as much as I want because I am not going to have it for a long time. Just to take advantage of it.

My grandma usually comes here on weekends. Over the summer she used to stay here for a couple of weeks. It was my birthday party, so she was baking a lot of stuff; I helped her with that. I enjoy the time we have together, she is really nice, very caring. We used to be close when I was little, because she took care of me for a couple of years before we moved to America. She raised me, I guess, I started school in her town and finished the first grade there. I don't get to see her that much now, because she lives in the Bronx, but we are still pretty close. Right now, I cannot really communicate with her, I mean we talk, but it is hard to explain things to her, because I sometimes forget words in Russian, and she cannot understand English that well. She does not understand how things work in America, and I cannot explain to her what is going on or what my friends do. When I call her, I tell her what's new, how my grades are, how is school. She always asks me about my friends, she likes my friend Michelle, the Chinese one, so I tell her about my friends. She asks me about my boyfriend, too. I tell her about the person I am dating, she doesn't know them, but it is still interesting for her. Whenever she sees me, she always compliments me, like, "Oh, you look good, did you lose weight?" My other grandmother, my father's mother, always nags my cousin, "Oh, you should lose weight, you are fat." It always bothers me, it's really negative, to say stuff like that to her. But she never says anything to me; she thinks I look OK.

My cousin, my other grandmother's daughter's daughter, she will be 16 in March. I think this is just the way she was raised, like *eat* and stuff. Maybe it was in her genes; on her father's side, the whole family is kind of overweight. Maybe she cannot help it; she tries to eat healthy and to exercise. She is not *that* overweight anymore, probably size 18, but she is still like, big. We always talk about it, because I always try to make her feel better, I tell her, "It's OK, it is not the end of the world. Don't listen to grandma Zoya," because I don't like it when she tells her that, why would she say something like that to her granddaughter? She should be supportive and say, like, "Oh, you look beautiful the way you are." I usually give her pointers, like, "You should exercise, like 3 times a week and eat healthier," and she does not get mad at me. She wants the advice, but the way my grandma says it, turns her off. She should say it in a more positive way.

When I lived with my grandmother, she stuffed me with food all the time. She still stuffs me, till today; grandmothers are always like this. She always makes me eat, asks me to eat, tells me to eat, encourages me to eat more. Let's say, I'll have a cookie or something, and she'll be like, "Here, have more!" And I am like, "I don't want any." And she is, "Come on, eat more, you are too skinny" or something, just like they always say, you are too skinny, just to make you eat. They just mean, "You are not fat, so why are you worried about your eating?" They think that I am not eating because I do not want to gain weight, but I if am not really hungry, I don't eat any more. When I want to eat, I eat. All the grandmothers I ever met are always cooking and always telling everybody to eat. I think that all they do is cook, so they want everybody to eat what they cook. My grandmothers, my friends' grandmothers; all Russian grandmothers I know. They always want everybody to eat. I keep telling her, "Stop asking me, you asked me three times already, I am not hungry." I don't know why she thinks that I don't eat, but usually because I am not hungry, I just tell her to leave me alone. She gets a little hurt, but she'll stop for a while. I guess it is nice when somebody samples your food and says, "Oh, this is very good." And I think she kind of gets upset if I don't taste it at least, so I try to taste it, but if she nags me about it, I am like, "Stop it!" She used to nag more, but not any more because, I guess, she thinks I am older. I really never like yelled at her for it, because I was young, but now, I just tell her firmly, "Stop!" My mom is also like that when my friends come over, she is like, "Eat, eat!" And I am like, "Mom! They don't want to eat!"

My parents have parties at home, and I am usually around when they have parties. When my parents' friends have parties, their daughter leaves, but I usually stay. I like my parents' friends, they are all Russian, I have known them for a while, and their kids—I am friends with them, too. We speak English to each other, and usually to the most adults, I speak English. My parents always go to Russian restaurants in Brooklyn for their friends' birthdays or something.

On weekends, I am always out with my friends, so usually we eat at a diner or McDonald's. My mom does not really mind it, but if I go often, she'll say something like, "Don't waste your money on it, it's not healthy for you," because it is really not, it is all fat and processed food. I always order a hamburger and French fries at McDonald's; I really don't order salads there. And I always order the same things in the diner, like chicken or mozzarella sticks. My friends eat the same thing basically, like French fries, hamburgers. None of my friends is worried about their weight. Usually I am mostly with guys, and guys don't really care. And one of my girlfriends, she is Russian, she is thin, but we went to a diner last night, and she just ordered a salad and coffee. I was eating chicken and I was looking at her. I guess she watches her weight more than I do, but right now I don't really care that much. If I gain weight, I'd want to lose it, but I would not go hysterical about it. I love eating out, not like those girls who starve themselves. I am so used to food, I like eating, so I don't think I am going to be able to starve myself. Probably I will exercise more.

I exercise whenever I decide to. I really don't have time for it, but whenever I have some free time at night, me and my mom jog around the block or walk fast. It usually lasts for a week, and then we stop, like we have other things to do. I try to do it every now and then, just to keep in shape. She wants to exercise, but she is always complaining that she doesn't have the time or she doesn't have anybody to exercise with, so I usually motivate her to come. I think my mom is fine for her age, but she complains constantly that her stomach and her butt are too big, so I say, "Let's exercise together," I want to help her out. And then we don't have the time to keep up with it, so we stop for a month, and then we have an inspiration and start over again, and then we stop. In school, I do cheerleading, it's not really sports, but it keeps me in shape, because we have to do the exercises and to stretch all the time, we do like dance moves. This season was over on Thanksgiving, but I could do basketball season in the spring. I decided not to do it, so for the rest of this school year I am not going to be involved in any after school activities, maybe I'll get a job instead. Last year I did both seasons, so that kept me in shape all year. When we are in gym, I am OK in every sport, like soccer or basketball, but I was never interested in any one in particular.

THE LEVINS

The Levin family consists of Marina, age 39, her husband, and her daughter Dana, age 15. The Levins have recently moved into a brand new house in Long Island. Marina's mother, Galina, lives in Queens, N.Y. with her husband. Marina came to the United States nine years ago from one of the Caucasian republics of the former Soviet Union. Galina and her husband came two years later from a large industrial city in the Ukraine. Galina chose to be interviewed in Marina's house, a spacious multi-level contemporary construction. That particular house was a model unit in a large development with manicured lawns and a large swimming pool. Lacquered modern furniture, pink and green carpets and matching window treatments looked picture-perfect. I interviewed Galina, Marina, and Dana in the large family room.

Galina

Galina, a tall, robust, attractive woman of 60, was an eager participant, willing to open her heart and to share her life story. Pouring out her worries and concerns in a continuous flow, she illustrated her stories with vivid examples and somewhat theatrical gestures. Her eyes filled with tears every time she was talking about her daughter's marriage, and her emotions tended to escalate rather quickly. She wore a bright pink housedress with short sleeves and matching open toe slippers. Bright red lipstick and rouge added color to her round expressive face framed by freshly cut and dyed blond hair.

Galina's Story

It is hard even to talk about my emigration. My husband did not want to go, he was terribly scared of leaving. He was in his mid-sixties, so he was afraid he wouldn't be able to find a job in America. In the Soviet Union, he had a job and, as people say, he was enjoying people's respect; he was a man in full. I lived with him for 40 years, how I could leave him and go alone? But since our one and only daughter left, we had to go, so I forced him. If not for Marina, I had no desire of my own for emigration. First of all, we realized that the language barrier would be too much for us to overcome. We knew it; my husband's brother wrote to us that it is not that easy and simple here. So we were preparing ourselves to a very hard and bad life; we left with tears in our eyes.

When we came here, we had a lot of hardship to bear. We were not young any more, and we were used to living separately. In the beginning, we lived together, and whatever was happening between Marina and her husband, reflected on us. Marina was attending a college far away, so she was getting up early and getting home late. I was a nervous wreck until I saw her back home; it was a tale of 1001 nights. My eyes were always red from crying. When it was midnight and she was not at home, I was going to pieces because she left at six in the morning. Then they had a terrible car accident, for me it was a torture and heartbreak. My husband became so depressed; he almost jumped out of the window.

We had to survive and to help our children. I could make some money babysitting our Korean neighbor's child. She would bring her in at 7:30 a.m. and pick her up at noon. She paid me $1.50 an hour, so I was making $50-$60 a week. Our granddaughter stayed with us, too, so I had to get one ready for school and to carry the other one in my arms; by nine in the morning I was dead tired.

Since Marina moved to this house, it became terribly difficult for me without her. First of all, I miss her badly; I worry about her and Dana all the time. Then I feel stressed out when I get a letter, I can't read it, even with a dictionary. So I have stress unlimited, my nerves are shot. It is even worse for my husband. A woman can always find something to occupy herself—laundry, cleaning, babysitting, this and that, and the day is gone, and what can a man do? Nothing. So he is depressed, till today. He can't go to a synagogue, and I cannot, either. It is not part of our life, we were not used to it from our childhood.

In our city, it was a horror to be Jewish, we were afraid to be seen on the way to a synagogue. There was one synagogue in the old outskirts, we had to get up very early to get matzos, and then we had to hide them so that nobody noticed, G-d forbid. The last few years before the emigration it was even worse. It was scary to be on a bus, the anti-Semitic hooligans would follow you and beat you up after you got off. When we were at home, they used to knock on our doors and windows. In 1992 it was especially horrible; I remember many scary events. One woman lived right across the street from us; she sold her apartment and was getting ready to leave for America. They killed the entire family and took everything; they killed the little child, too. This is the horror we lived in. Here we are safe and sure that nobody will beat us or call us names. And, of course, the nutrition is good here.

Our eating has changed a lot. I stopped cooking meat-based soups. There if you got anything to eat, you were happy already, and here it is so that you eat it all and in general you want salads mostly, things like this, vegetables and fruit, and nothing else. I like other things, too, but I don't want to cook them, because you gain weight eating them. I don't want to gain more weight. I feel very bad because of my weight gain, I feel uncomfortable, heavy both physically and emotionally, and in general, everything has changed for me here. I want to lose weight so much.

When I came here, I used to wear size 8, and now it is 18. My metabolism got screwed up because of the stress, my doctor told me this. I am in a terrible shape. For example, I call Marina and hear a difference in the tone of her voice; that is it for me, I already imagine that something happened to them, that she is not telling me every detail, so I am already all shaken up and I can't sleep all night. My head started shaking because of all the endless worries. Every day I call them in the evening to check if nothing bad happened. This is how the mother is; Jewish mothers, we are all like this. I do not eat a lot, but when I start worrying, I have to put something in my mouth. I just come to the refrigerator and take something. The most terrible part of it all is that I am eating and not feeling the taste of the food.

My daughter's mother-in-law is not so fat because she does not pay so much attention to her children. I think it is good in some ways, because she feels good, doesn't worry for a reason or without any reason; it is her great luck that she can control herself and take care of herself. This kind of people looks at things in a more rational way, they say that this is how things are and can't be otherwise, and that's it. I always think of something terrible that happened, I mean it is like I tune myself to bad things; I feel constantly worried. I am afraid of everything and everybody. When Marina used to live with us, her husband and she spoiled me, we would go by car wherever we needed to go; I almost never used public transportation. Now if I have to go to Manhattan or anywhere else, I am afraid of going. I would not go alone, even with my husband I am still afraid that we don't get off at a right stop or won't get what they are announcing. I can't speak English at all, and I don't get what they say to me. I can understand some pieces of conversation, like yesterday I overheard one woman talk to my son-in-law in English, I got some words, but this is not enough.

In the Soviet Union, I had a totally different lifestyle—I used to walk a lot, travel a lot. Here I move less, see people less. I believe that communication with people is the most important thing in life. There, I could not live without going to the movies with my friends, to the theater, to the opera. I participated in amateur singing groups at work. They gave me many awards and honor certificates there for my singing; I was OK. And here I feel simply that I am not needed. I hasten the day's passage, and if we did not have Russian TV, I would go totally crazy. When the children lived next to us, I could go see my granddaughter, do this and that, and the day was gone, and now we are like two stones together, and that's it. This is terrible. I cook dinner, I clean up, what else can I do?

I am trying to keep myself busy, I read a lot, follow the news. We have some friends, so we go for a walk, talk to them, but they are not the kind of friends we used to have there. If you are friends for many years, you know them and trust them, they are your tried and tested friends. I used to share with them things I could not tell my own daughter. You cannot trust the person you met here two or three years ago the same way, to be as open with them. There are moments when people need to open up, to share their pain. One poor woman said something to my neighbor, and now the whole street knows what she told her. It is difficult to find friends here.

I miss my granddaughter very much, of course. When we lived together, I used to spend a lot of time with her; she was mostly with me. The parents were taking classes, so they used to leave in the morning, and I walked her to school, from school, cooked, fed, served, took away the dishes, did the laundry. She would ask me, "Grandma, make me this, make me that," and I would make it. We never refused her anything, especially because she was born right before the Chernobyl disaster. As a newborn, she was very ugly; I was terribly upset about it. She was born wrinkled, like a monkey, her whole face was like a baked apple, and these long fingers, long and skinny, fearfully thin. When she was two months old, we did not know about the explosion and took her with us to the outdoor May Day celebration. We were happy, the day was beautiful, the sun was shining, and everybody went out with children. In two months, they made an announcement about the explosion when the city was already half empty. Everything you want was in the stores, and no people. It was scary, you walk in the street, and there is nobody around, and bread and everything is covered with cheesecloth, and there is plenty of everything. Everybody closed the doors, the windows; there was nobody to be seen. We were like on an uninhabited island. Everybody who could leave,—left, our government officials immediately sent away all their children and grandchildren, and we had nowhere to go, so we stayed.

We worried so much about Dana. When they brought her here, she was like a skeleton, she looked so scary—skin and bones. When she was born, she lived with us, but later they took her to live with them, and there they had nothing to eat at all. Whatever my husband and I were able to obtain, we would send them or bring them when we were visiting; we had a "wonderful" life then, too. To our despair, Dana was a bad eater, I think because of that accursed radiation. When they came here, my daughter's mother-in-law said, "My G-d, she is not a child, just a horror picture." She was so skinny that one could see blood vessels on her face. Now, thank G-d, she is OK, at least in this we are lucky. It was worth suffering everything only for this. Let our grandchildren be happy, we have lived our measure already.

When Marina was little, she was an absolutely wonderful child. She had thick hair with large curls, big expressive eyes. Now, of course, she does not look the same, she suffered so much. When she was six, she had a terrible accident. In kindergarten, she swallowed a stick. Her tongue was pierced, and she almost choked. After a very complicated surgery, they forgot to tie her to the bed, and she fell off. All her stitches burst open, and she developed peritonitis with blocked intestines. Her fever was so high that she experienced clinical death. After they revived her, she had three more surgeries. She spent a year in the hospital, and I was there with her. During that time my mother had her surgery for stomach cancer, everything happened at the same time. I learned how to change Marina's bandages; we were trying all the possible remedies. My brother obtained some terribly expensive medicine for her. We did not know that the side effect of this medication was hair growth. When she was eighteen, she was all covered with hair, so she was afraid to go to a beach or to wear a dress. It was terrible. Besides, the doctors told me that Marina would never be able to have children because her ovaries were all messed up by these surgeries. I was listening to them, and tears were filling my eyes. I was thinking about her and how it would be for her to never have a child. I took her to a good homeopathic gynecologist. She checked Marina and said that there was nothing wrong with her. She gave her some homeopathic pills, and my G-d! In a week everything was gone—her body hair, her liver problems, everything. When she got married, she gave birth to a normal girl.

When Marina got married, she moved to a different city. Before they left, I gave her some money and told her, "Rent an apartment and live separately." But her mother-in-law decided that living together was better, so they lived with her in-laws and her husband's brother. Marina had to take care of everything and to cook for the whole family; she learned the local cuisine very quickly.

My mother was a very good cook, and Marina always watched her and me do it. She loved cooking and did it wonderfully, but now she is tired of it. It is not easy to satisfy her husband. His mother could not cook anything, except for hot farina and scrambled eggs. He learned the taste of good food with Marina; of course, he likes it very much.

Marina's mother-in-law was not nice to her and stingy; she used to take from them all their money, his salary and hers. Here, thank G-d, she learned to wear clothes, but there all her life was in putting money on her saving account. She is a college-educated woman, not some kind of country bumpkin, but her control was a torture for Marina. She did not need to tell me. We are very close, and I always feel how she is. I know when she is happy and when she is sad. Even from the distance I could figure things out by the sound of her voice, even though she was protective of me. She did not want to tell me, knowing that I take everything to heart. But she had nobody else to share things, so willy-nilly she let some things out. When she was writing letters, there was meaning between the lines. At work, everybody liked her a lot, but when she would come home, it was bad. She was lonely there, in every meaning of this word; they were not nice to her, everybody, including her husband. Once when I was visiting her, I asked her, "Maybe you will go home?"

I was suffering because of our separation. We got used to each other and we could not live without each other there, either. When she first moved to another city, I was going crazy. I could not bear living without seeing her; I visited her many times a year. I used my vacation time to go there or took leave without pay, packed whatever I could obtain, because I knew they needed things. Then they got an apartment of their own, but they lived very tightly financially, because salaries were very small there. Then he lost his job and had no job at all, and she was stressing herself out doing extra shifts. Nobody helped her with the child. I felt terribly sorry for her, but I could not tell her, "Get a divorce." I am not that kind of mother who does it. A person has to decide for herself. It hurts me to look at Marina; I hoped that my daughter would live a better life. She has a very weak personality, she is kind, and it is not always good to be kind.

My own marriage was not so good, either. My husband's mother was a primitive woman; she never read books, never watched TV. She was like, "cook, wash, dust..." My family was different. When we returned home after the war, maybe we had nothing to eat, but we always had music, singing at home. There was nothing much to feel happy about, but we tried to tune ourselves to a positive tone. I liked things to look nicely. Maybe I had one skirt and one blouse, but they were always freshly washed, ironed, and I always had my hair done. My husband did not like it, and in general they were gloomy and suspicious people. His mother used to tell him, "If she has her hair done, it means she is having an affair." She kept pitching him against me, so I suffered a lot. When we got married, I was accepted to the musical conservatory, I had mezzo-soprano, but he said, "I don't need performers in the family." He persisted, so I quit. Now he understands what he has done to me, but it is too late. They terrorized me non-stop, I was nervous all the time, and it reflected on my health. My suffering caused neurological problems. When I was 25, my face became paralyzed and I lost sensation in my right arm and right leg. I spent six months in a neurological hospital.

When I first came to my husband's family, I felt bad for his mother that she had no husband, so I brought our salaries to her. She threw the money at me and said, "You will eat separately," and so we did. The room had 90 square feet in it, here was my bed, and here was her couch. She also told me, "Don't you dare to have any children." And I was so naïve; I did not understand these things. In my family we never discussed these things. I could not say them in my mother's presence. She was strict, but we loved her very much.

When we got our own apartment, I took my mother to live with me. She just had her surgery, so she needed care. She lived with us for thirteen years, the rest of her life. I did not even think of doing it any other way. I would not allow her to live alone. She did not know that she had cancer; I was protecting her. She was a smart woman, so she would say, "My surgery lasted so many hours; it means I had a tumor, was it malignant?" She had sarcoma, the most terrible one. The doctor said that she had one year to live. She was so sensitive, she understood everything from one look, so I told her, "Don't think these thoughts, you have nothing bad." She asked me, "How can you prove it?" I ate from the same plate with her, and my daughter would lie in the same bed. I am not talking about my life already, but I was risking my child's life to prevent my mother from thinking, G-d forbid, that she had cancer, and because of that she lasted 13 years. It was a gift from G-d. She was unique. When she was unable to lie down anymore, she would sit in bed and breathe from the oxygen tank. She kept herself so clean all her life. One day, she said to me, "Wash my hair and comb it." She forgot I did it the day before. I miss her very much, I would be happy to keep taking care of her for many more years, just to keep her alive. She was a great advisor; one could share anything with her. Neighbors would come to ask her advice, she was glad to help everybody.

When my mother was a widow, she did everything by herself. She could paint the whole apartment; sew by hand. When she went for her surgery, we were very much against it, we were afraid to lose her, but she said right away, "If it is my fate, I will live, but I don't want to torture you." She was sixty-five, and she weighed 80 pounds. She was a very smart woman, tactful; she could never hurt a person's feelings. When I took her and Marina home from the hospital, Marina had open wounds with drainage pipes sticking out of them. She would get up from her bed and grate carrots to make juice for her grandma. She loved her madly. When she started feeling better, the girls would call her from the outside, "Come out, let's go for a walk!" She would answer, "I can't go until my mother comes home, my grandmother is ill."

My mother was getting a pension for her husband and two sons who were killed in the war. Would she be able to survive on 13 rubles per month? She lived with me, and my brother would give her some money. My brother is an exceptional man, but he is unlucky in his family life. His wife is inhospitable; she doesn't like people. Nobody ever visits her, only relatives. She is spiteful; whatever you would say, she would say something to the opposite, just to irritate you. If she boiled some potatoes, she would keep them in the refrigerator for three days and feed them to her children and her husband. She was a terrible housekeeper, good for nothing. And in addition, she used to cheat on him, I knew it, I saw it with my own eyes. Of course, I never told him. He doesn't know, and let it be, what is there to talk about? She is ugly, too; some people are not so good-looking, but they have beautiful souls, one enjoys talking to them, but everybody wanted to run away from her. My brother found a job for her, but she was fired, because she could not get along with people, she always looked for something bad in everybody, got into fights, in general, she is an unpleasant person. What could he do? This is how they lived their lives, and now it is too late, they have grandchildren already. He never had a good day with her, and it hurts me, too. My other brother is in Israel, and I miss him. Our family is such that if one of us is suffering, we are all suffering, and if one of us is happy, then we are all happy. This is why it is so hard for me; I am far away from them, and from my daughter, too. I mean it is a distance, and we don't drive, and when it will become cold and slippery, I don't want her to visit me because I would lose my mind from worrying after she leaves.

Marina is a very good mother. Even when she was in a bad financial situation, she used to moonlight, she did everything possible to give Dana everything—sports, dancing; wherever she could find classes for her, she would take her there. She did it even here, in America. She made a special person out of her. They did their best, they drove her places after work, did not spare anything. They were falling off their feet, but kept driving her to the sports school—she was taking gymnastics. When they brought her there for the first time, she sat in the corner and started crying, "I won't do it, I am afraid." She was unsure of herself, afraid of everything. When she finally stood on the plank and made a full split and full turns, we were so impressed.

Her coach had a big influence on her. She became completely different—self-assured, she can go anywhere, talk to people. This is good, but we don't know what will happen in the future. G-d forbid, if she meets somebody wrong.

Our friends came here with two wonderful twin boys; they were 17 then. I knew them from the time they were born. The parents took great care of them, but the boys met some drug addicts in school, and that was it. For us it is a big tragedy, and this is why I am always afraid. I keep telling Dana, "Watch it, G-d forbid, don't let anything happen to you." And she says, "Grandma, what are you talking about? Am I some kind of a fool?" They weren't fools, either. They were smart boys, very good students. They started to shoot up; one of them got married, and during the wedding he made an injection and died on the spot. The other one followed him. One cannot imagine how these parents are now. They lived very well financially there and here, too. They gave the boys such a good upbringing, and here such a tragedy happened. So I worry terribly, because it is impossible to protect your child from the school, the street; all the bad things.

Even though people say that what a child does depends on the parents, I think that here things are different. When we lived in Russia, children were better supervised. Dana comes home at three; they come from work at six or seven, so she is alone for four hours. When they come home, they spend time with her, help her with homework, but they don't know what she is doing when she is alone. It is good if a child knows that one should not do this or that, but she has friends, and who knows what they are up to. I am always worried. At three, when she comes home from school, I call her, even though it is expensive; I am not at peace without it.

I am proud of my daughter. Everybody envies me, because she treats me very well. She tries to do everything for me, even more than necessary, over her abilities. It is difficult for her to visit me, but she cannot do without it. She calls me every day, there is not a day when she does not call to ask me how I feel even though she is so exhausted that she is falling off her feet. She takes care of everything on her own, she cooks and cleans, and does food shopping, everything, it is very hard, he does not help her at all. I feel sorry for her. When we lived next door, I tried to help her at least with some things, to make her life easier, and now I also try my best. Every Sunday, they drive Dana to

Queens for special math classes, so they visit me, for sure. I cook something extra, so that she can take some with her for Monday.

I think that Marina looks normal now, but she always felt terrible because of her full body. She is sure that she is the worst looking and the worst shaped of all. Besides, she talks about it nonstop in her husband's presence. Even if you are not beautiful and even if you have something missing or something is wrong with you, don't tell it to your husband. Even the best husband is still your worst enemy, in all aspects. It is absolutely true; nobody will make me change my mind about it. I have a cousin, he is a good husband, a family man, a good father, a good relative, and, with all this, he is his wife's enemy. His wife is staying with him all day long; he is a sick person. When she cannot stand it anymore and takes a five-minute walk; he starts worrying, going crazy, he is ready to tear her apart. He has to understand—she spends all her time with him and she gives him so much attention, but a human being needs a break once in a while. He should tell her, "Go for a walk, meet some friends," but he does not want to listen to me, I told him so many times. This is why I am absolutely sure that men are all the same—one is a little better, another one is a little worse, but in general, they are all in the same line of business. A woman should be careful when she talks to her husband, especially about her looks, and Marina is constantly looking for something that is wrong with her.

Maybe her attitude is the result of my upbringing. My mother had five boys, I was the youngest, the only girl. All my brothers were very-very handsome, everybody was saying this. My mother, she loved me, but she would say, "My boys used to be better looking." This hit me right into my heart. When I went to some places, everybody said that I was beautiful; I had dark skin, black hair, every braid was as thick as my arm. In the 10th grade my girlfriend envied me so much that she took scissors to them. I was sitting and talking to her, and she went to pour me some tea. She came up to me from behind and snipped off one braid; I had to cut the other one off. We are not on speaking terms till today. With all that I kept thinking that I am ugly, that my body is ugly, that I had this and that wrong. I always cringed when I was in a group of people; I used to sit somewhere in the corner. I even married the way I should not have to. Good and handsome men wanted to date me, but I thought that if I marry one of them, he would cheat on me or I won't be able to keep him. I was destroying myself.

I should have kept telling Marina, "You are beautiful; you are smart." I never said that, and my husband was always looking for what was wrong with her. We laid the wrong foundation, and this is why she is this way. She always thought that she was the worst in all aspects, and she keeps talking about it in her husband's presence. I think we were wrong, but now she tells her daughter too much in the opposite direction. She says, "I don't want her to be like me." I don't know if it is right or wrong. She is a happy child, yes, but if she keeps telling her this, it will go to her head. When somebody tells her, "You are smart," she answers, "I know," or "I know I am beautiful." So maybe at times it is not so good, in front of everybody. Let her know that she is all right, but not too much.

In Marina's family, her husband decides what to do and what to buy. He is the boss; he holds everything in his hands and gives orders. It is so hard for her to buy something for herself. When I was able to, I used to clothe them; I did everything I could. Now it is so painful for me that I cannot help her. I wish I could do much more. Her life is not the way she wanted in any way. She did not talk to me about it before, but she cannot hold it any longer. All of this together makes the mother feel so bad, and I suffer thinking about every little thing. We tried everything, even going to Teresa and Anastasia, they are some kind of clairvoyants or something; I saw them advertise on TV. So far I don't see any changes, even though Anastasia gave me some hope. Teresa was terrible, talking to her was worse than a total waste of money, but the other one was more like a counselor, not a village witch.

Maybe it is my upbringing, good or bad, I don't know what is good any more, but I taught Marina to be decent, true to him. She will suffer, but never cheat on him, never harm him. It was the same for me, never in my life could I cheat on my husband, even though everybody would say that I was more... attractive... and better educated than he was. Anyway, I could not do it; something would stop me. I imagined that if I, G-d forbid, allow myself something and then come home, how would I look in his eyes, how would I continue to live? I think that if things are not working out, one has to get a divorce, and then do whatever she wants. It reflects on children, too. In a good family, children are good, calm, well behaved, they learn from their parents.

When my son-in-law came to visit me for the first time, I was shocked by his manners. His mother is a teacher, how can he leave without a goodbye or not say good morning when he gets up? It is probably not his fault; he was brought up this way. When my granddaughter was with me, I told her, "It is good manners to say good morning when you get up and to say good night when you go to sleep." She used to do it all the time, but now I see the continuation of the old ways. Even though Marina is trying to teach her this, the child does what she sees in the family. I tell her, "You are a young lady already, never mind that your daddy doesn't say good morning."

Our family celebrates all birthdays at home, the same way we did in Russia—people come, and we cook. I don't like all this noise and merrymaking in Russian restaurants. You cannot hear yourself talk there. I love music, I love dancing, singing, all this. But when you come to a restaurant and meet people you have not seen for a long time, you want to talk to them. When five or six birthday parties are crammed in the same restaurant, I think it is not so good. I like American restaurants, it is quiet there; you can eat and talk to people there. Besides, it is better than to stand at the hot stove. If one can afford it; why not? Our son-in-law took us out several times when we stayed with them. I like Chinese food; it is tasty and less fatty than Russian food. Honestly speaking, you have a heavy feeling in your stomach after Russian food, and after Chinese food it is not so, you feel better, lighter. You are not hungry, but without the sense of overeating.

So far, things are good between Marina and me; what will happen later I don't know. Here children change. I see it by my neighbor. She does everything for her daughter; she spreads herself under her feet. But when she asked her daughter, a hairdresser, to give her a manicure and a pedicure, she said, "I don't have the time." She thinks that the mother has lived her life already and that she is stupid. She is the smartest woman, and she feels sorry for her daughter that she leaves in the morning and comes home late in the evening. On the other hand, she has two days off, so she can cook and clean, we managed to do it there. I always had dinner ready when my family came home. I would warm it all up and serve. If I came home late from work, I would still stand at the stove and cook, so that my husband and my daughter had something to take with them the next day. I always cooked something for Marina when she came home from school. We managed there.

This woman says that they lived very well there, that her daughter was very good to her, and here she is terrible. She had a birthday; so her mother made a complete birthday spread for her, she cooked everything. If you want to go to a restaurant with your friends, it is OK, young people want to spend some time without their parents, it is totally right. But to come home when your mother has cooked everything already and not to invite your mother to sit with you, to wish you a happy birthday? Your mother is barely managing on a meager pension, and if she saved two hundred dollars to give you as your birthday present, I think you should respect her. How can you refuse to sit at the table with her? You did not even have to do anything; your mother cooked everything herself. She invited you to her place, just come. They live in the same building, one on the third floor, and the other one on the sixth floor. But she did not consider it necessary; she went with her friends. Of course, the mother was hurt, she came to tell me, and I felt very sorry for her.

This woman never changed, even after what happened, this is how we, mothers, are. She still does everything for her, saves her every possible step. Her grandson had problems at school, he also got involved with friends who shoot up; she found out and suffered tremendously, the grandmother, together with that mother. They did everything to pull him away from them, they sent him to some private school; maybe he would do better there. Now, thank G-d, he graduated, so he is in college in Manhattan. He became a decent human being, more or less. She shared everything with you, good and bad, how can you be so unappreciative of your mother? She is selfish, that's it.

That mother is such a caring soul; we have a neighbor who paid so much in rent that she had nothing to eat, so she cooked something and brought her, she used to give her some clothes. This is the kind of person she is, and if the daughter treats her like this, then the son-in-law, too, and the grandson. Everything comes from the daughter. There are many tragedies in life. By the way, my son-in-law respects me and treats me well. He never said a rude word to me. When it was very hot, he called me and said, "Why are you sitting there? Come, we have a swimming pool, and it is cooler here, too." We live on the last floor, the roof gets so hot that one can die from heat; even the air conditioner does not help. He came to pick us up, and we were there for a week, my husband and I. I wish he treated her better and me worse, I would be happier. If I could sacrifice myself to spare my child, I would do it right away.

Marina

Marina's extraordinarily large velvety-dark eyes seemed fixed on inner, deeply painful thoughts; her clouded mood overshadowed the desire to be heard and darkened every word she uttered. Her thick, dark, shoulder-length wavy hair framed a soft round face with full lips and brilliant white teeth. When Marina smiled, charming dimples appeared on her round peach-soft cheeks, but her eyes remained sad. Her body was pear-shaped, with narrow shoulders and sizable hips and thighs. She willingly poured out her heart and shared her story with me, but when the conversation touched her marital problems, she said briskly, "I don't want to talk about it" and changed the subject. Her eyes watered and voice faltered when she was coming close to this topic on several occasions.

At the time of the first interview, Marina worked as an assistant librarian in a local library. She was unhappy about her job, but insisted on working until she finds a full time position as a software tester. She completed a training course a while ago, but so far her job search was unsuccessful. Marina's hair and fresh makeup suggested her interest in looks and beauty, but she appeared uncomfortable talking about these topics and turned the conversation to her family life. Dana's behavior and attitude were her special concerns, and she indicated that she agreed to participate in the study hoping to consult with me about Dana.

After the interviews, Marina invited me for a cup of tea in her spic-and-span modern kitchen, decorated with brightly colored ceramic dishes and Russian folk toys. Marina's husband, a tall, mild-mannered man in his mid-forties, was pleasant to me and tried to make a polite conversation, but tension between the husband and wife was almost palpable. They avoided eye contact and did not address each other. Marina's husband seemed to enjoy his new house and described its comforts to me in detail. He was especially proud that his house has two master bedrooms, so that Dana had her own complete living unit.

While Marina and I were having tea, Dana and her cousin walked into the kitchen with a cardboard box of doughnuts they just bought at the local shopping mall. The girls looked approximately the same age. Both were full-bodied, and wore loose clothes. Marina gave the box a disapproving look and said, "There are better things at home." Dana made an annoyed gesture, rolled her eyes up, and answered in a tense, high-pitched tone, "Ah, mom, don't worry." She offered the doughnuts to her parents and me, but Marina did not take any and kept drinking her tea with a dry cracker.

Marina's Story

I don't consider myself ugly, but I don't think that I am that beautiful because in order to be beautiful, everything has to be ideal, perfect, and I am not so perfect. I consider myself not beautiful enough. A beautiful woman is slim, with perfect facial features, tall, probably size 8, no more than this, I mean a woman my age. My body shape is especially bad, I am overweight and I would like to be better shaped. My legs are fat in the upper parts. No matter how much weight I used to lose, they were still fat. My bones are too wide, and my breasts could be better shaped, too.

My sense of myself depends on my inner state; it is coming from the inside. For example, I went to a party a while ago and I felt satisfied with my appearance. I was shocked; probably it was the first time in my life. I never had this feeling, and that time I was satisfied with myself. I had my hair set nicely, I was in a better shape, and my dress was good, so I looked—I saw that everything was perfect, the way I wanted things to be. I know I am very critical about myself, probably from family influence—my father is like this, he always criticizes everything, dislikes everything. I think it made an imprint on me; the father is the first man in a woman's life. He would always find something wrong with me, even now he always finds something in me he can criticize. I think that this is where my own self-criticism comes from. My father's attitude toward me is the root of my failures. My mother has never been satisfied with herself, either. And my husband, he never made me feel beautiful; not now, not before. I don't want to talk about him.

When I came to America, I gained a lot of weight, virtually right away—within the first year. There is so much stress here; besides, I have not achieved what I wanted here, I mean professionally. My organism is such that I eat constantly when I am nervous. I felt OK only during a few short periods here; this is why my weight is like this. I am trying at least not to let it climb again, but it is almost always the same here. I get as high as size 14, then I may go down to 12, but this is it, this is my limit. And when I came to America, I was size 8. So I think that this is a result of American stresses, because there is everything here to keep oneself in shape—the right food, possibility to exercise. When a woman is depressed, she stops paying attention to herself; she does not care about her eating, her looks. I used to go to a psychotherapist, and I learned that I have to look good to feel better. When a woman looks good, it is some kind of stimulus for her to overcome her depression, to get out of her bad mood. So I take care of my face, use good makeup; I never leave the house without sprucing myself up. If I don't do it religiously, I would neglect myself completely and look even worse than now, and feel worse, I mean my inner state would get worse.

I am on the brink of losing my job now, and this is killing me. I cannot imagine what I will be doing with myself without work. Now I work in the library and it is good for me, not that my job is so great, but I have to work, I have to go somewhere, I have to go away from myself, and then I feel good. When I stay at home, my inner state is horrible; I am unsatisfied with my life. I cannot find the job I would like to have, I cannot make the money I want, I cannot get the independence I crave; financially I am in chains. At times I start thinking that maybe I am sick inside because I have this nagging painful feeling—I am constantly dissatisfied, I long for something, I need to change, to become better. I want to take more classes and to try again to get a job. This job may not satisfy me emotionally and intellectually, but at least financially it will be better for me. I will know why I come to work and why I work there. I want to be independent; this is what I need the most at the present time. This is what I longed for my entire life.

When I feel good, I want to move more and I stop chewing, so I start losing weight. When I tried to diet, I realized that I gain more weight with it. The only thing I know is that when I sit down at the table, I should not eat as a normal person, I have to eat much less. I try to limit my eating, to eat no bread or sweets. At home, we practically do not keep sweets. If I feel like something sweet, I buy a little and eat it, and that's it. I know that I won't be able to stop myself, and all of it will stick to my body. So my diet is to try to keep my mouth closed as much as possible. When our pool is open, I will try to swim more, walk more.

When I was very young, I was involved in sports, but now I don't do any exercises, not at all. Before I got married, I did a lot of gymnastics, and here I used to attend an aerobics class. In general, I like movements that are similar to dancing. I never liked running, but walking fast is good. Now, I don't feel like doing anything or going anywhere. I have several tapes at home, so if I feel like it, I just turn the cassette on and exercise for an hour or an hour and a half. It also depends on my mood. I do it when I am in a better mood, two or three times a week. I don't know if I would go to a gym if I had more money or were in a better mood.

I am trying to prevent Dana's weight gain. I constantly talk to her about it, keep bugging her that she has to watch herself, that she should lose weight, that she should participate in sports. Anyway, she eats all this American food, all these hamburgers. Sometimes she does exercise. I used to take her to a sports school all the time—she did acrobatics, rhythmical gymnastics. When we came to New York, she was very little, so I tried to do for her what I wanted for myself, but could not have. She used to take dance classes. Now she stopped doing sports because we moved and she has a hard time getting adjusted to the new school, but she exercises at home, makes sit-ups; does some exercises for her stomach. She does work on her body. But I constantly remind her to watch herself, because I know it from my own experience that no matter what I tried, I stayed overweight. I want her to stay in shape.

In my childhood I had a very complicated surgery, so I was not able to exercise the way one should. I had an open wound, and my mother was extremely protective of me. Besides, I did not have an opportunity. I wanted to learn how to sing and dance, to join a chorus, to do rhythmical gymnastics. I was accepted into a special musical school for gifted children, but my parents worked all the time, they had nobody to take me there. My grandmother lived in a different town, and when she appeared, I was in a different stage. I was about 13 or 14, and the other grandmother, my father's mother, was busy with other grandchildren.

Dana came to a new school and was accepted into a very challenging class. In Queens she was at the top of her class, and now she is at the bottom, so she spends a lot of her energy on catching up. Besides, I have not found anything interesting here yet. In Queens, she was in a very good dancing ensemble. When she stopped dancing she gained a lot of weight. She was very thin all her life, like the first girl on your scale—arms and legs like sticks. I could never believe that she could gain weight, and now she has gained a rather hefty amount. Since she got her period, she started rounding up. When we moved here, I sent her to a sports summer camp. They had a very strong program, so she came back rather slim. And now again—bread, rolls, hamburgers, all this does not pass without a trace. I buy her all these potatoes, I don't want to buy them, of course, but I have to because she demands them and does not eat other things. Whatever is cooked at home, she wouldn't eat; I mean, she eats, but with a fight. She says, "I don't want to gain weight," but nevertheless she eats all this stuff. I don't like this food; I think it is bad for you.

Not all kinds of American food are bad. I see some Americans, they eat mostly salads, they don't eat bread and all these McDonald's and Burger Kings, I mean rich Americans. And in general, I think that here the marker for wealth is thinness. If you are thin, you are rich, and if you are full-bodied, it means that you are not so comfortable financially. There are all the necessary things to be thin, slim, and trim and to take care of your health in America. In the Soviet Union, my own attitude to my looks was the same, but only here I could get all the information about healthy eating and paying more attention to my body.

In the Soviet Union, we wanted to be trim, but we did nothing to achieve it. I always wanted to look good, but there it was not so significant as it is here, you would get a job anyway. And here the significance is in obtaining and keeping the job and that a person should look good for it. And since you are being compared with well-groomed and trim Americans, you also want to look as good as they do, you have your goal in front of you. When you come for an interview, you have to look trim and youthful. Besides your qualifications and experience you have to make an impression that you are healthy and can work and stay well. Americans are aware of this need to always have a marketable look, so they keep in shape to be able to compete on the job market. Their concept is that their appearance is their advertisement—a person must look beautiful, healthy, like goods in the store. Americans look like apples in the supermarket—shiny, shipshape.

Every woman wants to be beautiful; it is natural. In general, I did try to take care of my looks there, used good makeup; had my hair set nicely. The attitude toward one's body there was not like here. When you come to the beach, you can tell a person from the Soviet Union right away, just looking at her body. Even if the person is thin and trim, nevertheless, one can see it, definitely. Americans pay more attention to their bodies—they have tighter, better-looking bodies. I don't know the reason, but I definitely see the difference. In America, people exercise more, walk more, move more; they have this inner need for it.

I am not dieting and I cannot adhere to any system. I know a Russian couple here, they started separate eating in the Soviet Union, and they continue doing it here, too. I learned about separate eating in the USA, but from Russian books, because when you are reading American books you may miss something or not understand it right. I don't remember the author's name, but I know that Americans do it too. Personally, I don't see any benefit in doing it; I won't be able to stick to it. What I do manage—I buy low fat, low cholesterol foods, and when I cook, I try to cook with less fat. We eat mostly chicken, white meat mostly, and a lot of vegetables. I read somewhere that if you want to be trim, you should eat less fruit and more vegetables—fructose turns into fat easily.

In Russia I used much more fat for cooking. I stopped buying pork altogether, and I fry food much less. I cook now as much as I cooked in the Soviet Union, because my husband does not like eating out, he likes my cooking. He comes from the area where soup and an entrée were not considered full dinner, he wants several varieties—cheese pies, vegetarian dishes with walnuts, eggplant, herbs. I learned how to cook Georgian style, and now I am paying for it. When we lived together with my parents, I had to cook because he was not satisfied with my mother's cooking. Her food is heavier, more fatty, Ukrainian style. He does not cook at all, so all the work is on me. I make everything from scratch for parties, too, and he does not even help me, this is why I don't enjoy parties. I would rather have birthday parties in a restaurant. I love eating out a lot, I enjoy the whole process—I come, and they take care of me. At home, I have to take care of everything and everybody, and this is what makes me so tired.

Cooking has always been my hobby. I remember when I was still a kid and my father had a celebration, I cooked the whole spread for many guests all by myself. My grandmother was a great cook and an exceptional housekeeper. She had a great pair of hands; she could make something out of nothing. She was a Jack-of-all-trades. My mother told me that she even used to make shoes for the kids during the war. I learned how to cook from her, all the housekeeping. I remember visiting her before she moved to live with us; she made a cute little apron for me—I was very little then.

Our family liked to eat; our refrigerator was full all the time. My parents obtained "deficit" foodstuffs through connections. My mother cooked a lot, then my grandmother moved in with us, she did a lot of cooking and baking. We always had delicious baked things; her yeast cakes did not get stale for two weeks, she even baked bread. In Georgia, I used to bake very much, because one could not eat what was sold in stores—it was like poison. Here I stopped baking almost completely; I bake very rarely, only for special occasions.

I try to teach Dana to cook, but she has no interest in it, and generally speaking, I don't think she should. One needs to know how to cook, of course, but life here is so different. I think that the most important thing for her is to get good education, a good profession, to be completely independent. If you have money here, you can have anything you want without standing at the stove. If she is interested, she will learn how to cook later. If we stayed in the old Soviet Union, especially in Georgia, my attitude would have been different. It was considered important for a woman to be a good housekeeper, a good cook, the society was concentrated on it. And here you can buy anything almost ready, or order food in, or eat in a restaurant. I think that a half of American women cannot cook at all.

I leaf through American magazines, but not much. I am not so interested. In general, I have been living for a long time in the United States, but I still cannot understand Americans. I do not have American friends. We meet some Americans at the pool or in other places, but they never invite us to their homes, and I don't feel like inviting them. My experience with Americans at work was not too good. When Dana's friends come over, I do not have any contact with them—hi-bye, this is all. She has her own master bedroom and spends most of her time there. She does not have boys visiting yet, so by now this does not make me worried. When she starts dating, I would like her to date our boy—an immigrant from Russia or a child of Russian immigrants. It would be better for her and for us—we would be able to communicate with him and to have some kind of relationship with his parents. Common culture is very important—I want my daughter to become closer to me when she gets married, not more distant. I don't want to make an appointment to see her. I want to be close to her, not to live close, but to be able to talk to her often, to be there for her whenever she needs me, to give her some advice. If she marries an American, it will be terrible, they are so distant, so into themselves. My cousin is living with an American, so they have almost totally separate lives—separate bank accounts, separate things to do, and she is not communicating with her family, she became more like him. Her mother is heartbroken over this.

Generations relate differently here. In the Soviet Union, I used to be much closer to my mother than I am now. On the one hand, I visit her almost every weekend; I call her all the time, almost every day. I do it because I know that she cannot live without me, she lives through me, but at times these conversations are too burdensome. I cannot take it any more; at times I feel I am at the end of my rope. I have a different life now, and she is limited to her very small circle—food store and Russian TV, this is it, so I am her lifeline, and this is too much for me. In the beginning, we even lived together for a while, and then we rented an apartment for them very close to us. It was too much—my mother would spend 24 hours a day with me if she could. This distance is better. Here you can live your own life and not abandon your parents.

In Georgia, we lived like on a volcano; finally, we were practically thrown out. I did not want to emigrate; I knew that America is not a country for me. This country is for more independent, more active, more pushy people. I am a typical product of my country—obedient, lacking in initiative. Here a person has to be able to put her best foot forward, to be chosen over others and hired. I totally lack this ability. If they hire me, they will see that I can do my work well, but during job interviews I cannot sell my abilities, I cannot present myself in the right light. I know I have to be sure of myself when I go for an interview, but I am never sure of myself, in every aspect. I think it came from my upbringing.

Dana was very insecure too; it was a nightmare when she went to kindergarten in America. Every teacher wrote about her, "very shy person"—I felt terrible. Living in this country has helped her a lot. She is still not so sure of herself, but she is less uptight, less bound by conventions, more relaxed, I see a big difference. She still has some traits she inherited from me, but her overall personality was changed by the American way of life. If we stayed there, her life would have been a repetition of my ways, and this would be a nightmare. I consider it her luck that she came here. Have I grown up in this country, I would have been better off, too. It is so difficult for me here—the language, the job, everything.

Dana

Dana, a sprightly, plump girl of small stature, was ready to talk to me, but adamant against revealing her weight. Her large dark eyes had some resemblance with her mother's, but an angry, in-your-face assertiveness replaced Marina's velvety softness. Dana's body shape reminded her mother's significantly, as its upper part was much smaller than her hips and thighs. In spite of the hot weather, Dana came home wearing long jeans and a loose pink shirt. Her hair was brushed back into a long ponytail. She spoke in a quick monotone peppered with typical "teenage" slang.

Dana's Story

I don't like giving out my weight. I don't think it is important how much a person weighs. It is important how the person looks—the face and the legs—not too fat, not too skinny, either, not like someone who looks like a little stick or something, or who is big as a couch. Something, like, normal, between these two. For my age and height, I think, 115 pounds is good. When I watch TV, read magazines, look at movie stars, I kind of get what is a good body. I don't have favorite actors or actresses, probably my favorite is Michelle Geller, but she is too short.

In my family, we don't sit around the table discussing how people look; we don't do that. We talk more about what happened, how is life, my school stuff. Sometimes we talk about clothes. I like shopping for clothes. It's fun, it gets annoying, but it's fun. Sometimes the stuff looks good when it's hanging, but it just does not look right when it's on me. It might be too loose or too tight or just doesn't look right. Even if I change the size, I just look too big in it or too puny in it. I think I am normal, but I am not normal "normal," I think I am a little overweight. I don't like my figure or my legs, I don't like them. I think my thighs are too large; but everything else—I like it, it's just my legs—I don't feel comfortable about them. I don't like showing them. I like to wear jeans, long skirts; long dresses—because of my legs. In the summer, I am going to be in the pool anyway, and my legs are going to be hidden under the water. So I guess, bathing suits are OK since I am not one of those persons who just lie on the bench and just get a tan; I am more like a swimmer.

We have a pool in our development, and I go swimming all the time. We have gym in school; I love it, too. We play volleyball, not in a team, just in class. I don't have the time right now to do after school sports. I am in the eighth grade, and I have big tests this year, so I just don't have the time. If I had the time, I would take karate, it just seems cool to know it. I know how to fight, but it would be really cool if I knew even better than I do now, because now when I fight, I just hit, but I don't know what I am doing.

I don't remember Russia, I was really little, probably four when I came. I lived most of my life in Queens. We have been living here, in Long Island, since August, and for 8 years we lived there. Life here is really different from Queens. People are different, schools are different, education was much easier there; this is why I don't have any free time. People here are so snobby, they are just bitches—they have an attitude, problems with everything, and they are stabbing people in the back. They'll be nice to you one minute, and then they talk trash about you the next minute. Like if you go out with a lot of guys that year that means you have to continue doing that, and since I already went out with five guys this year so far, it means that I have to go out with at least two more guys. If you did not date anybody, then all of a sudden you start going out with like fifty people, then you are a slut. I have to go out, because this is what they expect from you.

There are a few people from Russia here, and I dated one of them this year. I dated Russian guys in Queens. They are not really different, except some of them; they try too hard to fit in. But for me there is no difference—when I go out with somebody, it's not about what religion they are, it's about how they treat me, how nice they are, if I like them or not. When I lived in Queens, my best friend spoke Russian; it was cool because we communicated with each other in Russian. We could talk about people, we could say, "Oh, he is hot, he is not," and nobody knew what we were talking about. That was cool, but sometimes all the friends that I had, all the girls were Russian, they backstabbed me; so I don't want like associate with them. They talked a lot of stuff about me, and I just did not like the way they were. I felt more comfortable with Americans or Russian people who were born here. People who just came are very rude. American kids were cool; they really accepted you.

And in this school, it is kind of confusing because practically everybody is Jewish, I mean American Jews. We hang out together, we talk; act stupid sometimes. We go to a park and hang out there; I am not big on restaurants. I like it, but it is not my idea of fun, that's more like my idea of family get together. My parents and I go to American and Russian restaurants; both kinds are OK because I like restaurants to have music. As long as there is music, like dance music, I am OK. I like American food more, I guess I am more used to it. I still like some Russian food, but American is just better, it's normal. When I am at home, I eat both, Russian and American food. My mom cooks Russian food, and I buy frozen food and heat it up in the microwave or throw a hot pocket in the toaster. My favorite food is pizza. I tell myself I got to limit myself, but I just keep eating.

I can't cook from scratch; it just doesn't turn out good when I cook. When I see somebody cook, I think I can do it, but I tried and it never turned out right. My mom cooks kind of Russian, and she puts spices and everything there, and sometimes she does it American style, like she steams vegetables or barbecues chicken. Whatever she cooks, I don't care, as long as it tastes right, I'll eat it. Sometimes I eat at home, and when I am not, I just go and grab something, like pizza or Mickey D's.

I don't weigh myself regularly, the less I see myself on the scale, the better I feel. When I see these big numbers, I am like, "I am not looking at it again." When I am eating, I am telling myself, "That's it, I am going to go on a diet tomorrow." And I keep eating, because I really don't care, if I am hungry, I am going to eat. I am just going to go to the fridge and get whatever I want... Sometimes I allow myself, like, garbage food, like Wendy's, pizza, ice cream, all that calorie stuff, but sometimes I tell myself, "Yo, you know," and I just take salad. I could pace myself if I wanted to, but I don't think I really want to, I am still a kid, and I think that dieting is for when you get older. So when I get older, maybe I'll work out or go on a diet, something like that. I am still growing.

When my body started changing, it was weird, because I was really skinny when I was young. I was really puny, and then all of a sudden I got fatter and fatter, and fatter, and I was growing breasts. It felt good because when I was little, I used to see my older cousins and my older friends, and I was just, "Oh, I want to look just like them." And when finally it happened, I felt good because I finally lived up to their expectations or to mine, really. I always wanted to look like them, and I guess I kind of do.

My mom is OK, I would like it if she were a little skinnier, but this is how our bodies are—the top is fine, our legs are humongous. I just don't like that. I don't want to talk about it with my mom; I don't think it's important. Hair and makeup are more important. I am beginning to use more and more now since my face is really breaking out.

In the morning, I need coffee to wake me up, I can't eat in the morning; I can't eat earlier than 10. I don't know why, if I eat anything in the morning, I feel like I am going to throw it up. It doesn't go there, feels like I am stuffed. As soon as it is 10, I am hungry. Then at lunch, I grab a drink, like a Snapple, and maybe two bags of chips. If it's good lunch, like tacos, I eat it, they really have good tacos; if they have baked potatoes, I'll eat it, and pizza, that's really it. Everything else there is not good, so I go home and grab something fast, like a bagel or something. Today I had two bags of Cheetos; I love them. I can't live without them. My mom hates all this stuff. She says I should be eating more healthy food, but it's too bad. I eat what I like. At seven I'll eat something like potatoes, spaghetti, something like that, I just grab something from the fridge. Sometimes we get together for dinner, but most of the time it's like we have our separate lives. We eat separately, but we do some things together, Like Saturday and Sunday we are always together. It's like weird, we have like family time; we go shopping, go to Queens, once or twice a month. We go there to visit my grandma.

My grandmother is getting really annoying right now. She is always in my business; I don't like that. She thinks she knows something, and she really messes things up. Like right now I am beginning to go clubbing and I come back smelling with cigarettes, but I don't smoke, and she started to make a big deal, woke my mom up, and now they don't trust me because they think I smoke, and I don't. Nobody asked her anything, and I just think she should mind her own business sometimes. She keeps intruding all the time; I don't like that. She comes over very often, and I try to be nice, not to lose my cool with her, but she is getting on my nerves, so I just walk away. When I was in Queens, she was always in my business, but it wasn't really anything bad because I was so young and I wasn't realizing she was doing it, but even then it was too much. My mom let me go there or here, and she started to be all over my business saying that she shouldn't, I just think she should shut up sometimes.

When I was little, my grandma used to make me eat; she still thinks I don't eat. She thinks I am supposed to eat every hour; sorry, I am not hungry every hour. I don't feel like eating every hour, and when I am in her house, she makes me eat, and eat, she just doesn't understand I can't eat that much. I just tell her I am not hungry, and she starts complaining to my mom that she is not feeding me. She pays too much attention to eating, and I don't like that.

I have a friend; she is Korean. She made a whole big scene out of nothing. She makes a big deal when somebody calls her fat even though she doesn't really care; she just tries to make a big deal. I remember she made a big deal so that people thought she was anorexic, so at lunch she would not eat anything because she said that she was too fat, and she is about my weight. That was such bullshit, because in school she made a big deal, and the principal was trying to make her eat and everything, and when I came to her house, she was stuffing her face. She likes to complain that her mom wouldn't let her have dinner, which is so not true. She makes all these lies, so everybody thinks she is anorexic and nobody would believe me that she stuffs her face more than I do. That's hard to believe because I can eat like five slices of pizza. I am serious, large. I can eat the whole pie. But on the other hand, I run around a lot, sometimes I act stupid, me and my friends, we really act stupid, we jump around a lot, we laugh a lot, I laugh way too much, I don't like sitting on my ass all day long eating. Even at lunch, I don't eat while I am sitting, I always walk around when I am eating; it is also kind of burning it off. My weight is like a roller coaster, it keeps going up and then it goes down, ten pounds there, five pounds here. If I see I gained ten pounds, I go ballistic, I tell myself I'm going to go on a diet, and then I don't.

THE WEISS FAMILY

The Weiss family consists of Minna, age 34, and her daughter Dora, age 15. They live in an old apartment building in Brooklyn. Minna's mother Golda, age 72, has her own apartment, several doors down the hall from Minna's. They came to the USA 10 years ago from Odessa, a large Black Sea port in Ukraine. Minna, a musician in the Soviet Union, is presently enrolled in a college where she is majoring in computer science. Dora attends a local high school, and Golda is receiving SSI (Supplemental Security Income). In the Soviet Union, she was a factory worker.

Minna's one-bedroom apartment was furnished in a modern style—shiny lacquer furniture, a large leather couch, mini-blinds, black Formica computer desk with a high shelf. During both interviews Minna was in college. She was unavailable for a meeting in spite of my several requests.

Golda

Golda, an outspoken full-bodied woman of 72, was a willing and eloquent participant. She mistook me for a journalist and started talking rapidly and passionately, enjoying the opportunity to express herself and to share her opinions. From the get-go, she introduced her own agenda, as she rushed to tell me about her neighbors without waiting for my questions. Golda's large shining hazel eyes, strong vibrating voice and expressive gestures added extra verve to her emotional narrative. She visibly enjoyed personal attention and rewarded me with a full theatrical performance, complete with speaking in different voices while quoting her friends and adversaries, banging her fist on the table, and demonstrating her body, dress, and gymnastic exercises. In spite of Golda's desire to treat me to her story as well as to her food, I sensed her tendency for embellishing things and her reluctance to talk about negative sides of her experience in the USA. She signed the consent form with her first name only.

Golda's short hair was dyed robust mahogany and set in candy-colored plastic curlers, as she was getting ready for the trip to the day care center she attends regularly. Bright red lipstick and freshly manicured nails were carefully matched. Her form-fitting dress of printed silk was trimmed with ruffles and decorated with large shiny buttons.

I interviewed Golda in her cozy, neat one-bedroom apartment. It was visible that Golda takes tremendous pride in it and has a loving relationship with every piece of its furnishing. The centerpiece of her living room is a polished "Helga"—a combination of a wardrobe and a breakfront—an item, popular in the Soviet apartments with their meager living space. Golda filled hers with crystal goblets, sets of dishes, and photographs of her children and grandchildren in large metal frames. Talking to me, she pointed at these pictures, beaming with pride. Her windows were adorned with lace curtains and embroidered drapes, color coordinated with ornate wallpaper and oriental-style rugs.

After her interview, Golda volunteered to walk me to her daughter's apartment, saying that she had to go there anyway to bring her today's dinner. When we entered, she gave Dora several instructions in low but intense whisper. I recognized a number of *don't*s in their stream. Dora looked rather annoyed and in no uncertain terms asked her grandmother leave, but with little success. Then Dora looked like she had enough for the day and said loudly, "I know, I know, enough already!" and deliberately turned to me. She switched the focus by asking me to help her edit her school essay after the interview.

Golda's Story

I cannot stop thinking about my neighbor. How can a mother be so weak and indecisive when she needs to act quickly, I don't understand this. She came to me last week crying because she found out that her daughter was pregnant. I was shaken when I was listening to her, and talking about it gave me the creeps—a Jewish girl got involved with some punk, and, hello, mommy, she is pregnant. She is only six months older than my little Dora; I could not close my eyes the whole night. Of course, I was scared for my little girl, too. In the morning, my blood pressure was so high I could not see straight. I went to this weakling of a mother and asked her, "What are you going to do about this business?" She did not say a word, just kept crying. Finally, two days ago, I could not stand it any longer and said, "When are you going to the clinic?" She looked at me as if I fell from the Moon, "What clinic?" I banged my fist and yelled at her, "You have to force her to have an abortion!" She started crying even louder, but what good did it do her? To make a long story short, I grabbed the kid by her arm and dragged her to the clinic. If her mother is weak, somebody had to take care of her so that she won't spoil her whole life. She is too young to think for herself, so I had to do it for her. In a couple of years, she will thank me for saving her from a horrible future.

My own youth passed during the war. I was not fourteen yet when the war broke. For what I suffered during the evacuation and then in Kazakhstan, I should have been under the ground for a long time already. We ran away naked and barefoot, left everything we had and lived in Kazakhstan on a distant collective farm, fifty kilometers from the railroad. It was a struggle for every piece of dry bread crust for four years. We used to go to the mountainside for wild berries and other stuff that grew there. First, we had to cross the longest, roughest river, then three kilometers of dry spiky land with snakes and turtles, walking barefoot. We had to go there to save ourselves, not to starve to death. There grew wild onions, so we would collect half a bag each; then we walked back across the river, and we had to orient ourselves on one particular bush—if we lost the sight of it, raging streams would carry us away. My mother, my younger brother, and I, we would go to the mountains together, and then we would cook this stuff in an iron pot, and we used to eat it, imagine what kind of food it was. Then I contracted malaria, and I had bouts every other day, and my mother had hepatitis, oh, we were so sick! On the way back home, I contracted dysentery, so I got into a hospital on the second day. My mother was so worried that we would miss the train... She would beg me, "Goldele, my heart, get up, tell them that your stomach is OK already, the train will leave without us." We went to a dusty railway station with our bags and our rags, and this is how we left.

On the way home, we stopped in a Ukrainian village and stayed there for two years, because we had no money to get back to Odessa. We were placed in the barracks for families. My mother and I used to share an iron army cot, head to toe; it was a nightmare of a sleep. I worked in the tractor group delivering water and filling the barrels of agricultural machinery. We were given two small plots to grow vegetables, so on one of them we planted a little bit of this and that— potatoes, corn, cucumbers. And on a more distant one we planted sunflowers and pumpkins; when we were leaving, we collected the crops. We exchanged sunflower seeds for oil, and I worked on a beet farm, so I was paid in sugar—forty pounds, and two hundred pounds of wheat. We sold it and bought railroad tickets. We were paid very little money—only 12 rubles a month, but we were not hungry there, we used to bake beets, potatoes in the open fire. In the fields, they used to cook borscht and deliver it to the field group, mashed potatoes, too. We did not have meat every day, but we ate, we weren't hungry. So we kind of hung on there, sold something, returned to Odessa, and in a month we have used up everything and were hungry again. And a loaf of bread used to cost 200 rubles on the market. My mother and I found work right away; we were sorting potatoes. Of course, we managed to take a few potatoes home. We exchanged some potatoes for corn meal and other things, and this is how we survived. Then I found connections and got accepted in a training program at a big candy factory. There I revived, of course. And then, little by little…we got on our feet. But all our lives it was hard anyway. Hard, and hard, and hard again. Very hard.

When we returned to Odessa, we had no roof over our heads; my mother went to the court to challenge some sailor who took our apartment. We got it back because we had all the papers that my father was killed during the war. The place was shabby, empty, no furniture, nothing. And this is how we started our lives again, from zero. Naked and barefoot, we bought some used stuff on the flea market, somebody gave us something, and this is how we managed… Our living conditions were terrible. We used to live in an old part of the city in an old house. We had two rooms, 200 square feet in both of them; they were not rooms, just boxes, a kitchen, and a tiny entrance hall. We had no running water there, no cooking gas, the only water pump was in the backyard. We had to carry water in pails to the second floor. And then we carried out the dirty pails, too. There was a toilet in the backyard, an outhouse, and the stink was so bad that it reached the street. Everybody dumped garbage in the middle of the backyard, and flies were flying around the pile. Just talking about it is like a nightmare. Seven or eight years after the war, they started carting the garbage away.

Right after the war, every spring—in March or April, especially before the 8th of March, the International Women's Day, Stalin used to issue the list of prices to go down. They did it for the most important stuff, like butter, bread, sugar, meat. And then little by little, collective farmers started bringing food to the market, so it was not so terribly expensive. Then we were able to afford a little chicken, one could buy a little, of course, not in the quantity to have your fill, just not to starve. For dinner I used to cook 300 grams of meat for five people. I would give a piece to my husband, and one piece to each child, and my mother and I, of course, had none. My mother-in-law used to say, "Golda, it is better than no meat at all. Even 300 grams of meat, but your soup was made with meat, so it has some taste. Add some herbs for flavor, too." This is how we lived. My marriage was not successful; I got divorced. I had two children, two boys. My mother used to cook for me in the morning. There was not much to eat then, we could not afford meat or cold cuts, so she would cook a pot of hot farina without milk and half a loaf of dark bread, this is what I would take with me to work. For dinner, she would make potato dumplings, some kind of soup, so this is how she helped me manage. Here, in America, vegetables are clean; they sort them out every day, throw away rotten ones. When we first came to America, I could not understand, did they wash them or what? We were used to buying dirty half-rotten potatoes, damaged by the spade, together with pieces of soil. They put them on a scale together with that dirt. And if you want to remove a lump or two, the saleslady would slap you on your hands, "Hands off!" She was in charge and dictated her rules, so half of it ended up in the garbage and very little was left for nutrition. And the same way it was with any kind of vegetables and fruit. I was never able to afford to pay three rubles per kilogram of… what do you call them… cherries… in the summer. Three rubles, and then it became five, I could never buy cauliflower, either, it was very expensive, and here—please, whatever your heart wishes. I go and buy this and that, according to my income; I can always find something for myself. There it was very difficult, very difficult, all my life. And it was even worse after the fall of the Soviet Union. Meat disappeared from stores altogether, even in the market there were long lines to buy meat.

I had my daughter by my second marriage; she is the light of my life. I loved her so much from the time she was born; I was going crazy about her. She was a desired child, I had two sons, and I wanted to have a girl so much. When she was born and they told me that it was a girl, I was crying hysterically and laughing at the same time because I was so happy. I did not know what to do for her. I used to dress her so beautifully, make bows and ruffles for decoration; I had talent for dressmaking. I have her photographs in a lace dress, with two long braids and huge white bows; she looked like a princess. I sent the picture to my aunt in Israel; she saw it and said, "My G-d, one cannot tell that she is from a poor family, looking at her picture one can say that she is a millionaire's daughter." In school plays, Minna always played the Snow Maiden, and I made her beautiful costumes, all by myself. I was going crazy, I did not know what else to put on her, if I could take out my own heart, I would have given it to her. And I love my granddaughter the same way.

When Minna was growing up, I worked, so my mother took care of her. I worked till three o'clock, and Minna was in school till two. When she would come home, my mother was there. I did a lot of cooking and dragging bags from the market, and my mother did a lot of cooking too. Like my mother, I helped my own daughter when she became an adult.

I worked at my factory for twenty years. There was a waiting list for housing there, so after twenty years of waiting my name came up. As a Jew, I got the worst apartment, on the ground floor. My supervisor moved to a better one, it had four rooms, and I got his old apartment. One bookkeeper from the accounting department said to me, "Golda, you will leave for Israel anyway." My second husband was not so good; he drank a lot, so they said to my supervisor, "She will not live with her husband anyway." They predicted my bad future just to snatch my apartment. When I found out about their tricks, I ran into the office, banged my fist on the table, I swear to you, and said, "It is none of your business that my husband is an alcoholic, he may be a bandit, too, but this is none of your business, do you understand? I have the rights for this apartment, and you don't, so you won't get it. Is it clear?" To make a long story short, they did give me this smelly apartment with moldy walls. And my co-workers took me to court because they claimed that I had enough room in my old apartment and didn't need the new one. I was crying all the time, I used to get up in the morning and shake and shiver from nerves; I was close to paralysis. I kept the apartment, two adjacent rooms, with a bathroom and hot water, but how much health I lost there, how many sleepless nights I had. Of course, I took my mother to live with me, how else could it be? She lived with me all her life, would I leave her to live alone in her old age? I slept in the middle of the room on a folding cot, my mother slept on a couch, and my daughter lived in the bedroom with her husband. The baby was born already, and this is how we all lived.

In that area, people were so anti-Semitic. In the morning, I had to run to work. Milk lines are long at 6 a.m.—people used to line up from 3, 4, or 5 o'clock in the morning to secure a spot, because there was not enough milk for everybody—one, two, three—and there is nothing left. I used to beg the saleslady to give me just a pint to make hot farina for my granddaughter. My neighbor used to yell, "Look at this sneaky kike!" because she would pour me a pint of milk. One neighbor we had, she was such a bandit. She would yell at my mother, "Close the door, you kike!" One day, my daughter heard her say it, so she ran out and grabbed her hair through her head shawl. On April 20, Hitler's birthday, they were distributing anti-Semitic leaflets. We did not sleep all night because we heard rumors that there would be a *pogrom* (mass lynching of the Jews by raging mobs) on the night of the 20th. We stayed awake, all dressed up, we were afraid to sleep. They were just terrorizing us, making us scared, but we believed it, of course, and this was the last straw. I am so happy that we left it all behind.

Thank G-d for my daughter. If not for her, I would have died there. It was her initiative to emigrate. She pleaded, "Mama, dear, let's go," and I agreed. When we applied for visas, she was fired on the spot. Then we got the papers and three of us left for America, my sons chose to stay in Odessa. By that time, we have thrown the pig out, I mean Minna's husband. Dora was a month and a half then. I was taking care of her, who else? Minna was studying, then working... All grandmothers help, how else can it be? Here grandmothers are such that they don't even want to come and touch the baby... They love themselves. I am not like this; I give myself completely, yes. I come and help, how else can it be? It is necessary to cook, to take care of them before they leave for school in the morning. I make tea with something for breakfast, like tuna or cheese sandwiches. Then they leave; I make their beds and go to my place. Then one comes from school, the other one comes from college in the evening; I have already cooked dinner... Usually I cook for two or three days to have it last.

When we came to New York, Minna went to a business school and she had experienced a fiasco there. She studied for half a year, and she was happy, she thought she would find a job, like for the government. The school turned out to be a fraud. At this time Dora got sick—she got asthma, a bad case of asthma, we almost lost the child. One day we went to a synagogue, and I said, "Minna, we have to fast this year. Look at the child, she has like dried out." We really fasted, and toward the evening, we left the synagogue already, and the child turned blue, and everybody was saying, "Look, your child is blue." We ran quickly outside, at that time it was very humid, and she started vomiting very badly, all over the new dress I made for her. We came home, I made tea; then she went to bed. We could not sleep, and in an hour—again choking cough—she was vomiting blood. My daughter and I had our fill of suffering then. Minna, this poor one, is not sleeping, and she has to go to work tomorrow... To make a long story short, I ran to our doctor. She told me a month later, "I was afraid to tell you then—you were close to losing the girl." We pulled the child out of the death's claws. And since then, little by little, we nurtured her back to health.

My granddaughter lives here from the age of five, she doesn't know Russian at all, she doesn't want to, absolutely. I ask her, "Dora, let me teach you something in Russian, maybe you will need it one day if you go to visit Russia or for work, or a business trip, or anything else." And she answers, "Grandma, leave me alone, I won't learn Russian." She does not want to eat dinner, either. I have much sorrow with her—she stopped eating borscht, soups, completely like Americans. She wants only American, everything American. Either Chinese food, or sandwiches... It is so bad for your health not to eat some hot soup. I am sure that one has to eat some kind of hot soup every day, as a law. I get sick without it; I must have hot soup every day. Sometimes I go to the day care center, it is very interesting there— they have concerts there, and a medical office, if you need medical treatment, you get it, food is not bad, I like it a lot. And they serve soup there too, sometimes pea soup, sometimes bean, or vegetable, or borscht. If I don't have any soup at home—I go there, of course, I don't go there every day—three to four times a week, and this is also a big stimulus for me. I get ready; at a quarter to four a bus comes, and I make manicure, have my hair set. I could not afford it in Russia. There I had one pair of nice shoes for all holidays—in November and in May, and for the New Year's, I wore them for many years. Of course I am very grateful to America that it accepted us, my G-d, what would we be doing there now?

My life here is very different, I am happy with my life. I am not hungry; thank G-d. I never had my own room, my own private life. And here, I am very happy and I should kiss the American ground, I swear, I live like a queen. I have a one-bedroom apartment. I am my own boss, I enjoy my life every day, every day I am happy that I am in this land, and I love my little apartment, so cozy, not so big, but pleasant. Everything is a little old already, but I like it. I bought this coach for $200 from some people, of course, SSI payments don't let you splurge, but thank G-d for what they give you. My son asked me, "Mama, if things got better there, would you return?" I said, "Never!" NE-VER! Recently one couple from our center went back to Odessa to visit, and they were very impressed. When they came back, they said that if Odessa were like this at the time they left, they would have never left to begin with. It is them; not me. They say that Odessa is beautiful now, and you can buy anything there, but I said, "And what about anti-Semitism?" They answered, "Yes, it is there like it was before." I don't want Odessa's beauty, I don't want these delicacies, here we also have very tasty things, and I like everything here, but the most important thing is that America is a country of immigrants. There is no chosen nation; I love it that all the nations are equal. My daughter and granddaughter have friends of different nations. I would like to go there for a visit, but I will die here. Here my mother died, and I will die here when my time comes.

I am happy for my daughter—she is almost finished with college. She is getting grants that cover her education; she will have a college diploma and will be able to get a good job. I hope to have happiness from my daughter and my granddaughter. My granddaughter is trying very hard; she wants to have a good career. She was chosen from her school to take special courses at New York University. They gave her a certificate, and now they are inviting her again, and they keep sending her papers to make her apply there. Of course, I am very happy. Now she is trying to get more credits, after school she stays for more classes, then she goes to another school to do some volunteering. She tells me, "Grandma, I will study a lot and suffer this year, but the next year it will be easier—they will send me to work at some law firm. When I graduate with G-d's help, I'll become a lawyer and have my secretary help me with documents." Of course, it is a big joy for me. She is very close with her mother and me—it is our luck that she is not secretive, G-d forbid, like that neighbor's girl. She has a good friend, a girl from Albania, also very serious. She always tells her, "Dora, we have to take these classes, we have to take this…" Dora is like, "Grandma, I don't want to be behind her, I want to go in stride with her." And she tells me everything, she trusts me. I always tell her, "Dora, my love, you have nobody closer to you than grandma and mother." Your mother and I are your closest friends. So she discusses all the things with us, asks for advice. And her mother helps her a lot. She is a lot with her, she is very busy, but as much time as she can spare… There is very little time in America for private happiness, private life. They don't get enough sleep, and I don't get enough sleep because of them. I know that I have to get up early, make breakfast, because they are rushing for a train, a bus, and go…

All mothers are crazy about their children, but my little Minna is very special, she knows it. She always tells me, "Mommy, you see me as if I were the only good looking person in the world. And I always answer, "No, it is not me, you are this way." When she is walking, she is like a queen—so beautiful. She has a beautiful face, she is tall, very well built, but she used to stoop. So I kept telling her, "Minna, straighten up, you will be elegant, attractive, you will be a beauty." She is not fat; she is watching herself. I think she is size 10 and Dora, too. G-d forbid if she gains some weight. She asks me, "Grandma, I lost some weight, right? Right?" I answer, "Dora, you are all right." Who needs this fat? She is very beautiful, body and face, tall, shapely. She goes to the gym sometimes, but it would not hurt if she straightened up her back at times. She forgets, and I tell her, "Dora, your back!" My daughter reminds her, too. When they are walking together, I walk behind and enjoy the picture—they are like two sisters. Minna is 34, and Dora is 15. They are of the same height, and the same body shape. I look at them and my heart fills up with joy. What else is important in life? I love my sons, too, of course, both of them, but the girls are different, they are younger, they are girls, I love them with all my heart.

I am watching my weight too, until today. I am already 72, and I am trying to keep my body in shape. Until today I know what it means to have a beautifully shaped body. I am not bad—size 16. I am trying... My friends tell me, "Golda, you have lost weight." I tell them, "One should eat less." Every morning I do my exercises, I would get stiff in my joints without them. In the day care center, they have an exercise group for us. I lie down on the floor and lift my legs. I can lift my legs like nobody else! I am trying to have a flat stomach; this is the most important part of looking good. If a woman is fat, with a big stomach, what kind of look is it? I am trying; as long as I live I don't want to be fat.

Whatever I sew for myself, I want it to look right on me. When I come to the center, everybody looks at me, and it makes me feel good. I always wear tasteful clothes, never flashy or shiny, like gold-colored sweaters. My daughter watches it, she says right away, "Mama, you bought wrong clothes," and I go change them. Everybody tells me, "You wear such tasteful clothes; you are so modestly dressed." Recently I bought an inexpensive outfit, I paid $8.99 for a jacket and $8.99 for the pants. But when I came to the center wearing it, everybody loved it. I like sewing, I sew myself dresses, knit berets for myself; I always have a fresh one...

Of course, it is not so simple to get used to the life here. My son is there; of course I miss him a lot. The language is different, and the life is different. You have to have a lot of willpower to always keep your spirits up and not to get depressed. I love concerts; there are some in the day care center, and in Jewish centers, too. I go there, I don't let myself sit within the four walls. I love dancing and singing; I sing in the chorus. I live by it, and I live for my children, to see them graduate, stand on their own feet. This is a big source of happiness for me, and when they are taken care of, I can live a little for myself. Last Jewish holidays our singing coach worked with us, so we sang many songs— we always have great concerts. In the spring we celebrated Jewish holidays and the WWII Victory Day—so we chose special songs for it. Our chorus sang last New Year's Eve, and this New Year's we are going to sing, too. This stimulates us, what can we do otherwise? Should I sit with gossipmongers on the bench watching who went where and to whom and who was wearing what? It is disgusting; I hate it.

In the center, we celebrated all the September birthdays. It was such a party! Not because there was food, not for the food, but because it was very beautifully organized. Out chorus leader and another guy, they made such a show, merrymaking with dances, jokes; they made us fill out questionnaires—what is your favorite book, favorite song. There was a singer, so she sang my favorite song, then they asked us what we would do if we had a million dollars each, you know, jokingly, to make everybody laugh. I said that I would build houses for my children and grandchildren, and for the remainder I would go to Bahamas. Then the question was to every birthday person, what is your favorite dish? So I said I love fresh fish, everything made of fresh fish. And also my very favorite is herring with potatoes boiled in jackets. By the way, I visited my friend at Bay Ridge and bought some gorgeous herring there, it is in my daughter's fridge. I ate it with baked potatoes; baked ones are better for your health than boiled ones. I am trying to eat healthier food, like salads, but in general, I love everything, everything I make myself. I love sweet *tsimes* (vegetable stew) with overcooked beans, fried fish. Oh, we used to have such wonderful fresh

fish in Odessa—flounder and bullheads—there were two kinds—
bigger, darker ones and tender, sand-colored ones.

My birthday was a couple of days ago, so my friends came, my
son's in-laws, they gave me a lot of attention. They gave me these
roses—so big, velvety, I have not seen roses that beautiful before. I
have good kids. I am always with a smile; I never give them trouble.
When I had my seventieth birthday, my children arranged my birthday
in the restaurant. But if it is not a special, round number, I celebrate it
at home. I cooked a lot of tasty food. Gefilte fish, first of all, everybody
loves my fish. I never adulterate it with white bread, farina, or crushed
biscuits, no, my mother taught me to make it—only fish, sautéed
onions, salt, pepper, and eggs. I also made gorgeous jellied meat; first I
cook cow feet and chicken, and then I strain it, put it in the refrigerator.
In the morning, I remove all the fat from the top. Who needs this fat, I
have too much cholesterol already—three hundred or more. Then I cut
up the meat, warm up the jelly with crushed garlic, and pour it over the
meat. Then I decorate it with slices of boiled eggs, it looks so good on
big platters. I stewed chicken livers with lots of onions; they taste great.
Then I made little flaky dough mince pies with turkey and sautéed
onions. I also made salads, potato salad vinaigrette and the second salad
with crab meat and mayonnaise, herring with black olives, decorated
with lemon slices, thinly sliced feta cheese, my own pickled tomatoes.
For main course I made my special schnitzel. I pound chicken breasts
across the fiber, finely chop 3-4 onions, mix them in a bowl with flour,
pepper, salt, and crushed bay leaf. I dip the meat into the mix, so that
onion bits stick to it. Then I dip them into beaten eggs, then into the
mix, twice in each bowl. Then I fry them on a small flame. They come
out wonderful—juicy and soft. My son's mother-in-law always says,
"Everything you cook is absolutely delicious!" For dessert, I bought
four flat honey-based gingerbread cakes and spread them with
homemade icing—sour cream, butter, and sugar whipped until the
mixture is light and fluffy. The cake is ready in an hour, and then I
decorate it with sliced kiwi, nectarines, preserved cherries, so it looked
like a fruitcake—stunning. It was light, cheap, and delicious! I also
served some grapes, watermelon, and a bottle of Manishewitz wine.
That's it; this was all!

Dora

Dora, a tall, blooming, very attractive girl of 15, was all fire and elan during the interview. She made no excuses for her "young and hungry" attitude toward life. Dora was ready and willing to talk to me. Well-spoken and passionate, she had strong opinions on many issues and made an impression of a person, well fit for the legal profession she chose for her future. My questions seemed to be far from the area of her interest, and she skillfully turned her answers into political speeches on the topics, dear to her heart and obviously contemplated before. When she was speaking, her huge gray eyes shone, her full bosom heaved, and her voice acquired impressive strength and depth.

Dora's Story

I came here when I was five, so I don't remember that much about Odessa. I remember having a few friends, like a girl with a caged bird. I liked the smells there, more than here, like the smell of the food, first of all, the quality of the food, and the smell of going out to the park and seeing more trees than one, not like over here. I remember being very wild as a child, like messing everything up, opening cupboards, spilling everything and getting yelled at and running away, and my grandmother, she could barely see anything, so I used to run away from her and hide between the sheets drying on the rope. It was really hard for her to keep up with me.

Here it became, like, a more superficial world, as soon as I came to school, the talk began, like everything that has to do with what you have, what you want to have, what kind of toys everyone is playing with, who is pretty, who is not. I think I fit this mold right now, like everyone in the school has a social place, like if you are popular, if you are not, but sometimes it's really hard dealing with that, even now. Sometimes it just gets to me, growing up in this society. It is really hard to fit in with people, especially coming from another country. When I first came here, there was a lot of prejudice against Russian people, and I had to go through this experience, like a whole class of people was against me. I didn't want to show up in school every day, I was constantly, like, tormented. I wanted to get away from my past life in any possible way, to pretend as if I was from another country or to make up some other lie, just to get away from that. I just wanted people to stop looking at me and pointing at me, saying, "Look at her, she is

Russian, Russians do this, and this, and this." They have these stereotypes that Russians are dirty, and if I am Russian, it automatically means that I am probably dirty and I am dishonest and that I think I am cool and good-looking when I am really not very good-looking. They have stereotypes for different people, like Italians and pasta. I remember coming to a classroom and having everyone like, laugh at me; tease me, literally torture me just because I was Russian. I mean now I don't have a Russian accent or anything, but when I first came, I was trying to learn the language; of course, I had an accent.

Now things are better, because in high school people choose their groups, like Russians hang out with Russians, and they are proud of their cultures, and if Arabic people are all proud, why can't I be proud, too? Just because of that experience, I developed a sense of hiding myself, of putting up fronts for other people, like I am not, like, sensitive, or anything, not to let them see me cry. It was very hard. I think that these experiences made me a stronger person, able to withstand things. But I am still very sensitive, and my self-esteem is not so high.

I guess my family helped me survive all that pain. I have someone to come home to every day, someone at least to, like, relieve most of my problems, if not everything, because I did not want to worry them, at least most of the things. My mom, she always stood up for me. My grandma, she was here to talk to me and tell me that everything is going to be fine, that I was going to make a lot of friends in high school; that everything is going to change for me. She said that I was going to become better looking, that I shouldn't worry about how I look, that people are good on the inside and if they can't notice that, then they are not people that are worth to deal with. They were supportive, very supportive. I could just come to them with any problem I had, and they would usually understand because my mom had similar problems growing up—she was the only Jewish person in her class. And everyone used to make fun of her that she was Jewish, so it's like history repeats itself. She would probably understand me even if she did not go through that, but it gave her this extra anger inside. She, too, did not want to come to school, see these faces again; have them laugh at her. My great-grandmother died two years ago, G-d bless her soul, she used to come to school and embarrass her. She said a few words in Yiddish or speak like, "Minnele, come here!" They could tell by her accent, right away, that she was Jewish, so my mom tried to also, like, cover it up and say, "No, I am not, what are you talking about?" But they could always tell if someone was different.

Now I have a lot more friends, boys actually like me, and not only Russian friends, but also Italian friends, and Spanish friends, and every nationality one can think of, and they don't criticize each other. Like in high school, they all accept each other, because it is such a big school, and everyone is from such a different background, so the only thing we have in common is that we are all so different. My best friend is Albanian, and my other best friend is Chinese. They are great friends.

My friend Stephanie was with me through junior high school. And her family has money problem because she has a lot of siblings, and we have money problem, so we can relate to that, and my other best friend—we go to the same school, we have the same visions in mind what to be when we grow up. We want to go to the same colleges, our grandmothers are very similar, like they use these remedies, milk and baking soda to drink when you have a cold, and all these things, which definitely, totally do not work, but they try that anyway. I go to her house, and her grandma came from Albania to visit, and she was making us eat, and there was so much eating, and I was, like, OK, go ahead.

I was very well fed as a child, and I used to not enjoy eating at all, but now—sure. I look forward to the next meal. I never wanted to eat, that time when I actually had to eat was like death to me, "G-d, oh, no, now grandma is going to call me to eat this disgusting, disgusting, disgusting soup. And she would say, "You have to eat your soup because you are going to ruin your stomach, and you are going to get an ulcer or other things. And my great-grandmother, too—she was like all grandmas, they worry if you ate or not, it is the only thing on their mind. If you had a six-course meal an hour ago, right now you are hungry. And if you are not—you still are. It doesn't matter—you still have to eat, and there is no argument, like, you can't argue because they'll either yell at you or they'll annoy you until you give in. They used to scare me, but now, I am just like, "Hey, food! I can eat again!"

I think when I have kids, which will be, in, like, I hope, in another fifteen years, because I really don't want to have kids now. I don't see myself like that, at least I have to be thirty or something to have kids, but when I do have kids, I am sure I am going to make them want to eat also, just like she made me. I'll definitely continue the tradition, live on her memory with her food. She is going to write down some of her recipes for me; I asked her to. I am not planning to be a housewife, but you need to cook for your family sometimes. We still live in a male-dominated society, after everything women have been through, so we still have to cook anyway, a man is not going to be able to. If it comes to cooking, my grandma is the expert because she cooked just about anything. Everything my mom cooks came from my grandma, and then she makes her own creations—she adds something, like a little more sweet, like her borscht is sweeter than my grandmother's, my grandma's has more salt in it. My mom gives it a little more zest, like herbs and spices, so it is her own creation. I am not a good cook—so far, I can make an omelet and I can boil some macaroni; that's basically it.

I eat so much, like when I go to a restaurant or something, I order something, and I feel like it is my obligation to finish it. When I was little, my grandmother used to tell me, "If you leave leftovers, they are going to bother you all night, they are not going to let you sleep." Oh, yeah, she always said, "Your leftovers are like what makes your brain, so if you are not going to eat them, you are not going to be smart." I got into that habit, so whenever I order food, I don't even know why, it is silly to say it is just because of her, but it's just like this, "I have to finish it, I don't want to leave any at the end..." Maybe it's an excuse... I guess it is both—my grandma and that I enjoy food. I don't like eating too much Russian food, well *zharkoe* (beef stew) is OK, *pilav* (lamb stew with rice) is OK, but I cannot eat any of her soups, none of them. She makes these roll-up things with goat cheese and layered dough, actually I tasted them in my Albanian friend's house, and her grandma gave me the recipe. Now my grandma makes them for me.

When I first came here, I used to love pizza. I could not live a day without eating a slice of pizza, it was my favorite thing, and then I got introduced to Chinese food. I started really liking that, like sesame chicken, and sweet and sour chicken, Chow Mein, Low Mein, all these Chinese things, and I love Thai food and Japanese, too. We go out every weekend, so I am used to that. My grandma sometimes buys me, like Chinese food. Usually I come home late, and she goes to some place, like a sanatorium, so she leaves some food for me. I love food, American food. If I ate only at home, I'd still eat a lot, but going out makes me really eat. At a Chinese buffet, there are, like, a bunch of things to choose from, and I take all these things, and I eat them, and then I feel really-really full and I can't move for, like, an hour. Then it settles down, and I think, like, "Hey, umm... maybe I am hungry again," and then I eat again. I enjoy it, but I run around a lot, so I don't really gain that much from it. I don't just sit around and create fat cells. But if I eat at night—that's it, then I wake up with, like, extra 3 pounds. I weigh myself every day. I try to watch my weight.

I am good and plenty. I consider myself overweight and I would like to look thinner, definitely. Sometimes I attend a health club. My mom signed me up there for my birthday present, I asked her to. First three weeks I went every day. I was so committed, I lost like 5 or 6 pounds, and that was it, I went on vacation and started eating again. Then I came back to school, and now I am so busy—community service, homework, and everything... I just can't. I was supposed to go yesterday, but then I had homework to do. I can't really exercise now, maybe over some vacation, like Christmas. I want to, but my schedule is way too filled to consider that. My mom used to attend gym regularly. Now she is very busy with college and everything, so I think she slowed down in going, but mostly she does it pretty often. She has a pretty good body, she is not flabby, she weigh less than I, and she is an inch taller, so she is OK. In school, I take weight training to tone my body, to get muscular, like Arnold Schwartzenegger. I want to be able to beat someone up, like a guy. I don't want to be picked on by my husband or anything. I see all these movies about women being abused and read all these statistics, like one out of every four girls is raped by the age of 20. It really scares me, I don't want to be one of these statistics; so I am trying to become stronger and to be able to defend myself if the situation like that arises.

A lot of Russians talk about their weight, "Oh, my G-d, I am not allowed to eat this, and this, because I don't want to be fat." They do it just to impress you, but usually they are not even skinny. Usually they just worry about it and talk about it, and make other people feel bad. They like to show off, like, they hardly have any money, just like African-Americans. They might be living in the streets, but have the nicest sneakers you can buy. And Russians are like this, too—they'll be on welfare and walking around in Versace and driving, like, Mercedes and Porsches, and Ferraris, and meanwhile you come to their house and everything is, like, falling apart, they are just putting up the front. I guess this is where they get part of their bad reputation.

Americans are down-to-earth people. They have the usual family, I mean the father, the mother, they have this big Buick station wagon, they put their family there, they go on vacations like once a year, they have a family pet. They are not trying to dress nicely, especially mothers. I am scared here, because here, once you reach, like, thirty, you start making kids—that's it. You start wearing these, like, raggedy things and walking around like a bum. That's it, that's the usual American attitude toward getting older—like, they don't care—once you have a husband, it's OK to put on weight. When they are teenagers, they are really good-looking, a lot of them. Then, after 25, it's like... "What is that? What did I marry?" That's why the average American marriage lasts like a year, with all these people becoming fat. This is a superficial world, so their husbands would go out and cheat, of course, because the husbands usually don't really change that much. After the wedding usually the women become fat, they don't care any more, they go like, "Well, I have a husband, he loves me, he'll never leave me, he'll never cheat on me..." Guess what? They find out that he has been sleeping with one of his co-workers. That's it, and then a divorce, and you date again.

It is like a law in America; when you are around 26, you have to get married. Weddings are so special here, people are calling on the phone and telling all the friends, "Hey, I'm getting married, come to my wedding!" I think it's the hype; marriage is just like an institution, I don't think it is that necessary. That's why people break up so easily, because they date for six months, and women start talking about marriage. They get married, and then they are like, "What? I didn't know she was supposed to look like this when she wakes up" and "What is he doing? Why is he walking around like that? It is disgusting." People have to get to know each other; they should live together for a year before they get married. On dates you talk about political issues or some minor problems, you try to be profound, to make yourself look good in front of them, and maybe, maybe once in a while you have a really big problem. It is crazy to think you can decide all these matters right away—money, what you want to be, views if women should stay home or how many children you want to have, or if you want to have any children. If I had a choice, I wouldn't even want to have children, but mostly men—they want to have children to carry on their name or something else, I don't know. Our world is overpopulated, people live in the streets, so people should adapt children, there are so many of them in shelters. If they don't get the love they need, they are going to grow up like killers, like all these convicts that we don't want on our streets, so we better take care of them while they are small.

I think I'd rather adopt a child. When children grow up, they are going to leave you anyway. It doesn't matter if you are their real mother or how good a mother you are. Everyone wants their own life, they don't want people from the past tie them down. They want to make their own family, to get married, to have a job, and they don't want to look back. I love my mother a lot and my grandmother, too, but I have to say it—I am going to go to college the year after next. I definitely want to leave, because I also want to have some independence. I mean, I've been living with my mom this long, and my grandma on the same floor, it's getting so tiring—them smothering me. Of course, they don't want me to leave. My grandma said she's going to go crazy if she won't have the responsibility of taking care of me, and my mom also—she wants to enjoy some time together with me. She is almost finished with college, so she wants to go to work and then to come home to be with me. But I think that I'll be able to expand my social horizons if I get away. I just want to get away; I cannot stand it anymore. I have to be home before certain time, even on weekends; in order to go to some kind of party, even some religious gathering, I have to discuss it with my mom, like, million times before she actually even considers it. I mean I understand it is really hard raising a child here, especially in a big city, like New York, but I need to have some space. I am going to grow up sooner or later, and if she is just going to wait until I am eighteen and to throw me into the world, I am not going to be ready for it, it is going to be overwhelming for me. I want to go to Boston University for a pre-law program, like political science. If not Boston, then Massachusetts or Michigan.

From my mom, I got this music thing; like, I think I can sing. I started thinking of a conservatory, but then it was like no, I am not going to let it happen to me like go to musical college and then have to switch careers and go to college again. She could not make a living as a singer here. It is better just to choose something solid, long-term, something you can fall back on. Maybe I can take music as a hobby later.

Sometimes I read these magazines where everyone is telling you how to become a perfect 10, how to dress right, how you can exercise and what you need to eat, and what mask you need to put on your face, pimple cream, antibiotics, suntan lotion, the shampoo, herbal wraps, spas. You read it all, and then one day you sit down and realize—you are never going to look like these people. You should just give up because you are wasting your time thinking that it is going to change anything, because you are just going to be yourself. And then you think maybe if you put on as much makeup as these people have on them, like while they are taking these pictures, I think it makes just anyone look pretty. I guess magazines and movies make you think like this. If you are ugly, I mean their definition of being ugly—an overweight person, you cannot get a guy, some basketball star or football quarterback. You have to be a cheerleader, you have to have blond hair and blue eyes, and you have to be pretty by their standards—very thin, and you have to act like you are dumb, to speak in this manner, "Oh, my G-d, gee, I am a girl! Want to go make out or something?" The standards are already set for you. Some of the stuff in these magazines, like YM, Seventeen, is pretty interesting, like stories about kids who get abused or molested at home and how they become better people, and the horoscope. I read about the signs and what's going to happen. I also like it when they talk about movie stars and how they are in real life. Sometimes it makes me a little jealous—like when I read about Tori Spelling. Just makes me mad. It is difficult to become like them. First of all, she is an actress. If she were just a pretty person walking down the street, she barely would have anyone anyway. She has the right connections, she has money, she has a rich daddy that provides everything for her, and I just wish that, like, for one day, I could have the experience of having everything handed to me. Just because her father is some famous writer, he writes these plays and she has roles in all these shows. Just because of that she gets so much fame, she is a millionaire, her life is set for her; she doesn't even have to work hard. If she wants to, she can spend every single day staying home, watching cable TV for the rest of her life. I have to work for things, I have to do these extra programs, and I have to spend late nights doing homework and not going out, because I have stuff to finish. There are kids in my school with fathers who own oil companies, they know a representative of Harvard and they know they can get accepted even if they have a grade average of 60 with SAT scores of 900. "Hey, my kid over here, you know him, he is a great kid, and here is fifty thousand dollars, (whispers) accept him." So he is accepted to Harvard, and for me, "Hi, you can go to Brooklyn College." "Thanks, I really want to go to Brooklyn College." I can't stand it; it hurts so much. Why do I have to work hard, why do I have to be born like this, why can't I have it all? I believe in reincarnation, like in every life you can become like three times better. I guess, I am still at a low stage, and maybe in my next life I'm going to become someone better, and then still better, and eventually I will become a queen of the world or something.

For me happiness is having a great law career, working in some office in Boston or Manhattan, having clients, getting up every morning just to know that you are going to make a difference in someone's life, and you are going to help someone. OK, you have to have money, of course, and you have to have a nice car and a good-looking husband who also works on Wall Street, and you have these almost perfect kids. I never wanted to be a doctor. My grandma always goes, "Oh, she is going to be a doctor, your mom passed the chance of being a doctor, you know, you should be one, you should be the first doctor in our family." And I am just like, "No, I don't like blood, I don't like touching dead people." I like writing; I have a very active imagination. When I started realizing what kind of person I am; I felt that I could be a lawyer, I can speak well. I even took some courses at NYU last year, like these law courses; I got picked from my school with my best friend. This year we are going, too, to this advanced program. Last year we took introductory courses and we had mock trial. I was a lawyer for the prosecution; it's pretty fun. This year, from the last quarter of school I signed up for mock trial also, it takes a lot of time after school, and I have community service, too, so I have to manage it all somehow, but I think it's worth it. If I work hard this year, then the next year, I may relax more, like in my senior year. In two weeks I am taking the PSAT, in another few months I am taking the SAT. I have to go for Princeton Review courses and study with a math tutor. I am doing this *Teachers of Tomorrow* Program, you teach first graders drama, or art, or science. I don't want to be a teacher; I just want to have it on my college transcript. I am going to start this government internship, and I really want to do it. The next year I hope that I can join this co-op program where you work in a law firm and you work there, like answer the phones, make copies, type things. I am really looking forward to this, I want to finish this year the things that I must do, so the next year I can do the work-study program.

I am trying to get ahead in life. I don't want to have ten million children and get divorced, and have my husband leave me with nothing, because he had everything, he provided the family with everything. I want to be the breadwinner. If I had a choice—either I work, or my husband, I'd say, "I'll work, let him stay home." I want to have the lease of the house, in my name. I want to have a prenuptial agreement, so he cannot walk away with everything that is dear to me. With all these things that are going on—marriages last such a short time, and the woman is getting bankrupt. And with all these people marrying for green cards, like green card marriage; that is just sick, I think. They may fall in love with you and then say, "Oh, thanks, that was my green card, OK, now I have to go, meet my girlfriend who is much better looking than you." So I want to be protected from all kinds of things, definitely. I want to be respected as an older person. Here, in America, older people barely have any respect at all. They make fun of them on TV, old people with their fake teeth. I don't want to be subject to that. If I am going to be someone important, like a lawyer, my popularity is not going to die with my looks, and I am going to have my reputation for my ability, not for how I look and how I talk. I am trying to make something permanent for myself, something I'll have even though I may not have anything else.

I want to have my revenge on these people that teased me, I think they gave me my drive. If they weren't talking down to me, telling me that I would never be any good, that I am going to be stupid and clean toilets for a living, I would be another one of these lazy teenagers who lie around all day, like, "Oh, G-d, what am I going to do now?" They go out and have parties, and get high, and smoke, and do drugs. I don't do these things, I want to come back to a high school reunion with a rich husband, in a fancy car and fancy clothes, and I want to show them what I became. I want to see them working at a gas station, married to some Seven-Eleven worker. That's, basically, my dream. I want them to be, like, wow! I want them to feel bad for doing that to me and making fun of me. I don't want to be a criminal lawyer, but if that does happen to me, if I get thrown off track, I imagine one of those people is getting tried for some homicidal thing, and I have to defend them. I would be like, "Hi, remember me, I am Dora, the girl you made fun of, the dirty Russian girl. Now look what I am going to do to you." I also want to make my mom proud of me, my grandma; I want them to be happy. I want my grandma, when she does go, I want her to go in peace, to make her know that at least I am taken care of for the rest of my life, that I am someone. She can tell her friends, too. You know how these old people are - all they have left is their memories and what their children do. They sit around in a circle and go like, "Well, my daughter does this, and my granddaughter does this, and she looks like this, and when I was young, I was like this." They live by their memories and by their children. They live vicariously through them. So I want to give gratification to my grandmother. Also I want to give my mom a car for one of her birthdays. Or something, like, wow! She always tells me that I am talented, I am beautiful, like all these things to make me feel good about myself, and I just want to show her that all that pays off one day.

CHAPTER 4

Major Themes

The following are major themes, which emerged from the analysis of the interviews with participating women. Themes are affect-laden statements, which appear frequently across interviews or seem particularly relevant and important. Themes are organized into categories. The order of presentation reflects the participants' expressed order of priorities.

Category I: Social Issues
    Theme 1 Work/Achievement
    Theme 2: Collective/Individual

Category II: Family Relationships
    Theme 1: Mother/Daughter
    Theme 2: Grandmother/Granddaughter
    Theme 3: Men/Women

Category III: Self
    Theme 1: Body Image
    Theme 2: Taking Care of Self

Category IV: Food and Eating
    Theme 1: Eating Habits
    Theme 2: Changes in Eating Habits

Category V: Losses and Gains of Emigration
    Theme 1: Losses
    Theme 2: Gains

CATEGORY I: SOCIAL ISSUES

Work/Achievement

Subtheme A: I Worked all my adult life (grandmothers and mothers)

A conflict between career and family never appeared in any of the interviews. All adult participants have always worked full time and spoke about it without a shadow of a doubt that it could be otherwise. Moreover, when I asked them, "How did your life change since you came to America?" three grandmothers and three mothers started talking about their work as a source of self-respect and self-definition. Greta described her mother's and her own long teaching careers in detail and with pride. She said that the inability to continue her work in the former Soviet Union played an important role in her decision to emigrate. She also reported her hopes for finding work in the United States and suffering from her inability to do so:

> I was not able to return to work, I had practically nothing to do, even though I love my profession very much and here I suffer a lot because I cannot find any use for my teaching abilities. Even if it sounds funny, I packed my textbooks and some of my own works in phonetics. I hoped that something may happen and I would get so lucky, even though I realized that I would need to learn English.

Greta repeatedly stressed professional achievement as a major source of self-esteem for her and her family, and her conclusions about the challenges of emigration are based on this mindset. Speaking about her daughter, she said, "I think that the middle generation is having the hardest time here. It is so difficult to establish themselves professionally, to prove themselves again." Genya, also a teacher, described her work as labor of love, a major source of satisfaction in her life:

> I worked in schools for seventeen years... I had students graduating from the tenth grade, with such emotional good-bye. I had a hard life, but very interesting. We were friends, my students and I, and we stayed friends after graduation. And

then I started working in a kindergarten. I taught the children
to listen to the music, to move to the rhythm. I gave them a lot.

Success or failure in their work was a significant part of the
mothers' self-esteem. When I asked Greta and her daughter Maya how
their lives changed since they arrived to the United States, they both
started with their work, defining themselves primarily by their
professional achievements. Greta said,

> Of course, my life here differs significantly, in principle.
> While living at home, in our country, we all worked. I worked
> as a teacher of Russian language for forty years. My career
> spans from the first to the tenth grade. I also taught in a
> college for elementary school teachers and at the university
> level, training high school teachers of Russian language. This
> is my list of accomplishments.

Maya considered her professional achievement to be a major part
of her self-image, "When I arrived in the United States, I considered
myself a middle-aged woman. In the Soviet Union, I had worked
already for a sufficient number of years after the university, and I was a
professional of a certain level." Several other participants also defined
themselves by their professions. Marlena talked with pride and
satisfaction about her present situation and reported her self-doubt in
the Soviet Union:

> In the Soviet Union, I was extremely unlucky with jobs, I even
> developed a complex that something is wrong with my head
> that I had to change a lot of them—there were different
> reasons. And here I was lucky from the day one. I am very
> respected and appreciated, even though they had their measure
> of trouble with me.

She explained her ambivalence about emigration by her fear of not
getting a job in America, "If not for Chernobyl, we would still be there.
We were afraid that we would not be able to find jobs here." Marina
reported disliking her present job and feeling depressed by her lack of
achievement, but explained her need to keep this work for emotional
reasons:

> I am on the brink of losing my job now, and this is killing me.
> I cannot imagine what I will be doing with myself without

working. Now I work at least four hours a day, and it is good for me, not that my job is so great, but I have to work, I have to go somewhere, I have to go away from myself, and then I feel good. When I stay home, my inner state is horrible; I am unsatisfied with my life. I cannot find the job I would like to have. I cannot make the money I want.

She described her plans for the future and expressed hopes for achieving a better, more rewarding career, "I want to take more classes and to try again to get a job. This job may not satisfy me emotionally and intellectually, but at least financially it will be better."

Minna, a non-participating mother, attended college at the time of the interviews. Her mother Golda reported Minna's determination to graduate and to obtain a good job. Talking about her hopes for her daughter's future, Margarita started with work, "I want her to have an opportunity to study well and to have a good job later on. Then, I want her to marry better than I did." The importance of work and professional achievement appears to be a dominant theme for all the adult participants of the study. Even though the granddaughters were only 14 to 16 at the time of the interviews, the influence of their mothers' and grandmothers' "work first" attitude was noticed in their stories.

Subtheme B: My work is more intense in America (mothers)

Three of the four participating mothers reported feeling more stressed at work and having less free time and energy as compared to their work in the Soviet Union. Their reasons fell into several categories: the need to work in a new language, higher intensity of work, longer working hours, and longer commutes in the United States. Maya concluded that work was easier for her in the Soviet Union:

Work is more intense here, besides, we have to work in a foreign language, practically. There, I did not have to search for words, I didn't need to control what I was saying, and here it is absolutely impossible. I would also say that there is much more responsibility in your work. This intensity is not only physical; you feel it mentally at times. Sometimes when I come home I not only lack strength to do something, but I don't feel like moving a finger or saying a word.

Margarita also reported feeling exhausted after work. She believed that the need to travel to and from work and doing overtime on a regular basis deplete her energy:

> There the town was small. I used to work in a walking distance, about 5 minutes. Now I spend about 2 hours a day on the road, so my life is more complicated now. I work a lot. Today and yesterday were two very rare occasions when I came home on time, and when you spend 10 hours a day sitting at the computer, you already don't want anything. I have no energy left; I get very tired there.

Talking about her daughter and her immigrant peers, Margarita stressed their determination for "making it" in the new country. She compared their situation with that of "young people from the provinces" of the former Soviet Union who had to take any kinds of jobs and to suffer all kinds of privations to be allowed to stay in the capitals and to "claw their way up." Musing on the subject, Margarita made a wider generalization. She said, "Emigration makes us work ten times harder." Marlena reported coming home from work at seven or seven-thirty in the evening and feeling "lazy" and tired.

Even though Marlena's and Maya's husbands work and make comfortable living, it did not seem to occur to them that they might work part-time and spend more time taking care of themselves or their daughters.

Subtheme C: I want to be smart and rich. I want to be a lawyer (granddaughters)

Talking about their plans for the future, four of the five teenage granddaughters demonstrated the influence of their mothers' and grandmothers' attitude toward work and achievement. Interestingly, three of them indicated their strong interest in the legal profession, probably identifying it with power and affluence. They demonstrated detailed knowledge of academic qualifications and personality traits, necessary for this career. When asked about her plans for the future, laconic Dosia said few words, "I want to be smart and rich, I want to be a lawyer. In school I am a member of a debate club, and I can do it well, I like it. It is a little too long to study for it, so what?" Expressive Dora made her achievement of happiness contingent on her career:

For me, happiness is having a great law career working in some office in Boston or Manhattan, having clients, getting up every morning just to know that you are going to make a difference in someone's life, and... OK, you have to have money, of course, and you have to have a nice car and a good-looking husband who also works on Wall Street, and everything, and you have these great kids.

It is not surprising that a husband and kids come after the career, money, and a car in Dora's list of priorities. Growing up in a family of divorced women who valued self-reliance and financial stability, Dora developed a survivor's attitude toward her own future. She expressed anger and jealousy toward those who have "everything prepared for them" and sounded determined to do everything in her power to achieve her goals. Talents and hobbies appear to get sacrificed on the road to a secure and lucrative career, as well. Both Dosia and Dora talked about their decision not to develop their musical abilities in search for a more stable career. Described as "overly serious" by her musician grandmother, Dosia said, "My grandmother played the piano and I tried to sing. I used to like it. Now I am more interested in college and in the debate club. I think it is more important for me." Dora brought up her mother's example as a basis for her decision:

I think I can sing sometimes... and I started becoming interested in this kind of musical conservatory, and I was thinking, like, no, I am not going to do what my mom did and go to musical school and then have to switch careers and go to college again. I don't want to go through that, so it is better just to choose something long-term, something you have to fall back on.

Contemplating her daughter's single-minded thirst for success, Margarita makes broader generalizations:

Our children are very ambitious and working hard to achieve what they want. And the older was the child when he came here, the harder it was for him to get adjusted to this life and the more motivated he is to pull himself out of this. The person who is in a tough situation has more drive to succeed, and the one who is relaxed, who gets things easily, is less motivated. Our children, who do not have everything ready for them, like American children, are very motivated.

A strong desire to achieve through hard work and the best possible education seems to have been absorbed by the granddaughters from their mothers and grandmothers. Their learning takes precedence over other interests and needs when they have to make a choice. Dana reported loving sports, but having no time for it, "I love gym. We play volleyball. I don't have time now to do more than this—I am in the eighth grade and I have big tests this year. If I had the time, I would take karate, it's so cool." Dana's mother Marina supports her daughter's choice:

> She did acrobatics, rhythmic gymnastics. Now she stopped participating in sports because we moved and she has a hard time getting adjusted to the new school. She was accepted into a very challenging class. In Queens, she was at the top of her class, and now she is at the bottom, so she spends a lot of her energy on catching up.

Marina stressed her preference for Dana's education and career over other pursuits, "I think that the most important thing for her is to get good education, and good profession, to be completely independent." Other mothers and grandmothers were no less interested in the girls' careers. The consensus of opinion on this particular issue was strong and clear.

Collective/Individual

Subtheme A: It is difficult to find friends here
(grandmothers and mothers)

All participating grandmothers and mothers stressed the value of friendships in their lives and reported feeling frustrated by their difficulties establishing close social relationships in the United States. Galina considered this lack of social connections a major source of her depressed mood:

> I think, communication with people is the most important thing in life. There we had friends, we used to go to the theater, to the movies. Here it is different. I hasten the day's

passage, and if we did not have Russian TV, I would go totally crazy.

Galina reported missing her old friends' support and understanding. She explained her difficulty in forming new friendships by the need to build trust over time. For the Soviet citizens, trusting the wrong person could be deadly. Their paranoia was based on the macabre reality of the Communist regime. Galina elaborated on her suspicious attitude toward new connections:

> We have some friends, so we go for a walk, talk to them, but they are not the kind of friends we used to have there. If you are friends for many years, you know them and trust them, they are your tried and tested friends. I used to share with them things I could not tell my own daughter. You cannot trust the person you met here two or three years ago the same way, to be as open with them. There are moments when people need to open up, to share their pain. One poor woman said something to my neighbor, and now the whole street knows what she told her. It is difficult to find friends here.

In the absence of other support systems during the Communist regime, many Soviets looked to their friends for advice, guidance, and for emotional relief. For this reason, friendship took on greater significance for many former Soviets. Galina was not alone in her tendency to merge friendship and therapy. Greta quoted her granddaughter's disapproval of her tendency to air her home issues with her friends, "I don't want you to discuss all my problems, my relationships with all your friends. I know you report everything to each other." Nevertheless, when the problem arose, Greta did exactly that:

> We had a dilemma—Hunter, or Stuyvesant, or The Bronx School of Science. The father was immediately yelling, 'NO! That's it! NO!' Daniela said, 'It is I who will study there, not you. I have to decide.' From our house to the Hunter is two hours by train. Of course, I quietly talked to Maya; my friends gave me advice that he should drive her there. Let her take a look where she wants to go, what kind of commute it is. That was it; the problem was solved.

Describing her new friend's problems, Galina demonstrated intimate knowledge of every detail in that woman's life. She expressed angry criticism of her friend's "selfish and ungrateful" daughter. In her fervor, she started addressing the "bad daughter" directly, as if she were facing her in person:

> My neighbor does everything for her daughter; she spreads herself under her feet. But when she asked her daughter, a hairdresser, to give her a manicure and a pedicure, she says, 'I don't have the time.' Then her daughter had a birthday, so her mother made a complete birthday spread for her, she cooked everything. If you want to go to a restaurant with your friends, it is OK... But to come home when your mother has cooked everything already and not to invite your mother to sit with you, to wish you a happy birthday? The mother gave you $200.00 as a present; if she managed to save two hundred dollars from her meager pension to give you for your birthday, you should respect her.

In another case, Galina does talk directly to the "offender," trying to teach her cousin how to treat his wife right:

> He has to understand—she spends all her time with him and she gives him so much attention, but a human being needs a break once in a while. He has to tell her, 'Go for a walk, meet some friends,' but he does not want to listen to me, I tell him so many times.

Golda expanded her understanding of friendship and its responsibilities even further. She felt obligated to act for the "good" of her neighbor even though the woman came just to share her problem with her, not to ask Golda to solve it for her. Unable to limit her participation to advice alone, Golda described the order of events:

> How can a mother be so weak and indecisive when she needs to act quickly, I don't understand it. She came to me last week crying because she found out that her daughter was pregnant. I was shaken when I was listening to her, and talking about it gave me the creeps—a Jewish girl got involved with some punk, and, hello, mommy, she is pregnant... I went to this weakling of a mother and asked her, "What are you going to do about this business?" She did not say a word, just kept

crying. Finally, two days ago, I could not stand it any longer and said, "When are you going to the clinic?" She looked at me as if I fell from the Moon, "What clinic?" I banged my fist and yelled at her, "You have to force her to have an abortion!" She started crying even louder, but what good did it do her? To make a long story short, I grabbed the kid by her arm and dragged her to the clinic. If her mother is weak, somebody had to take care of her so that she won't spoil her whole life.

For Greta, friendship is a source of joy and satisfaction with life. She spoke with admiration about her new friend Gita, valuing her support and emotional strength:

I found wonderful friends, we get together, have a good time, enjoy the activities. Gita, my best, closest friend, my soul mate, is such a special person. We go to the center for gymnastics classes, so one day I told her, "No matter how I am trying to run away from being old, it catches up with me. Now, my leg hurts.' She stopped, looked at me, and answered, 'Madam, you are not sixteen. Are you walking on your own? Can you see the sun? Say thank you. What else do you need?' She is an optimist and such a wise human being. She has the unique ability to convince you that every little thing in life is valuable, to teach you to enjoy it and stop thinking about your losses and your past. She stimulates my energy, helps me go on living.

Gita herself was more concise, but expressed similar feelings, "We go to a literary club, very interesting, we enjoy each other company, see interesting people."

While grandmothers sounded content with having almost exclusively Russian-speaking friends in the United States, the mothers appeared uneasy about their limited social contact with Americans. They blamed Americans for being unapproachable, probably trying to stave off their own feelings of inferiority and discomfort over crossing the cultural and language barriers. Maya juxtaposed her relationship with colleagues in the Soviet Union and in the United States:

Of course, I know my colleagues, but there is no such closeness as we had in the Soviet Union. And people are not striving for it. There are a few colleagues with whom I am closer, with others I am less close, but to openly tell them everything that worries you, of course, not.

Describing her unpleasant feelings of alienation, Marlena attributed her lack of socializing with Americans to her limited mastery of English:

> We have no American friends. At work, I am on wonderful terms with everybody, but no friendship. I mean everything is nice, we talk, share our news, but there is no friendship. I have no friendship with our neighbors, either; it is difficult for me to communicate with them. I mean, they don't want to, and I don't, either. I feel scared to go to Dina's school. If things are OK, I don't want to force myself and talk to them, to communicate.

At another point of the interview, Marlena returned to her feelings of alienation in the new culture, attributing the impossibility of satisfying communication to her limited English mastery:

> It is impossible when you cannot speak fluently the language of the country where you live. We cannot be like Americans; it is impossible. Anyway, there will be a chasm that you cannot cross. At times you catch yourself thinking that you are a kind of guest here.

Marina reported similar feelings about her difficulties in forming friendships:

> In general, I have been living for a long time in the United States, but I still cannot understand Americans. I do not have American friends. We meet some Americans at the pool or in other places, but they never invite us to their homes, and I don't feel like inviting them. My experience with Americans at work was not too good.

Margarita's feelings about difficulties in forming friendships in America were consonant with those of the other mothers. Her recollections about the friends of her youth are filled with romanticized, exulted longing for "ideal," soulful connections:

The friends I had in my childhood were the only true friends I ever had in my life. They understood you before you finished your thought and responded to your subtle emotional tone. We sensed each other's inner state by our skin, ears, everything.

Margarita described her parting with school friends as a dramatic event, charged with danger and endured with stoicism:

I told them not to come to the station to see me off; it was dangerous during these times. And all my friends came anyway, all of them. I was standing, smiling, talking; I was controlling myself. I did not want them to see me crying.

Contemplating her nostalgic feelings, Margarita concluded, "Of course, I do not miss the country, just my friends. Probably this is what motherland is about, not that damned stove." Describing her present situation, she sounded unhappy and lonely, "Here I do not have so many acquaintances, and decent people are hard to come by." She sounded resentful of competitiveness and insensitivity of her fellow immigrants. Margarita painted an unappealing portrait of vain and presumptuous Russian immigrant women she met in New York, "Here women from the Soviet Union are like that Russian fairy tale character—it was not enough for her to be a princess, she wanted to be a queen. It looks ridiculous and ugly." Margarita's anger probably stems from her envy of better provided for married women, but her observation appears to be keen an accurate, as it suggests strong competitiveness among former Soviets who have to prove themselves in the new country.

Margarita believed that language problems and cultural differences in America prevent her from forming the type of friendships she longs for:

It was a very strong friendship; I don't have it here. As it became clear to me, here it is very difficult to find friends. Probably not only here, but also when you are well past 30 and you have grown up in certain conditions, and people around you have grown up in others, any word uttered by you or them may be misunderstood or not understood correctly.

Even though the participating mothers talked about cultural differences between the United States and Soviet Union, they appeared unaware of the sources of their attitude toward friendship. The analysis of their interviews suggested that strong friendships were necessary for survival during the Communist regime as they served as an informal support system. Margarita's side remark summarized this attitude. "We became very close friends. I know that if something happens, I can lean on him, which is a difficult thing to say about anyone here." The need to "lean on" somebody in the time of need appears to be one of the factors that strengthened friendships in the Soviet Union.

Subtheme B: American society is focused on individuality (grandmothers and mothers)

"Analytically oriented," Maya was the only adult participant who conceptualized the basic difference between the individual orientation of American society and the collectivism of the former Soviets. When she compared the two school systems, she realized that the "collective" was a means by which the government pressured its members into obedience. From a very young age Soviet children were collectively brainwashed into functioning as worker ants for the government's interests. Mundane and boring tasks, such as collecting scrap paper, were romanticized and turned into a collective pep rally.

> I was so shocked when we just arrived—every year children, starting from a very early school age, are moved from one class to another. It is not like it was with us—you graduate practically with the same group of students you started with in the first grade. This system develops close contacts. American society is focused on individuality; not we, but I, as it differs from the former Soviet Union, 'We, the collective of the 9-B class decided to collect and deliver this much scrap paper for the national economy.' Here nobody needs this, and a personal opinion is to be developed on every issue. Americans don't need to fit in like we did.

Maya considered pros and cons of both attitudes at different points of the interview. When she talked about her work, she seemed to prefer the Soviet-style "stable working collective" as it provided emotional support for its members, "There were 20 people in my collective; we used to know each other very intimately. We knew each other's families, parents, children, closest friends." Describing her youth, Maya reported her preference for intellectual aspirations and attributed it to the "collective" norm of valuing intellectual over material pursuits, "There I did not have such a need to assert myself on the sole basis of my appearance. Probably we asserted ourselves by other means—we had more of other interests. Purely intellectual needs were more stressed." Margarita's phrase, "Like all the Soviet children, we read very much" supported Maya's opinion. On the other hand, her story suggests awareness of the repressing, anti-individual pressure of "collective" opinion,

> I remember the mother of one of my classmates. She paid very much attention to my friend's looks; she wanted to dress her better than others and to make her stick out. She kept telling her mother, 'Stop it, mom, everybody is this way, and I want to be this way.'

Maya's mother Greta noticed the new attitude in her granddaughter Daniela, and it seems to be difficult for Greta to accept it. Sharing her distress over the family conflicts, she described to me the situation that arose when her granddaughter had to choose a high school and considered a distant one:

> The father started yelling immediately, 'NO! That's it! NO!' She says, 'It is I who will study there, not you. Why are you deciding for me? I have to decide." You see, it is already American influence, her position, she is an individual; she plans her life for herself. And her father is right too—the school is too far.

Other adult participants mentioned "collective" and "everybody" matter-of-factly, probably having internalized some of the dominant Soviet attitudes toward the benefits of "living as a collective." Talking about Marina, her mother Galina said, "I am proud of my daughter, everybody envies me because she treats me very well." Genya sounded happy describing her students and her friendship with them, "When my students were graduating, it was such an emotional goodbye for the whole group. They were like family to me and to each other, we kept the ties after the graduation, ten years together is not a trifle." When Margarita and Marlena discussed weight loss methods, their reports suggested pervasive character of these fads as if masses of people agreed to starve themselves into shape one day a week. Attempts to lose weight in a group with others made the task feel easier for Marina. The price for the comfort of group support, according to Marlena, is the norm that dictates putting the interests of the collective ahead and above the interests of the individual. Contemplating the new for her, American concept of "loving oneself," Marlena compares it with the self-sacrificial nature of Soviet collectivism:

> I understood that here you have to live in a new way—you have to think more about yourself, you have to do what you want. I do not mean anything bad, but in general, you should think more about yourself and live the way you want and think less about others and how they will think about you.

Self-sacrifice, giving up one's own needs and interests for the sake of others, appears to have been instilled into the minds and psyches of all participating mothers and grandmothers. They spoke with pride about their sacrifices for the sake of their children and grandchildren. The question, "How else could it be?" seemed to reflect their unquestioned acceptance of this cultural norm. Having grown up in the society based on control, they seemed unaware of their own controlling tendencies and considered governing their adult children's and grandchildren's life a normal payoff for their sacrifices.

Subtheme C: I have friends of different nationalities (granddaughters)

All five participating granddaughters spoke fluent English and reported having "mixed racial people" as friends. Dora spoke about her enjoyment of such relationships:

> I have a lot more friends now, and not only Russian friends, but also Italian friends, and Spanish friends, and every nationality you can think of. My best friend, she is Albanian, and my other best friend, she is Chinese. And I am able to find common ground with both of them. I am very happy about that; they are great friends.

Dina spoke about feeling comfortable with a "different variety of people" even though she expressed a preference for having Russian friends "because it is just easier to bring them home to your family. They will be able to communicate better with my parents." Living in the suburbs, she described the limited opportunity for communicating with Russian peers, "I really don't have too many Russian friends here in Westchester; here in the neighborhood or in school, so I don't get to be around Russian people that much. I am always around American people." Dana, another participant living in the suburbs, spoke about her new school where "everybody is Jewish practically, American Jews." At another point of the interview, she talked about her Korean friend. For both granddaughters, the cultural background of their friends appeared to be unimportant.

The granddaughters who lived in areas with sizable Soviet immigrant population, such as Brooklyn, Queens, or the Bronx, talked about an opportunity to "hang out" with people of the same or similar ethnic background. Dora said that she finally felt good when she regained her ethnic pride after "being tortured for being Russian" in elementary and middle school:

In high school, they all accept each other, because everyone is with such a different background, so the only thing we have in common is that we are all different. In high school, Russians hang out with Russians, and other people have their own groups, and they are proud of their cultures. I am thinking if Arabic people are all proud, why cannot I be proud, too?

Daniela's early experience was not traumatic, but she reported a similar change:

In junior high school, I mostly had American friends, and in high school, I started mingling with the Russians, and most of my friends are Russians. I still have a few, like within school grounds I am very friendly, I am friends with a lot of mixed racial people, different nationalities, but outside the school, if I am hanging out, they are mostly Russians.

Dosia, another granddaughter living in the outer borough of New York City, reported having "Russian friends and Chinese ones." Only one granddaughter, Dora, spoke about her reason for seeking out a friend with a similar cultural background:

Albanians and Russians are very close because they both are, like, Slavs, I think they are. So our grandmas are very similar. I go to her house, and her grandma came from Albania to visit, and she was making us eat.

Dana was the only participating granddaughter who expressed strong negative feelings against Russian immigrant youngsters:

> All the friends that I had, all the girls were Russian, they backstabbed me, so I don't want, like, associate with them. I felt more comfortable with Americans or Russian people who were born here. People who came, they are very rude right now.

However, her impressions about American peers were strikingly similar, "The people here are more snobby, they are just bitches—they have an attitude, problems with everything, and they are backstabbing people."

In general, it seems that having grown up in the United States, the participating granddaughters experienced no difficulty forming satisfying friendships with people from the larger American society. As they spoke fluent English, their inclination for socializing within their own ethnic group appears to stem, for some of them, from their desire to accommodate their families and for others, from their interest in common cultural roots.

CATEGORY II: FAMILY RELATIONSHIPS

Mother/Daughter

Subtheme A: I would not leave my mother (grandmothers)

Four participating grandmothers reported very close connections with their mothers throughout their adult lives. Two of them never lived separately from their mothers, and the other two returned to living together when the mothers needed care. None of the mothers reported questioning this arrangement or seeking an alternative solution. Galina spoke about her mother with emotional intensity and passionate longing:

> After the surgery, I took my mother with me. She lived with me for thirteen years, all the rest of her life. It would not have occurred to me to do otherwise. I could not allow her to live alone. She was unique. I miss her very much, I would have been happy to keep taking care of her for many more years, just to keep her alive.

In her adoring portrayal of her mother, Galina stressed that she "was a very smart woman, tactful, she could never hurt a person. If she knew something would hurt you, she would never touch upon this theme, she would never say a word." Saying this, Galina appeared to have blocked out her earlier recollection, "My mother used to say, 'My boys are better looking.' This hit me right into my heart. All my life I thought that I am ugly, that my body is ugly, that this and that was wrong with me." Even though Galina was aware of the destructive impact of her mother's criticism on her life, she spoke about 13 years of care for her ill mother a "gift from G-d."

Greta reported loving and enjoying her work, but she expressed no doubts about her decision to retire when he mother needed care, "I retired early because my mother became very ill. I could not leave my mother alone because she became blind, the last twenty years of her life she was blind."

Regardless of the cramped space in Golda's new apartment, she took her mother to live with her. This is how she described their living conditions:

> All my married life I lived together with my mother. When I received a new apartment, of course, I took her with me again, how else could I have done it? She lived all her life with me, and in her old age I would leave her to live alone? I slept in the middle of the room on a folding cot, my mother slept on a couch, and my daughter lived in the bedroom with her husband, and the baby was born already. This is how we all lived.

Gita talked about her mother with love and gratitude:

> When my mother died, she was ninety-two. She lived with me all the time. When I got married, my father died, and I could not leave her to live alone. She was a very calm person, never meddled in our business. She helped me a lot when my children were little. She always stayed with them, cooked.

Other three grandmothers also reported that their mothers took care of their children and cooked for the family. Golda said, "I worked, so my mother took care of my children. My mother did a lot of cooking, too." When she talked about helping her daughter Maya take care of Daniela, Greta stressed that she did what her mother did for her:

> I am a teacher; she was also working in school, so we managed to set our schedules so that we did not have to leave her. It was the same with my children. My mother was a teacher, so we arranged our schedules in such a way, that I could bunch up my kids and take them to my mother's house. Then after work I would come to my mother, pick up my children and run home.

Genya, a war orphan, was given no chance to take care of her mother, but her story included a hair-raising episode of filial devotion:

> My grandmother and her other daughter Fira lived in their old house in a tiny room. When the war started, my father's mother was evacuated with us, and my mother's mother returned to our city. She came to the railway station with us and said, "I have no strength to go; I will stay." Fira went back home with her. My father's brother was in the motorized division, so he left the city with the last trucks. He was passing their house, so he stopped for a moment and begged them to come with him, he told them that everybody who stayed would be killed. My grandma was in bed, she had no strength to get up, and Fira said, "I will not leave my mother." They were close, in life and death.

Talking about her sister, Greta described an episode, illustrating the self-sacrificial nature of maternal and filial devotion:

> My sister's younger daughter left for Israel in 1990. When she was expecting a baby, my sister hurried to get there for the time for her daughter to give birth. My sister has always been a very sickly person, but her physician told me that emigration hastened her death. On July 17th they left Moscow for Israel. Exactly in four months, on November 17, she died. The only letter I received from her from Israel was full of joyous descriptions of her tiny granddaughter, how happy she was to see her. On the other hand, she wrote that she would never forgive herself for not being there for our mother's funeral.

The participating grandmothers and peers they mentioned in their stories, seem to have internalized their mothers' attitudes, applied them to their relations with their daughters, and expected their daughters to continue the tradition. Their ties and sense of mutual obligation formed the glue that held the families together.

Subtheme B: I came here to be with my daughter, this is my mission in life (grandmothers)

All five participating grandmothers stressed that the main reason of their emigration was their desire to be with their daughters and to help them as much as possible. Two mothers emigrated together with their divorced daughters; the other three joined their married daughters within a short period of time. Genya said:

> Margarita wanted to leave, especially after her divorce, and I was afraid to let her go alone. I said, 'I will not let you go with the child. If we are to go, we all should go together.' My husband did not want to go, but we came for her sake and for her daughter's sake.

Galina also had to overcome her husband's resistance. According to her report, she had only one reason for emigration—her desire to be with her "one and only" daughter Marina. In a dramatic tone, Galina described how she suffered their first separation, "We could not live without each other there, either. When Marina got married and moved to another city, I was going crazy." Marina's emigration was an even harsher challenge for Galina, since she was not able to "visit her all the time," as she used to do in the former Soviet Union. Most of the information Galina had about immigrant life in the United States at that time was negative, "My husband's brother wrote to us that it is not that easy and simple here." Nevertheless, her desire to emigrate was strong enough to overcome her own fears and to "force" her husband who "did not want to go," fearing the loss of status he was enjoying in the former Soviet Union.

Lavishing praise on America and its pleasures, Golda expressed her gratitude for her daughter's insistence on emigration, "I am so happy that I left that part of the city, I mean Russia in general. All this is thanks to my daughter, 'Mama, dear, let's go.' If not for her, I would have died there. Golda described her household activities in detail, beaming with pride:

> I come and help, how else can it be? I cook, take care of them before they leave for school in the morning. Sometimes I make them juice, sometimes just tea with something they have for breakfast, like tuna or feta cheese. Then I make the beds and leave for my place. Then one comes from school, the other one comes from college in the evening, and I have already cooked dinner.

Greta's report was similar:

> Now my mission is to support my family as much as possible. I came here for it, to help them, to support them in their hard life. All the housekeeping responsibilities for my daughter's family I took upon myself. I live with my daughter, and I must cook dinner. This *must* is defined by me; so I must clean up and do the laundry.

All grandmothers stressed that in the United States they continued the family tradition of supporting their adult children by giving them money and taking household responsibilities upon themselves. They did the same in the Soviet Union, considering no sacrifice too big. Describing their first years in America, Genya said, "My granddaughter lived with us for a while, so that Margarita was able to work and to study." She explained her decision to move back to her despotic and cruel husband by her desire to help her daughter:

> When Margarita got married, they lived with me until I moved back to my husband, so that they could have the apartment for themselves. I returned to him for her sake. We have to help our children, we love them; how else can it be?

More than once, Genya stressed that her behavior was typical for her peers, "This is how we came—following her, together with him, for their sake, as it usually is among us." And on another occasion, "I am not an exception, all the mothers I know do as much as I do."

It was interesting to observe that the grandmothers described their household responsibilities only when I asked them, considering these common knowledge. All of them replied, "You know how it is" in response to my questions. In their spontaneous conversations, the participating grandmothers and mothers tended to mention their household responsibilities only when the exceptions to the rule occurred. Marlena explained her need to cook for her family in the Soviet Union, "I did not live with my mother, we lived in a different town; so I had to cook." Marina complained about her "spoiled" husband, "When we lived with my parents in Queens, I had to cook, because he was not satisfied by my mother's cooking."

All participating and non-participating grandmothers chose to live with their daughters rather than sons. Three participating grandmothers have sons, but their connection with the daughters was obviously closer and stronger. This difference in attitude toward male and female children was nicely summarized by Gita, "My daughter is my special child," even though her son was living with her at the time of the interviews. Talking about her children, Golda sounded proud of her hard-working and loving sons, but she reserved her great passion for Minna, "My daughter is the light of my life." The same emotional division between female and male adult children was considered natural in all the families described by the participants. Gita compared her relationships with her two granddaughters, "We are so close [with Dina]. Not with my other granddaughter, because I was not taking care of her when she was growing up, the other grandmother did. I have not seen her for five years." As her son's daughter, the "other" granddaughter was less of a priority for Gita. This difference probably has its roots in the cultural tradition that expects a daughter, not a son, to take care of the elderly parents.

All five grandmothers reported that upon their arrival to the United States they lived either with their daughter's family or in very close proximity. They experienced the changes their daughters made in these arrangements as personal affronts and felt hurt. Generally positive and soft-spoken Gita expressed unusually strong feelings about her daughter's departure for the suburbs, "In the beginning I got upset and said, 'How can it be? I came here to live with my daughter." Gita's daughter sounded guilty when she talked about this decision and described the arrangements she made to diminish, at least to some degree, her guilt and her mother's hurt:

> Of course, I wanted to live next to my mother, but we could not live in the Bronx. And for my mother, living in Westchester, I think, is not good. Let her live long and healthy

till 100, but when she needs it, of course, I will take her here and she will live with me, but while she is on her own legs, she does not need it.

Galina sounded devastated by her daughter's move, "Since my daughter moved to this house, it became terribly difficult for me without her." Even though she reported feeling "dead tired" when she took care of her granddaughter and the child she babysat, Galina attributed her depressed state to the loss of these responsibilities:

I hasten the day's passage, and if we did not have Russian TV, I would go totally crazy. When the children lived next to us, I could go see my granddaughter, do this and that, and the day was gone.

Galina also reported being upset by her inability to help her daughter financially. She recalled wistfully, "When I was able to, I used to clothe them, I did everything I could. Now it is so painful for me that I cannot help her. I wish I could do much more."

Talking about her daughter and granddaughter, Genya reported "taking care of them on all fronts" and "thinking about them most of the time." As the grandmothers consider all their efforts and sacrifices a given, their expectations of filial responsibility and obedience became an outgrowth of their overall concept of the family roles. When their daughters failed to fulfill these expectations by adhering to new lifestyle demands, the participating grandmothers reported feeling "left out" and "not needed any more."

While the participating grandmothers stressed that they felt responsible for taking care of their adult daughter's housekeeping and child rearing needs, they seemed to have extended their control to other areas of their daughters' lives as well. Their narratives contained stories about other mothers who felt entitled to control the lives of their adult children, considering this power the obligatory payoff for their sacrifices. Galina talked with resentment about her domineering mother-in-law who "forbade" her to have children. She reported perceiving herself as not being "that kind of mother who could tell her daughter, 'Get a divorce.' Nevertheless, she did give Marina this advice, albeit in a softer tone, "Once when I was visiting her, I asked her, 'Maybe you will go home?' Addressing her neighbor's "ungrateful" daughter, Galina stressed the sense of mutual obligation:

Her son had problems in school, he also got involved with such friends who used to shoot up, and she found out and suffered tremendously, the grandmother, together with the mother. They did everything to pull him away, and now he became a human being, more or less. I mean she shared everything with you, good and bad, how can you be so unappreciative of your mother? One shouldn't be like this.

Genya recalled the pressure her mother-in-law exerted on her and blamed herself for not following this woman's example, "I always feel guilty that I was not like my mother-in-law who opposed my divorce for the sake of my child. I triggered Margarita's divorce, and I blame myself for it all the time. Dosia is fatherless because of me." Golda described her loving relationship with her children, praising her unassuming attitude, "I never give them trouble. I never demand anything from them." Golda's choice of words suggests her sense of entitlement to the rights she professes not to exercise.

Greta reported feeling responsible for keeping peace in her daughter's family and sounded distraught by her inability to do so, "My daughter is suffering terribly; she is constantly between two fires. At times I am desperate, simply desperate—I am there and cannot help." Greta's complaint about her son-in-law and his child-rearing ideas revealed the extent of her sense of entitlement to give advice, "In this aspect, he is damaging her because the girl is not accustomed to overcome difficulties, and when I tell this to them they do not change anything."

The grandmothers whose daughters moved away from them considered their daily telephone conversations and frequent extended visitations a norm. Talking about Marlena, Gita said, "I visit her whenever I want to. She calls me every day. I have a very good daughter. When it is very hot here, I go there, they have a pool in the backyard, and I stay in the pool all day long." Galina chose to be interviewed in Marina's house as she reported visiting her on a regular basis. Both she and Genya also reported their daily telephone calls as a necessity. Galina declared, "Every day I call them in the evening," and Genya said, "I am not always able to come, to see them, but there is the telephone—if I don't call them one day, I do not feel right." She reported her conversations with Margarita in a manner suggestive of her deep involvement in every minute detail of her daughter's life, "I necessarily have to know what is going on. I ask Dosia, 'What did mom cook?' Then Margarita comes home from work and asks me, 'Mama, why isn't she eating peppers?' So I answer, 'She won't eat them on the third day.'"

It appears that in the United States, such emotionally charged ties became even more necessary for the participating grandmothers due to their increased social isolation. On the other hand, they became too onerous for the participating mothers. Marina reported her efforts to satisfy her mother's need for connection, "I visit her almost every weekend, I call her all the time, almost every day. I do it because I know that she cannot live without me, she lives through me." She spoke about Galina's desire to "spend 24 hours a day if she could" with understanding and compassion as she was aware of her mother's reasons for it, "She is limited to her very small circle—food store and Russian TV, this is it, so I am her lifeline." Nevertheless, Marina reported her satisfaction with the distance afforded by her move to the suburbs, "The distance is better. Here you can live your own life and not abandon your parents." But even with this distance, she feels exhausted by her mother's constant telephone calls, "At times these conversations are too burdensome. I cannot take it anymore, at times I feel that I am at the end of my rope."

As the participating grandmothers reported expecting their daughters to maintain the emotional intensity of their attachment, the mothers seemed to perceive their failure to meet these expectations as causing the grandmothers excessive stress. For the grandmothers, the "Americanization" of their daughters seemed to become a personal tragedy.

Subtheme C: I can worry myself sick (grandmothers)

The participating grandmothers repeatedly spoke about feeling "like a fish out of water" in the strange cultural environment; their adult daughters became a "lifeline," connecting the participating grandmothers to the larger world. All grandmothers reported their difficulties negotiating many aspects of their new environment, such as using public transportation, dealing with bureaucracy, or getting necessary services. Greta summarized their new sense of helplessness by a colorful simile, "I am like that proverbial dog that understands everything, but cannot speak." Galina said, "When I receive a letter, I feel stressed out, I cannot read it, even with a dictionary. So I have stress unlimited." The sense of new dependency and the fear to lose this vital connection appears to have been exacerbated by real and media-amplified dangers of living in the metropolitan New York area. For the participants, who came from mid-size cities with few cars and stable population, the dangers of living in the big city seem especially frightening. Three participating grandmothers reported being tormented by constant worries about their daughters and granddaughters. Galina talked about the whirlwind of fears and imaginary horror scenarios, raging in her mind, "I always think of something terrible that happened, I mean it is like I tune myself to bad things, I feel constantly worried." When she and her husband lived in Marina's apartment, Galina's "eyes were always red from crying" as she reported being "a nervous wreck until I saw her back home" every day. Living separately did not bring relief to Galina. Her vigilance for hidden signs of trouble seemed to increase her worries.

> I call Marina and hear a difference in the tone of her voice. That is it for me, I already imagine that something terrible happened to them, that she is not telling me every detail, so I am already all shaken up and I cannot sleep all night.

Every negative event in Marina's life is a "torture and heartbreak" for Galina. She reported feeling that she can "lose her mind from worrying," and that it "reflects on me terribly." On the other hand, she insists on being informed about every possible detail, including her daughter's sex life, "For a woman, sex is also important, and she is not getting what she should have gotten, and this is not so good, either. And all of this together makes the mother feel so bad."

Galina is even more worried about her granddaughter Dana. In her infancy, the girl may have been exposed to radiation, released by the Chernobyl catastrophe. The family worried about her health and ascribed her "bad eating" to "that accursed radiation." Dana's thinness was considered a sign of her poor health as Galina's in-law described her as a "horror picture." Galina's description is no less dramatic, "She looked so scary—skin and bones. She was so skinny that one could see blood vessels on her face." Dana's entry into adolescence gave Galina another reason for worrying, "We don't know what will happen in the future. G-d forbid if she meets somebody wrong."

Even though Galina is reasonably satisfied with Dana's progress and feels proud about her achievements in sports and in character development, her mind is unable to rest. She looks for scary examples from other people's lives and worries that similar things may happen to Dana. The tragic story of two young men who died of drug overdose threw a dark shadow over her mind and pushed her imagination into a frenzy,

> For us it is a big tragedy, this is why I am always afraid. I keep telling Dana, 'Watch it, G-d forbid, don't let anything happen to you. I worry terribly because it is impossible to protect your child from the school, the street, all the bad things.

Galina reported calling Dana every day to alleviate her worries:

> Dana is alone for four hours, and her parents don't know what she is doing when she is alone. It is good if a child knows that one should not do this or that, but she has friends, and who knows what they are up to. I call her, even though it is expensive. I am not at peace without it.

Galina's mind is not at peace even when things go well. On the one hand, she reported having a very good relationship with Marina, "I am proud of my daughter, everybody envies me because she treats me very well." On the other, Galina dwells on her neighbor's complaints about her "selfish" and ungrateful daughter and fears that similar things may happen in her own family, "So far, things are good between Marina and me, but what will happen later, I don't know. Here children change. I see it by my neighbor."

Galina reported being so nervous that it reflected on her health, "My head started shaking because of all the endless worries." She believes that her significant post-emigration weight gain is also a result of her nervousness, "I do not eat a lot, but when I start worrying, I have to put something in my mouth. The most terrible part of it all is that I am eating and not feeling the taste of the food."

Greta, another participating grandmother, "worries herself sick" even though she lives in the same apartment with Maya. In spite of Maya's efforts to accommodate her mother's desire to know where she is at any time, the slightest unexpected deviation from Maya's stated plan causes Greta intense suffering:

They told me that they would be back soon. They left at noon and returned at six. Starting from three o'clock and until six I was dead from worry, and my idiotic personality is such that my mind immediately gets flooded by a million of "pleasant" pictures, a car crash or something of the same kind.

Like Galina, Greta is also preoccupied with fear for her granddaughter's future:

I love the way Daniela looks, no doubt about it, but my heart aches all the time. She is beautiful, with a great slender body, and smart, too. But I know from the experience that it is better to be born lucky than beautiful, so this is why I am very tense inside. I am scared all the time, I am afraid for her. The morals are so lax here.

At another point, Greta contemplated Daniela's near future, "I am sure she will run away from home. The question is how she will do it. She may do some wrong things. I worry terribly about her and about my daughter." Galina's fears of being abandoned by her daughter seem to have materialized for Greta. On the one hand, she criticized her son-in-law for being unable to "understand the new mentality, new circumstances and requirements of life here," on the other hand, she talked with longing about "the way it used to be in our family before" and was hopeful to have it back. For Greta, the changes in her daughter's and granddaughter's attitude, their striving for little privacy are a source of tremendous pain, "What really makes me suffer is that both my daughter and my granddaughter have changed very significantly. I don't get enough of their warmth, especially from my granddaughter." Grappling with the new limits of her involvement in her children's life, Greta reasoned, "I understand that their family is their family and they should have and do have their own problems, issues they want to discuss only with each other, without my participation." Nevertheless, her report suggested that she feels hurt and left out, "I don't think that there is a necessity that my daughter tell me absolutely everything, like what is going on in her life, but at least something. I think that many things are not absolutely secrets."

Genya seemed to be even more intensely involved in her unmarried daughter's life, as if she was trying to overcompensate for the harm she felt she caused her daughter, triggering her divorce. She sounded especially sad when she was talking about her daughter's situation, "She got divorced there, and this was also stressful for her, of course. And here it does not work out for her, either. She is thirty nine now, it is not so easy, my heart aches for her." With all that said, Genya also complained about suffering from her daughter's lack of warmth and understanding, even though she tried to switch the blame from Margarita to her husband and to her own unfairly high demands for her daughter,

My daughter took a lot after her father; I suffer from the lack of warmth in her. There is no heartfelt closeness between us. At times, she does not want to listen to me, she does not understand me at times; she should be kinder to me. Sometimes I feel hurt by the tone of her voice or by her choice of the conversation topic or she would not listen to me. I cannot open my heart to her, cannot confide in her. Probably a mother should not confide in her daughter, it is not right.

Greta and Genya reported feeling lonely in spite of having families, probably due to their "Americanizing" daughters' emotional distancing. Golda tried very hard to sound optimistic in her interviews, but her description of her daughter's first "fiasco" resonated with the other participating grandmothers' feelings of deep involvement in their daughters' every step and intense worry about her future. In general, the participating grandmothers take their children's affairs to heart even more than they did in the former Soviet Union. The reason appears to be the combined effect of the grandmothers' increased social isolation and their daughters' newly acquired sense of privacy.

Subtheme D: It will be a disaster if my child forgets me in my old age (mothers)

The need for connection with the daughter and fear of "losing" her when she grows up, appear to be even stronger for the participating mothers than for the previous generation. The mothers appear to be caught between the demands of two cultures. On the one hand, they seemed to maintain the traditional attitudes of their mothers, as one can hear in Margarita's interview, "I am very devoted to Dosia and give her everything I have. Everything I have and everything I do is for her. If I am trying to achieve something, it is not for me, but for her, to help her have a better life." On the other, they demonstrated awareness of the new tendencies their daughter acquired from the new environment, especially going away to college and marrying outside of the émigré community. Three mothers talked about these "dangers" directly, still hoping that their daughters retained enough of their original culture to maintain the connection the mothers crave. Considering the changes in her life, Marina said, "Generations relate differently here. In the Soviet Union, I used to be much closer to my mother than I am now." Yet when the conversation turned to her own daughter, Marina sounded more willing to retain the old norm:

> When she starts dating, I would like her to date our boy—an immigrant from Russia or a child of Russian immigrants. It would be better for her and for us—we would be able to communicate with him and to have some kind of relationship with his parents. Common culture is very important—I want my daughter to become closer to me when she gets married, not more distant. I don't want to make an appointment to see her. I want to be close to her, not to live close, but to be able to talk to her often, to be there for her whenever she needs me, to give her some advice. If she marries an American, it will be terrible, they are so distant, so into themselves. My cousin is living with an American, so they have almost totally separate lives—separate bank accounts, separate things to do, and she is not communicating with her family, she became more like him. Her mother is heartbroken because of this.

Marlena's fears and hopes were strikingly similar:

> If Dina marries an American, I am afraid we will have no communication with him and his parents. It will be, "Hello, good-bye, how are you doing? How is work?" but never a close relationship. This is why I hope that she finds some Russian immigrant and marries him.

Going away to college was another item on the participating mothers' "worry list." Marlena said, When Dina goes to college, I don't know if I am going to see her as often as I want to see her. I will see her as often as she will want to see me." Even though Maya chose not to discuss this topic, her mother's account sounded convincing enough, even if Greta significantly dramatized it, "Now Daniela is talking about going away to college, but she is the only child. Without her they would be lost. She is the meaning of their life. They can't survive five minutes without her." Trying to justify her decision to go away to college, Dora complained about her mother and grandmother "smothering" her. She made an assured comment, "Of course, they don't want me to leave," but left an impression of having her mind set on a distant college.

Margarita sounded hopeless about her chances for remarriage. Probably this was her reason to be particularly frightened by her daughter's "Americanization":

> I hope that my daughter will give me more time and attention in my old age than American children do for their parents. I hope my daughter will keep her Russian attitude in this respect, I am afraid that it can be otherwise. Honestly speaking, she is the only soul I have in this world, she and my parents, and they, unfortunately, are very elderly. I have no hope to get settled some other way, so I don't plan things I cannot realistically expect. For me it will be a disaster if my child forgets me, I am scared even to think about it.

Trying to alleviate her fears, Margarita compares two cultural attitudes toward family closeness. She finds solace and hope in her daughter's upbringing, "Dosia is a combination of Russian and American ways. She was brought up by her grandmother and grandfather, they don't speak English; they will never be Americans." Margarita even spoke with nostalgic tenderness about the abominable living conditions she recalled with hatred on other occasions:

> Americans do not have such strong ties like we do. Yes, we were squeezed into a bunch in one apartment, it was like a noose on one's neck, but we were so much closer to each other, everything was passed from one generation to the next.

A combination of a traditional Jewish view on children as an extension of parents and the mother's desire to have a second chance in life through vicarious enjoyment of her daughter's life appear to further strengthen the mother's need for connection. Talking about her hopes for the future, Margarita said, "I want her (Dosia) to marry better than I did, it is very important." Describing her daughter's childhood, Marina said, "When we came here, Dana was very little, so I tried to give her an opportunity to do things I always wanted for myself, but could not

afford. She was in a dance class in Queens and in gymnastics."
Marina's mother added a dramatic note to this report:

> She made out of her everything she could. Even when she had
> it very hard financially, she used to moonlight; she did
> everything possible to give her everything—sports, dancing,
> here and there. They did their best, they drove her after work,
> did not spare anything. They were falling off their feet, but
> kept driving her to different places to make her good in
> everything.

Marina also reported her efforts to help Dana escape the repetition
of her weight problems, "I constantly remind her to work on her body,
because I know it about myself that no matter what I did, I was
overweight anyway, I could never lose weight. This is why I want her
to stay in shape."

The participating daughters appeared to be aware of their mothers'
hopes for their continued closeness and of their own guilt about the
future separation. Their choice of college will become the testing
ground for their ability to negotiate the cultural conflict between
American independence and the expectations of their families.

Grandmother/Granddaughter

*Subtheme A: Let our grandchildren be happy, we have lived our
measure already (grandmothers)*

All participating grandmothers considered deep involvement in every
aspect of their granddaughters' upbringing as well as being their
primary caretakers a moral imperative and the pivotal element of their
lives. Reporting that their granddaughters suffered from life-threatening
illnesses, three grandmothers sounded no less involved in their care
than their daughters. Galina said about her granddaughter, "We never
refuse her anything because she was born when Chernobyl disaster
started. We worried so much about her." Describing her
granddaughter's dangerous condition, Golda sounded as if she were in
charge of the situation:

> Dora had a bad case of asthma; we almost lost the child. And
> one day we went to the synagogue, and I said, "Minna, we

have to fast this year. Look at the child—she has like dried out." We really fasted, and toward the evening, we left the synagogue already, and the child turned blue. She was coughing and vomiting blood. I had my fill of work with her, suffered so much—don't ask. My daughter and I—we both had it. This poor one is not sleeping, and the other one has to go to work tomorrow. I ran to the doctor and showed that phlegm and all to her. Dora was in the hospital for a month, and this is how we pulled the child out.

Genya talked about her granddaughter's illness with the similar sense of sharing the responsibility for her health:

When Dosia was seven, she got very gravely ill, she had acetone in her urine. She lost a lot of liquid, so I ran to my cousin, she is a pediatrician. She said, "Don't even try to treat her by yourselves. You may lose the child." To make a long story short, we saved the child.

Genya spoke about her involvement in Dosia's education, too, "We could send the weakened child to school, but we decided to keep her for another year in kindergarten." She continued taking care of Dosia's education in the United States. This is how she described the first years of her emigration:

To say it briefly, we took care of our granddaughter. I used to give her all my time; who else would I take care of? I did not go to English classes; I did not have the time. I did not know one English word, so I used the international transcription system. We used to study, study, study... We used to do homework together, solve problems. We used to sweat a hundred times over until we understood the verbal problem. Now we can help her in mathematics. I am interested in it, I cannot let my granddaughter's education pass by me. I have to stick my nose, "Dosia, what are you learning now?" I see she is doing angles.

Genya expressed the belief that she "gave her a right start and direction in life," so Dosia became "especially good—she needs no pushing to study hard, she is a serious responsible girl." Genya also talked about efforts to keep Dosia's Russian language active, but admitted that it was a losing battle, "When she lived with us, we used to read with her. We have a bookcase filled with Russian books, and a lot of them are for children. Now she reads Russian the way I read English." Talking about "taking care of them on all fronts," Genya concluded with the question, "How else can it be?"

Another grandmother, Golda, started talking about her granddaughter with the question, "I took care of her, who else?" In general, she made little distinction between her daughter and granddaughter:

> Minna is 34, and Dora is 15. They are of the same height, and the same body shape; they look like sisters. I look at them and enjoy it; my heart fills with joy. What else is important in life?

Speaking about her love for her daughter, Golda used a passionate, dramatic metaphor, "If I could take out my heart, I would have given it to her. And I love my granddaughter the same way." For Golda, like for other grandmothers, loving means taking care of in every possible way. Golda defined her *must* herself, without being asked, "They don't get enough sleep, and I, too, next to them, don't get enough sleep. I know that I have to get up early, to make breakfast, because they are rushing for a train, a bus, and go."

Besides feeding and cleaning, Golda stressed her emotional closeness with "the girls", valuing the atmosphere of trust and openness:

> She tells me everything, she trusts me. I always tell her, "Dora, my heart, you have nobody closer to you than grandma and mother. Your mother and I are your best, closest friends." So she discusses all the things with us, asks for advice.

Golda's insistence on such openness had an overtone of control as she hinted to the "abortion" story she told me before the interview, "Dora is very close with her mother and me—it is our luck that she is not secretive. That girl I told you about was secretive, G-d forbid." Control appears to be a significant issue for another grandmother, Greta, as well. She sounded distraught by "lax" American morals and by Daniela's attitude toward her comments:

> When she goes to school with a bare navel, I cannot accept it, but all her peers do the same, so I have to keep silence. And she is such a girl that does not tolerate any negative comments

about her. One cannot even say a word, she gets offended right away, explodes, and a fragile peace is immediately broken.

Greta's report about Daniela's "Americanization" sounded highly emotionally charged, "This movement away from cultural life upsets me tremendously because I believe that intellectual aspirations of my daughter and granddaughter are suffering significantly from it. For example, my granddaughter has practically lost her Russian, which makes me very unhappy." Golda's report about her children's progress sounded equally emotionally intense, albeit positive, as evidenced from her involvement in their lives:

> My daughter... I am happy—America is helping her complete her education. She will have a college diploma and will be able to get a job in some company. I hope to have happiness from my daughter and granddaughter. Dora is also trying very hard; she also wants to have a good career. She was chosen from her school to go to Columbia University for the summer, she took courses there, they gave her a certificate, and they keep sending her papers to make her apply to their college. Of course I am very glad and happy.

In their desire to live through their children and for their benefit, the grandmothers appeared to fully agree with Marlena's words, "In Russia, 40-45 was considered a woman at sunset. At fifty she is a grandmother, and that is it—all her interests, all her life must be in grandchildren, and she has to forget about her own life." Galina expressed the same concept in a more dramatic tone, "Let our children be happy, we have lived our lives already."

The participating grandmothers appeared to strive for the continuation of the traditional norm of living with their adult children, for their children, and through the children. They did not seem to mind sacrificing their own interests in the process. Rather, the disruptions of this pattern caused them discomfort and distress.

Subtheme B: Looking at the granddaughter, one can see the grandmother, not the mother (mothers)

All participating mothers reported their mother's significant role in all aspects of their daughters' upbringing as part of a cultural norm. They touched upon feeding and babysitting only briefly and reported in more detail the grandmother's contribution to the granddaughter's personality development. Maya recalled her own childhood and her grandparents:

> We used to go to the Baltic republics, to Moscow, and this was because they had the means and, what is the most important, they had the desire and the need to do it. Not just to babysit, not just to wipe the grandchildren's noses, but to take them along and to show them something interesting.

When Daniela was born, Maya's grandmother was blind. Nevertheless, she left a lasting legacy of love and culture, "Daniela remembers that she knew an absolutely unbelievable number of poems by heart and she used to recite them to her since she was unable to read to her." Maya's mother Greta babysat Daniela and continued the tradition of "not just wiping the grandchildren's noses". Maya recalled, "She used to take her along when she would go to other cities to visit friends, to the theater. I remember she used to take her to the theater many times." She concluded, "She took an active role in her upbringing." Maya reported being shocked by the difference between American and Russian grandparents' attitudes. Her tone was highly disapproving while making the comparison:

> There is a man in my office, he has a son and two grandchildren. This man says, "We don't babysit the children, only if they have to go somewhere for two or three days, then we would take them. But most of the time they have babysitters." They live separately, so probably they visit them, but to do it or to *offer*—I did not hear any special excitement in his voice.

Maya's last sentence was highly indicative of the source of this specific cultural norm—the grandmother is supposed to *offer* her assistance, not just provide it.

Margarita's report was very similar. She recalled her mother taking care of her infant daughter so that she could work before the emigration. When they arrived in the United States, Dosia lived with Margarita's parents for some time for the same reason. Sharing her regrets about Dosia's lack of exercise, Margarita reported, "When we came here, we could not afford gymnastics classes and we had no car to take her there. I was happy that my parents were able to pick her up after school and to feed her." Margarita talked about her mother's role in the development of Dosia's musical abilities, "My mother tried to stimulate her interest in music. Dosia has it all—she can sing well, too. She likes Russian songs, even Ukrainian ones." Margarita was aware of her mother's feelings about Dosia's musical education, "My mother is always upset and cannot forgive me that she is not taking musical instruction." The grandmother felt resentful about her daughter's decision to allow Dosia to make her own choice and not force her to pursue the interests she chose for her. She summarized Dosia's relationship with her grandparents, "The grandmother used to spend a lot of time with her, now they are less in contact. It is natural that if a child sees them every day, they have a big influence on the child." Margarita's mother Genya talked about music as a spiritual connection between her and her granddaughter. She regretted her inability to give Dosia the most valuable gift she could:

> I want my granddaughter to also have some inner emotional, spiritual plank that will help her in times of hardship. She has musical talent, appreciation of classical music, so I feel very sorry that she is not getting formal training in music. She sings in the school choir, brings the notes to me, participates in concerts. This is our point of contact, and I am happy for it.

Other participating mothers also reported very strong emotional connection between grandmother and granddaughter. This connection extends into a more intellectual realm as well, such as listening to classical music, reading, and going to the theater. Reporting her mother's feelings about her move to the suburbs, Marlena said, "It was very difficult for us and for my mother, because my mother has brought up Dina, one can say. She brought her up and gave her a lot until she was 8." Marlena described her mother's relationship with Dina:

> Dina was my mother's favorite granddaughter, and she always took care of her. When we applied for emigration, my mother wanted to spend more time with her. She asked us to let Dina live with her. We agreed, we thought it would be easier for us to take care of all the paperwork, but it took longer than we planned—two years. My mother came to America three years later after us, and we lived together in the Bronx, and they became close again. Then we moved to an apartment nearby,

so my mother visited us regularly. Dina was still young, so my mother cooked, spent time with Dina, took her places, picked her up from school.

Gita's report about Dina's participation in dancing and sports inferred her continuing involvement in her granddaughter's life:

> In Russia, she took ballroom dancing for a year; she liked it a lot and did very well in class. I used to take her to the town culture club, waited until the class was over. Marlena lived far away. When Dina's partner moved to another town, she switched to the modern dance group; one did not need a partner for it. She swims very well; I used to take her swimming very often. And here, she is in some kind of group; it is like dancing and gymnastics to the music.

Marlena recalled her own grandmother in the tone that reflected the cultural norm, "My grandmother lived with us all the time, so she took care of us, kids." She also mentioned her mother-in-law who "virtually takes care" of her granddaughter, Marlena's niece.

The absence of a grandmother was stressed by the mothers because it created a hardship and forced them to use creative ways of managing or to forgo some desirable activities altogether. Recalling her own childhood, Margarita said:

> My mother had nobody to leave me with. I had a grandmother, she was very good, but she lived very far from us. I have no maternal grandmother; she died when my mother was 12. So she took me along to the musical college, and I would sit somewhere at the end of the hall and listen to their studying, singing. I did my homework, and they were practicing.

Another mother, Marina, complained that she was not able to pursue her interests because her grandmother lived far away:

> I also wanted to join a chorus, I wanted to sing very much, I wanted to learn how to dance, to do rhythmical gymnastics, but my parents worked all the time. I was accepted into a special musical school for gifted children, but my parents were not able to take me there, either. My grandmother lived in a

different town, but when she appeared, I was in a different stage.

According to Margarita, American children she knows demonstrate bad manners and compare poorly with immigrant children in terms of upbringing. Reflecting on the causes of this problem, Margarita concluded:

American grandmothers do not spend much time with their children, and it was a norm in Russia. Instead, American mothers have babysitters. As a result, there is a general lack of good upbringing. A babysitter is a stranger, she does not care what the child is doing; she just watches the child. When grandmothers took care of grandchildren, it happened that children had a better upbringing. Parents are always more busy than grandparents, and this is where manners, culture, general orientation were coming from. One could see what the grandmother is all about by looking at the granddaughter, not the mother.

Margarita sounded upset by another aspect of American lifestyle—distancing of generations. She said, "Here generations are very much separated" and presented a vignette that impressed her as unacceptable, "I cleaned one elderly American woman's apartment. She had several children, tons of grandchildren, and they used to take her home once a year for holidays." Margarita justified the adult children's behavior by the tradition, started by their parents, "Since parents spend little time with their children, when they grow old, their children spend little time with them. They have nice relationships, but they may live for years without seeing each other, just talking on the phone." She concluded that in spite of all the Soviet hardships, the benefits of sharing apartments were obvious, "Yes, it was terrible, like a noose on one's neck, but as a result, we were closer to each other."

All participating mothers appear to have internalized traditional Russian/Soviet attitudes toward the role of a maternal grandmother in her grandchildren's upbringing. An active participation of the grandmother in all aspects of her grandchildren's lives was reported as a norm, and an absence of such involvement spawned special comments and explanations.

Subtheme C: I want to give gratification to my grandmother (granddaughters)

Three participating granddaughters talked about close emotional ties they have with their grandmothers. Dora attributed her motivation and resilience to support and understanding her mother and grandmother gave her in times of hardship. She recalled being teased in elementary school:

> My family gave me the strength to overcome all this. I have someone to come home to every day, someone at least to, like, relieve most of my problems... My mom, she always stood up for me, and my grandma, also she was there to talk to me and tell me that everything is going to be fine, that I was going to make a lot of friends in high school, that everything is going to change for me... They were supportive, very supportive. Every problem that I had I could just come to them, and they would usually understand...

Dora's gratitude was mixed with the sense of obligation. She spoke with eagerness about her own desire to achieve in life that was reinforced by her desire to reward her mother and grandmother, to make them happy. She appears to recognize the sense of her grandmother's desire to live through her children:

> I want to make my mom proud of me, my grandma; I want them to be happy. She can tell her friends... You know how old people are; all they have left is their memories and what their children do. They sit around in a circle and go like, "Well, my daughter does this, and my granddaughter does this..." They live vicariously through their children.

Dora used her grandmother's love and willingness to sacrifice her own interests as a basis for a broad generalization. She compared Russian and American family attitudes in a vignette:

> The grandmothers and grandchildren, most of all it shows the difference. My mom and I were on a cruise. There was a grandmother who took her granddaughter along to show her Alaska, so it is good. We had a late sitting dinner; it started by 8:30 p.m. The kid was probably nine years old, by this time

she was tired already. She did not feel well, so the grandmother gave her some pills, and the girl fell asleep right at the table. The grandmother enjoyed her dinner, finished her dessert; then she chatted with us about the sightseeing trip we took that day. Then she woke up the child, and they went to the cabin. I know for sure that my grandmother would have carried me there, put me to sleep, and she would have stayed with me, not have the dinner.

Her grandmother's attitudes seem to have become an integral part of Dora's character, and she spoke about her plan to continue them in her family life, " When I have kids, I am sure I am going to make them want to eat also, just like she made me. I asked her to write her recipes for me in a book. I will definitely continue the tradition, live on her memory with her food."

Daniela praised her grandmother's support, "We have good times a lot, she is very easy to talk to, she understands more than my parents, maybe because she is a grandmother and she is used to raising families." She also talked about her grandmother's role in her intellectual and emotional growth:

I am sure she has a lot of influence on me. She was a Russian teacher; when I was younger, I did not want to learn anything, but now, sometimes I take a book and read on my own, I mean a Russian book. And she calms me down because I am a very hot-tempered person. She has an influence on the whole house.

Another granddaughter, Dina, spoke about her grandmother with warmth, "I enjoy the time we have together. I like spending time with her; she is really nice. She is very caring." Dina's grandmother Gita sounded happy when she talked about their closeness:

She was always very open with me, there and here, about who she likes, who she doesn't like, she tells me about the boy she is dating, shows me the photographs. She doesn't understand how it is not to tell her grandmother. We are so close.

Nevertheless, Dina was the person who broke painful news to her loving grandmother, probably without much awareness of the effect of her words, "Grandma, you know, here in America people don't live with their parents. So when we move to a new apartment or buy a house we will live separately from you." Dina appeared to be aware of the growing distance between her and her grandmother due to the increasing cultural and linguistic gap. Her perception of their closeness differs significantly from her grandmother's report. She sounded guilty when she spoke about it:

> I don't know about now, but we used to be close when I was little. She took care of me for a couple of years before we moved to America. She raised me, I guess... but right now... I cannot really communicate with her, like I can communicate, but it is hard, because I sometimes forget words in Russian, and she cannot really understand English that well, so it is kind of hard to explain everything to her. She really does not understand everything in America, like how it works and I cannot explain to her what my friends do, it is difficult for me, but we are still pretty close.

The reports of Genya and her granddaughter Dosia are similarly discrepant in their perception of closeness. Genya said:

> Dosia and I are very close, too. She tells me everything, yes. Yesterday I asked her, "Tell me in detail what is your school like? What are your difficulties in?" She told me everything with pleasure. She used to carry tons of books, such thick volumes. And now they have lockers, so they take home only what they need for tomorrow. She told me all the details, she doesn't hide anything from me, I think so, and she doesn't have anything to hide yet. Maybe later she will. She always tells me, "Grandma, I love you. Don't worry, I love you." She is such a good girl.

Dosia said with the tinge of guilt, "We used to spend a lot of time together, and now I don't have the time."

> The participating granddaughters appear to have benefited from their grandmothers' love and support, especially during their pre-emigration and early emigration years. Acculturation, however, has brought its challenges to the grandmothers as well as to the granddaughters, since the younger generation's fast adaptation to the new culture made them the major agents of change in every participating family.

Subtheme D: My grandmother is getting really annoying right now (granddaughters)

Not all emotions expressed by granddaughters in relation to their grandmothers were positive. Three granddaughters described their grandmothers as people obsessed with food and feeding to the point of being oppressive, stressing that this is the common trait of all grandmothers they know. Talking about her own grandmother and great-grandmother and her friend's grandmother, Dora made broad generalizations as she resigned to their insistence,

> Grandmas worry if you eat or not, this is the only thing basically on their mind, it is not like if you had a six-course meal an hour ago, right now you are hungry. And if you are not—you still are. It doesn't matter—you still have to eat, and there is no argument, because they'll either just yell at you or they'll annoy you until you give in.

Dina's experience is strikingly similar, but she reported it with the added sense of guilt for resisting her grandmother's efforts,

> All the grandmothers I know, all of them, are always cooking and always telling you to eat. When I was younger, she always nagged me to eat, and eat, and eat. I really never, like, yelled at her for it, because I was young, but now, I just tell her firmly, 'Stop!" or I just tell her to leave me alone. She gets a little hurt, but she'll leave me alone after that.

Dina's mother Marlena described her own grandmother in the same vein, but her motherhood experience gives us a perspective on transmission of this custom along the generational line,

> My grandmother had such a principle—to feed, she loved those who ate well. She cooked very well, and, of course, she stuffed us with food like all grandmothers. I mean all the children were stuffed with food the same way; my daughter was stuffed constantly by my mother and me, and my mother-in-law.

As adolescence brings about much change, the childhood conflict around feeding gets overshadowed by other pressing issues. Every participating granddaughter reported her growing resentment of her grandmother's desire to be involved in every aspect of her life. Being brought up by their Russian Jewish grandmothers and absorbing American attitudes toward privacy seems to have created the inner conflict, as they feel pulled by these different paradigms. Dana was the most outspoken and angry about her grandmother's intrusiveness,

> My grandmother is getting really annoying right now. She is always in my business; I don't like that. She thinks she knows something, and she really messes things up. Like right now I am beginning to go clubbing and I come back smelling with cigarettes, but I don't smoke, and she started making a big deal, woke my mom up, and now they don't trust me because they think I smoke, and I don't. Nobody asked her anything, and I just think she should mind her own business sometimes. She intrudes all the time; I don't like that. She comes very often, and I try to be nice, not to lose my cool with her, but she is getting on my nerves, so I just walk away. When I was in Queens, she was always in my business, but it wasn't really anything bad because I was so young and I wasn't realizing she was doing it, but even then it was too much. My mom let me go there or here, and my grandma started to be all over my business saying that she shouldn't. I just think she should shut up sometimes.

As reported by Greta, her granddaughter Daniela sounded less angry, but firm in her desire to set the limits for her grandmother's involvement in her life, "Daniela said to me very straightforward, 'You know, grandma, it is not your fault, it is my fault, but it is my business." Aware of her grandmother's feeling of being entitled to know everything that is going on in the family, Daniela used the word "fault" to excuse her grandmother and to switch the blame onto herself when Greta was prying too deep for her comfort. "When I ask her, 'What were you talking about with Vickie?' she says, 'I don't want you to discuss all my problems, my relationships with all your friends."

Another granddaughter, Dora, described her plans for the future and expressed her strong desire to get away from her "smothering" family and gain some independence despite her mother's and grandmother's strong feelings against such plans,

> I definitely want to leave because I also want some independence. I have been living with my mom this long, and

my grandma right upstairs; it is getting so tiring. I am so tired sometimes of them smothering me. My grandma said that she is going to be crazy because she won't have the responsibility of trying to take care of me, and my mom also—she does not want me to leave. I just want to get away; I cannot stand it anymore.

Daniela's plans for the future are very similar as reported by her grandmother Greta, "She is talking about going away to college. She said it many times that as soon as she graduates from school, she'll run away from home. Simply will run away."

Another source of intergenerational tension for the participants was the difference in attitude toward cultural pursuits. Grandmothers sounded angry reporting their granddaughters becoming culturally Americanized, and the granddaughters' reports were permeated with guilt. In the Kogan family, Greta reported her serious concern about Daniela's interests, "My granddaughter has practically lost her Russian which makes me very unhappy. Of course, she speaks and understands, but it is not fluent, and she has no desire to go see a drama production, to read a book, she has no desire to go somewhere to see something." Daniela is well aware of her grandmother's feelings, so she sounded guilt-ridden in her description of her and her friends' leisure activities:

We hardly talk about school, I guess, clothes come up, we go shopping a lot together, it's like our quality time, guys, I guess, too. That's it. We don't really get to the museums or anything. In the summer we went even to the city, to some museum collection, art collection.

In the Arber family, Genya takes pride in owning a large collection of Russian books she brought to America for her granddaughter's benefit. Her granddaughter Dosia prefers watching TV. She reported her guilt about the changes in her relationship with the grandmother, "At times I am not too nice to her—like if I am busy and she would call, I would yell at her, and then I apologize. ... She used to play the piano, and I tried to sing. We used to watch Russian movies, the old ones." Daniela sounded very similar to Dosia in her regrets about her treatment of her grandmother:

When I am tired I don't want to be bothered, so I go to my room and finish my homework, and she is always, like, 'How

are you, how was your day?' So sometimes when I had a bad
day, I take it out on her, and I feel bad when I think about it,
but I cannot do much about it when she wants to talk.

Overall, the participating granddaughters appear to view their
grandmothers as a significant source of strength and resilience in their
life even though they struggle with the question, "how much is too
much?" in defining their emotional and cultural boundaries within their
family structure. Going to college appeared to be a big decision that
conflicted with the desires of the participating granddaughters'
families, increasing their guilty feelings and testing their determination.

Men/Women

Subtheme A: Even the best husband is still your worst enemy
The majority of the adult participants expressed overwhelmingly
negative feelings about their husbands. At the time of the interviewing,
three out of the five grandmothers were divorced, and two were open
about being unhappily married. In general, the participating
grandmothers either avoided talking about their husbands or portrayed
them as insensitive and controlling dictators.

The divorced grandmothers said close to nothing about their
former husbands, trying to cross them out of their memories and to
move onto the issues they considered more important. Gita, the most
positive of the participating grandmothers, mentioned her divorce in a
concise phrase, "Children, of course, were supportive of me," implying
that her adult children sided with her as the wronged spouse. Her friend
Greta was equally brief in talking about her husband, "At that time I
became so to say a free lady—I got divorced from my husband and
moved back with my mother," thus equating her divorce with freedom.
Golda mentioned her two failed marriages only while talking about her
children or describing her struggle for an apartment. She angrily yelled
at her adversaries who schemed and plotted to take away her small
apartment with wet walls, "So what if my husband is an alcoholic? He
may be a bandit, too, but this is none of your business." When she
finally secured the apartment, she moved there with her mother,
daughter, granddaughter, and son-in-law. She did not mention her
second divorce and made no further comments about Minna's father.

Golda's life story is prominently devoid of any spousal warmth or support. Laconic Gita, loquacious Greta, and outspoken Golda were equally reluctant to talk more about their former husbands and eagerly switched the topic of the conversation away from them. Compared to the divorced grandmothers, two married ones were much more open about their husbands, releasing their pent-up anger and resentment. They sounded especially unhappy about their husbands' demands that they behave exactly the way they were used to in the former Soviet Union—as housekeepers with few needs and wants of their own. Galina went right to the crux of the matter, evaluating her marriage as "not so good, either." Her husband and mother-in-law were "gloomy and suspicious people" who emotionally "tortured" young Galina "nonstop" and drove her to a nervous illness that resulted in facial paralysis. Galina's husband forced her to abandon her career of choice, opera singing, "I was accepted to the conservatory before I got married, but my husband said, 'I don't need performers in my family.' He persisted, so I quit." Galina's tendency for looking to others for support of her beliefs, brings to light the jealous, insensitive, and selfish husband of a friend who throws angry fits when his wife allows herself a ten-minute break from taking constant care of him. The only reason Galina found for not leaving her own husband was the length of their marriage, "I have lived with my husband for 40 years, how could I leave him and go alone?" She did not give any indication of other emotions involved in making this decision. At the time of the interview, Galina summarized her married life by a vivid metaphor, "We are like two stones together," indicating that her husband's emotional state is worse than hers. Left without purpose in life, her husband appears to be utterly needy and depressed, making Galina feel obligated to drag him along as a heavy stone.

The second married grandmother, Genya, openly regrets her miserable and hurtful marriage, "Why did I get married? I was better off without him." She talked about her deep feeling of being shortchanged by life, "The deep sense of being cheated by life, my whole miserable life." Reevaluating her life when she "finally started understanding things," Genya considered her marriage a grave mistake for which she has been paying all her life. Besides being unfaithful to her, her husband was neglectful or totally absent from her life in times of need and hardship, "When we finally moved to our own place, the walls in the room were so wet that I did not know where to put the child's bed. My husband picked himself up and left us, he went to live with his mother." Fatherhood did not change his selfish ways, "When Margarita was growing up; I had to claw things for her out of him. I could not clothe her on my salary." Genya did not talk directly about physical abuse, but her casual remark, "if my mother-in-law did not step between us, I would have had a concussion" strongly suggests its presence.

Recalling her aborted attempt to leave her husband, Genya presented the reasons for her return, "My mother-in-law came to me and said, 'Do you want to leave your child fatherless?' She ran away from her own husband herself, but she used this pressure on me, and I gave up." Genya's mother-in-law probably wanted to spare her granddaughter from privations and indignities her own children suffered as a result of her divorce. Realizing that, Genya returned to her torturer for purely material reasons. Not a sound was uttered about Genya's own feelings or needs, the scary ghost of her mother-in-law's past was sufficiently convincing, "She had to work in a student canteen filling plates with food for the self-service line. She could take the leftovers home and feed her three children." Genya believed that her decision to return to her torturer were based on the need to survive, "Why do we, women, suffer from it? We never have enough money to feed the children or a decent apartment." Many years later, when Genya decided to move in with her husband after 18 years of semi-separate life, she was motivated by the desire to help her daughter, "I moved back to my husband and left the apartment for Margarita. I had nowhere else to go."

Emigration does not seem to have changed Genya's personal life; it is still full of misery and loneliness:

> We live in our separate rooms, and I have no table in my room, so I have to write letters on my lap. His table is covered with his papers, and if I sit down at it, he would yell, "Don't touch my letters!" When Margarita bought me a television set, he was livid with fury, "I allowed you to buy an air conditioner, and now you want the TV, too!"

In her marriage, Genya has many responsibilities and no benefits, "It is my responsibility to cook and serve. He would be happy to have me spend my whole life in the kitchen, and then, 'the dinner is served.'

This is the lordly manner of our Russian men." She described her husband as the one who is unable to give her emotional support, cold and uncaring toward her, "When I have a heartache, he does not understand. He would never ask me how I feel or what is bothering me. Now he has it himself, so I am trying to help him as much as I can." Genya's list of complaints is long, and she summarizes her married life by a painful metaphor, "He put his heavy paw over my whole life."

Two other women mentioned by the participants, have miserable marriages as well. Genya dismissed her brother-in-law as a good-for-nothing lout, "There were no alcoholics in my family except for my sister's husband. He drank himself into nothing. We left him in the institution for treating alcoholics." Another non-participating grandmother, Marlena's mother-in-law, is still married. Marlena's description of this woman is full of admiration of her stamina and willpower. She mentions her father-in-law only in connection with eating, as his expectation of sticking to old-fashioned ways is an additional burden for his wife, "He eats exactly the way he did in Russia, he eats whatever he liked there—sweets, dough, fatty food, fried cutlets. She cooks all this stuff, but she does not touch it, they eat separately.

Overall, divorced grandmothers, having removed their husbands from their lives and minds, made an impression of being happier than married ones. They reported participating in pleasurable activities and spending less time on household chores, learning to value their time and discovering the pleasures of eating out. Married grandmothers' reports about their marriages conveyed a strong feeling of being suffocated. They seemed dragging them along as a heavy and unpleasant burden, carried out of obligation or tradition.

Subtheme B: I am unhappy with my daughter's marriage (grandmothers)

Every participating grandmother seemed to have continued the tradition of speaking negatively or saying nothing at all about her son-in-law. Gita mentioned her son-in-law once in a relatively neutral tone, "I love swimming. When I was staying with my daughter, I went swimming many times a day, so my son-in-law said, "my mother-in-law has probably grown gills." Typically expressive Golda was brief and did not mince words speaking about her son-in-law, "By that time, we had thrown the pig out of the house, I mean my son-in-law."

Usually soft-spoken Greta put her guard down when the conversation touched her daughter's marriage. She was seething with hatred, scapegoating her son-in-law for her daughter's and granddaughter's perceived shortcomings, "I get very upset that my children move away from cultural pursuits, they are not interested or have no time for it. I keep thinking that my daughter is getting more and more influenced by her spouse who is pulling her into his philistine mire." She made a brave, but short-lived attempt to cover up her anger and to empathize with her inflexible and controlling son-in-law, "As a mother, as a woman, I feel sorry for my son-in-law. He does it all with the best intentions, but I don't know why he does not understand the simplest things. He has to retreat a bit, give her some freedom. He cannot go on like this." Greta blames her son-in-law for creating a difficult situation for her daughter and for the whole family, "We have terrible conflicts and explosions all the time. My daughter is suffering terribly because of this, she is constantly between two fires, and I am afraid that she will not be able to continue this way."

Galina reported her strong disappointment with her daughter's marriage, "I suffer because I hoped that my daughter would have a better marriage." She blames her son-in-law for his failure to protect Marina from his mother's dominance, "His mother is a very stingy woman, all her life was about putting money on her saving account. It was different in our family, we did not waste money, but we lived like people. So it was very difficult for her. And he did not protect Marina from this." Galina harbors a lot of resentment of her son-in-law, "All the money is in his hands, he controls everything, and it is difficult for Marina to buy something." She seemed to be uncomfortable when she felt obligated to admit her son's-in-law humane behavior toward her, "He asked us to come to stay with them when it was very hot." Galina sounded more comfortable when she could rant and rave about her son's-in-law shortcomings, especially pitching her granddaughter against him, "I tell her, 'you are a young lady already, never mind that your father does not say good morning. You should do it anyway.'" Galina reported her teaching Marina to be honest and faithful toward her husband, "Maybe it is my upbringing. I always taught her to be true to him." However, her suspicious and angry stance "the best husband is your worst enemy" appears to negate these attempts as she resents Marina's tendency to admit her weaknesses to her husband.

Genya sounded as negative about her former son-in-law as other grandmothers, but, on the other hand, she spoke with regret about her daughter's "fate" of not being "settled" yet. She stressed her guilt in initiating the break up of Margarita's marriage, "I did not preserve Dosia's father; I am guilty of it." Having suffered her own bad marriage, Genya still has hopes that her daughter finds a mate. Golda, another divorced mother of a divorced daughter, sounded happy and proud when she reported to me during the second interview that her daughter's boyfriend of several years "has finally bought an engagement ring for Minna." What was it for these women, "the triumph of hope over experience" or realistic expectations of securing providers for their daughters?

Subtheme C: My husband never made me feel good (mothers)

Even though the participating grandmothers hoped for better marriages for their daughters, these women ended up in unsatisfying marriages as their mothers had. Two out of five participating mothers are divorced, one described her marriage as unhappy, and two avoided talking about their husbands. Yet every detail in all of their life stories suggested marital discord or, at best, a lack of communication and support in their marriages. Marlena appeared the least unsatisfied with her marriage. She even attempted to find an excuse for her husband's insensitive and controlling attitude, switching the blame onto herself,

When the weekend comes, I feel lazy, I don't want to cook, but my husband is a homeboy, he does not like eating out. He says, 'Why do we have to go out? Let's have something quick at home.' I answer, 'Quickly means that I have to stand and cook, and I want to relax. I don't feel like cooking on weekends.' He doesn't get it. If it were up to me, we would eat out much more often, five or six times more often, than once in two weeks, but the man is the head of the household.

For Marlena, having a house party means more work, but, again, she feels she has to cook, "my husband likes house parties, probably because he does not cook. I do the cooking, this is why I like eating out." Marlena's elegant home was hardly suggestive of a strained financial situation, and she reported having "a good job with a nice salary." Nevertheless, she sounded resigned to cooking "something fast" after a full day's work and spending weekends "making soup and something more substantial for my family." It appears that no matter how financially comfortable the family is and no matter how large the wife's financial contribution, the husband still dictates that she continue to perform the traditional responsibilities of a housekeeper, even if there is no apparent need for it.

Marina's feelings about house parties are similar to Marlena's, "I have to cook for parties, this is why I don't like them. My husband does not cook, he does not even help me." This complaint is the mildest in Marina's long list of grievances. A strikingly beautiful woman, Marina said bluntly about her husband's attitude toward her, "He never made me feel beautiful, not now, not before." She reported disliking her part-time job, especially the low pay she is getting, but she feels compelled to work, "I have to leave the house, I need to get away, otherwise my emotional state gets worse." Work helps her avoid sinking deeper into depressive thoughts about her unhappy married life. Marina talked at length about her dissatisfaction with her life, her marriage, and herself. She concluded, "Financially I am in chains. I crave financial independence."

Marina's husband "controls everything in his family" even though he has never been the sole breadwinner in the family. Her mother Galina spoke about the period in his life when he lost his job after the fall of the Soviet Union and Marina was "killing herself moonlighting, doing extra work." What was her motivation for staying in her painful, loveless marriage? Probably it was her adherence to the social norm that dictated that women should stay married at any cost for their children's sake.

Usually eloquent and "analytically oriented" Maya chose not to discuss her marriage, but according to the reports of her mother and daughter, her husband is hardly more supportive or less controlling and rigid than the other men described in this study. His constant yelling matches with their daughter Daniela leave Maya desperate and exhausted. Greta described the situation, "He explodes immediately, and he loves his baby madly. I don't know if there is anything in the world he would not do for her, whatever he can do, he would. He is destroying her this way."

Margarita seemed to have married a man painfully similar to her father in his cold selfishness and total lack of caring for his child, even in times of dire need, "I lost my job, and could not find another one.

My husband did not care; he did not want to see us. I would come and pick up alimony payments, and this was the extent of our contact." Unsatisfying married life seemed to have repeated itself in the second generation of the participating women.

Subtheme D: my father's attitude toward me is the root of my failures (three generations)

For most of the participants, their fathers' attitude toward them had a long-lasting damaging effect on their lives and on their attitude toward men in particular. Only two mothers mentioned their fathers, again, in highly negative tones. Marina believes that her low self-esteem was formed by her father's constant criticism, "A father is the first man in a woman's life, and my father has always been very critical of me. He was always looking for something wrong in me, so I grew up believing that I am ugly and no good. My father's attitude toward me is the root of my failures." Describing her difficulties in finding a job, she bemoans her fear of being interviewed and concludes, "Probably there is something wrong with me." Margarita appreciates her father's "passionate tenderness" toward her daughter, but in her own life story there is no room for him. Margarita's paternal grandmother had the same negative opinion about her son:

> My grandmother had pity on my mother for two reasons. First, she was an orphan herself, and also because my mother suffered from her son. My father has a very difficult personality, and my grandmother probably realized how it was for my mother.

Margarita's mother Genya was the only grandmother who talked about her father with warmth and love, praising his interest in her education and welfare. Nevertheless, even the orphan's wistful longing for a father cannot prevent her from painting a portrait of a petty tyrant, distrustful of his young daughter, "My father wanted the best education for me. He used to lock the piano after I finished doing my homework. There was a theory that playing by ear may spoil my playing." Two more grandmothers reported being orphaned by WWII and suffering from abject poverty as a result of losing their fathers.

Only one daughter, Daniela, initiated the conversation about her father, describing his oppressive, controlling personality. She admitted that her father loves her, but she described their relationship as stormy,

"My father thinks I am the best, but he gets very annoying sometimes. Me and him; we have very similar personalities, so we don't get along a lot of the time. It scares me because I don't like how he is, annoying, and he is always thinking about what I am doing, I don't want to do the same thing when I grow up." Dosia never mentioned her father during the interview. According to her mother's and grandmother's reports, she does not know him as her parents were divorced during her infancy and she had no contact with him afterwards. It seems that neither the cold uncaring father, nor the passionately loving one was able to influence his growing daughter in a positive way.

Subtheme E: I hope my daughter marries one of our boys (mothers)

Two mothers expressed hopes for their daughters to marry "our boy, a Russian immigrant or a son of Russian immigrants." This desire may sound paradoxical, considering the mothers' own disappointing married life. Their reasoning, however, is substantiated by two factors—first, the mothers have limited information about American men in general, as they all reported difficulty forming friendships with Americans. Secondly, the elements of American national character they are informed about, such as valuing independence and self-sufficiency, tend to scare the mothers and to strengthen their desire to keep their daughters within the Russian-speaking community. Even though their teenage daughters are far from marrying age, the mothers were already fantasizing about their future sons-in-law in the hope to keep close connections with their daughters.

Marina equated having an American son-in-law with losing contact with her daughter, "I don't want to make appointments to see my daughter. My cousin lives with an American man and she became like he, so distant. Her mother is heartbroken." Marlena expressed similar feelings about her future son-in-law and his family, "If Dina marries an American, I am afraid that we will have no communication with him and his parents. It will be, 'Hello, good-bye, how are you doing? How is work?' but never a close relationship. This is why I hope that she finds some Russian immigrant and marries him." Common language and similar cultural background appear to be important for the other two mothers as well, as reported by their daughters.

Subtheme F: I want to be able to beat someone up, like a guy (granddaughters)

Even though all the participating daughters are dating or have been dating, none of them seemed interested in sharing this side of their life with me. Typical for many teenagers, distrust of adults was probably strengthened by my belonging to the same age and cultural group as their mothers. Some other reasons could have been the negativity toward men they learned at home or their focus on things they consider more important, such as career planning. It was instructive to note that two "fatherless" teenage daughters, Dosia and Dora, demonstrated these two tendencies more prominently than the girls whose parents were married.

Generally described by her grandmother as "too serious," Dosia was straightforward when I asked her about her vision of herself in the future, "I want to grow up smart and rich; I want to be a lawyer." A man was not included into these plans, and Dosia seemed to treat dating as an impediment to her career plans. Becoming a rich lawyer was the major part of Dora's plans for the future as well, but her attitude toward men was more militant than Dosia's. Even though she described the boys she dated in relatively neutral tones, her motivation for sports was highly suggestive of her pent-up anger against men and of her perceived need to protect herself from their aggression, "I take weight training to get muscular, like Arnold Shwartzenegger. I want to be able to beat someone up, like a guy. I don't want to be picked on by my husband." Interestingly, despite the proliferation of female bodybuilding and muscular actresses of Linda Hamilton's type, Dora wants to be identified with no less than the ultimate male power symbol. She wants power in more than one area of life, "I would like to work and have my husband stay home and I want to have the house to my name." A voracious reader, Dora tends to pay attention to the reasons for divorce and wife abuse, piling up unpleasant examples with the passion of a collector. For herself, she appears to have her mind set on "something that will keep me when my looks are gone." Nevertheless, when Dora stepped down from her public speech podium, she sounded resigned to serve the very man she is planning to dominate financially, professionally, and physically, "I am not planning to be a housewife, but you need to cook for your family sometime. We live in a basically male-dominated society, still after everything women have been through. We are still going to cook sometimes anyway, a man is not going to be able to, so I asked my grandmother to write down some of her recipes."

Three daughters were rather brief and neutral in their reports about boys and dating, but they indicated an inclination to date boys of the same ethnic background to accommodate their families. Daniela reported having "mixed racial people" as friends, but being inclined more towards dating boys of Russian origin, "I guess now I have more preference toward Russian boys, because I know my parents would approve of them more. One of my best friends is a guy, and he is Russian, it is better—my parents can talk to him, my mom loves him, and we can communicate better, and his mom likes me because we are both Russian and it is easier to communicate. For me it is all the same, but it is just family stuff." Dina's response is similar to Daniela's even though she lives in the suburbs with very few Russian families around:

> I don't have too many Russian friends here in Westchester, but if I have a choice, I would go for Russian friends, especially boyfriends, because it is just easier to bring them home, to your family. They will be able to communicate better with my parents. My parents would feel more comfortable.

All the participating daughters spoke fluent English and reported speaking to their Russian friends and boyfriends "in English with some Russian words we put in once in a while."

The younger generation of participants appeared to have assimilated rather quickly in most of the social aspects of American life, but when family matters are considered, they prefer cultural closeness even though their experience of Russian men is far from positive. This tendency appears to be based on their desire to accommodate their families' desires and on their more limited acculturation in the areas of family life and gender roles.

CATEGORY III: SELF

Body Image

Subtheme A: I think I look normal (grandmothers)

All five grandmothers reported that they liked slim body shape and disapproved of fat and "extra flesh." Nevertheless, they appeared overweight by mainstream American standards. Their reported body sizes ranged from 14 to 18 with size 14 considered acceptable, "I think look normal," and size 18 considered too large, "I am fat and I suffer from it." Two grandmothers, who talked about being "rounded," still sounded rather relaxed about their bodies.

Golda, who reported being size 16, sounded comfortable with her body. She said, "I am trying to keep my body in good shape. I am trying to have a flat stomach; it is the most important part of looking good. As long as I live I don't want to be fat." Only one grandmother, Galina expressed strong negative feelings about her body size. Even though she did not look much heavier than Golda, she said, "I feel very bad because of my weight gain. I feel uncomfortable, heavy both physically and emotionally, and in general, everything has changed for me here." For Galina, extra weight seems to symbolize her depression and to exacerbate her negative feelings about herself.

Another grandmother, Greta, attributed her weight gain to aging, so she sounded more resigned about it:

> I never welcomed it; even now being so round irritates me, too. But I am at the age when it is not so easy to shed kilograms. Now I weigh as much as I weighed before the emigration, but prior to this I used to be thinner and in general I was always slim. I started gaining weight after fifty-five.

Gita looked more plump than her friend Greta and she made an impression of a person who can enjoy life and accept herself the way she is to a higher degree than Greta. She reported liking her granddaughter's slim body and laughingly said about her own, "I am not so thin myself." Nevertheless, she reported eating as much as she wanted and not gaining much weight, "I did not gain weight in America. I am in the same shape as I came five years ago; I can wear the same dresses. I am not limiting myself—I eat whatever I want."

Genya was also aware of her being "not thin" and sounded satisfied with it. She compared her body with her mother's, "She was like me, not fat, not thin. And I consider that I am in a good shape, normal." Genya's daughter Margarita attributed her mother's taste to the general standard of the time of her youth, "My mother was formed by the pre-war years. All the actresses of that time, not one of them was thin." Genya's story suggests another explanation—unforgettable starvation during the war and intermittent food shortages afterwards. She mentioned her emaciated state at the time of her arrival in New York and compared it with her sister's condition, "They were able to make it to here, but in what condition—very emaciated. We also came not such beauties, but we have eaten and filled out into shape a little." In Genya's mind, thinness is still connected with deprivation and beauty is being "filled out."

Most of the participating grandmothers appeared to accept a wider spectrum of body shapes than their daughters and granddaughters. The main reason for this attitude appears to be their experience of starvation and severe food shortages during their formative years.

Subtheme B: She was so horribly thin (grandmothers)

For the participating grandmothers, beauty seemed to have a lower priority than health. Since three of them reported starving during WWII, their reports suggested that in their minds, thinness is related to malnutrition and poor health. When I asked Genya about her attitude toward her daughter's body, she said:

> My heart used to ache for her, always, for her health, that's the main thing. It never occurred to me to think about her in terms of liking or disliking her looks or body, I was solely concerned about her health.

Genya's daughter recalled gaining a lot of weight in her youth and her mother's approval of her full body, "She liked it, she used to tell me later, 'You were exactly right—very good.' When I lost weight, she said, 'What do you look like? You have only your nose left." Talking about her daughter and granddaughter, Genya expressed similar feelings:

Margarita looks very well now. She stopped smoking and gained some weight, and she looks better this way. She feels healthier; she was pale, very thin, so my heart used to ache for her. And Dosia is too thin, too... But she is growing; I take this factor into consideration.

Dosia's illness was still fresh in her grandmother's memory. Genya still associated thinness with dangerously poor health:

We almost lost the child due to acetone in her urine when she was seven. She had food poisoning, so she was vomiting all the time. She looked like a skeleton and was unable to walk. Margarita had to carry her to the hospital.

Golda reported feeling that her granddaughter looks "all right," implying that Dora was in good shape. In contrast, Dora defined herself as "good and plenty" and said that she weighed 147 pounds. The difference in these women's definition of "fat" suggested a significant change in the body ideal between the members of two generations.

In Galina's story, a thin child was a "horror picture." Addressing her granddaughter's possible exposure to radiation, she seemed to associate her "poor" appetite with its consequences. She described little Dana in dramatic tones, "When they brought her here, she was like a skeleton, she looked so scary—skin and bones, a tall skinny child, so skinny that one could see blood vessels on her face." Galina's report suggested that she was pleased with Dana's rounded figure, "And now, thank G-d, at least in this we are lucky. Only for this—our emigration was worth the suffering."

Marlena recalled the general cultural attitude toward feeding children in the Soviet Union. She explained it by the connection between eating and health, "We used to think that if a child eats, she will be healthy, and if a child stays hungry, she will have less health. This was the opinion of everybody around me." Even though Marlena's mother Gita said she liked her granddaughter Dina's slim body, Dina's report about Gita encouraging her to eat sounded very convincing, "My grandmother always encourages me to eat more. Let's say I have a cookie or something, and she'll be like, 'Here, have more!' And I am like, 'I don't want any." And she is, 'Come on, eat more, you are too skinny." Since all the participating grandmothers were, at least for a while, primary caretakers of their granddaughters, it seems reasonable to expect that their attitudes had significant influence on these girls.

Subtheme C: I gained a lot of weight in America (mothers)

All participating mothers and one grandmother reported significant post-emigration weight gain. Galina complained about going from size 8 to size 18 in less than seven years. Maya said, "I gained about 25-30 pounds since our arrival seven years ago." Margarita's response was more vague, "Now I am afraid to step on the scale because I know I weigh much more. I think by at least 15 pounds, for sure, or even more." The participants attributed this change to a variety of factors, including the availability of a wide variety of new kinds of food in America, chemical and hormonal additives to food in the USA, eating as a way to alleviate their stress or depressed mood, lack of exercise, and aging.

Galina reported her physician's opinion that her "metabolism got all screwed up because of the stress." She complained about her resorting to eating when nervous, "When I start worrying, I have to put something into my mouth. Besides, I used to move more there." Galina's daughter, Marina reported a similar pattern of response to emotional challenges, "When I came to America, I gained a lot of weight, virtually right away—within the first year. There is so much stress here; besides, I have not achieved what I wanted here, I mean professionally. My organism is such that I eat constantly when I am nervous. When I feel good, I want to move more and I stop chewing, so I start losing weight."

"Analytically inclined" Maya also considered several factors that contributed to her weight gain:

> Because of my occupation, I have a sedentary lifestyle; I mean I sit all day long. I know for sure that I need more physical activities and some limitations in food consumption, too. Changes in the housekeeping are demonstrated in more caloric, tastier, and more readily available nutrition. With time metabolism slows down, and all of this is stored in the body.

Marlena explained her own 20-pound weight gain by the changes in her lifestyle. She reported eating more, especially in the early period of her emigration, and exercising less in America. She said, "When we first arrived, it was such a temptation—there is more food here and all of it looks so beautiful, we wanted to taste it all at the same time." Marlena believed that her difficulty shedding extra weight was a result of aging, "My body is not managing, if earlier I could lose 5 to 10 pounds by adhering to a diet or starving a little, now it is very difficult, very." Marlena also expressed her concern about food additives and their dangers. She believed that significant obesity of some Americans is a result of these, "Here people are very fat; it is just a disaster. Probably it is not the food, it is some kind of chemicals in certain kinds of food." Margarita's point of view is more radical:

> I have gained weight here because food contains something, I don't know what, but here you gain weight too easily from everything. I think I gain weight here by eating salads because they contain some kind of chemicals. And then meat— chickens here are so stuffed with hormones, they are grown on hormones, you ingest them willy-nilly. When you take a container from a supermarket shelf, just read what is in the product—some kind of carbohydrates, then some kind of strange names of chemicals, like flavorings, it is not the aroma only. I think people gain weight from eating these.

Even though Margarita reported an extremely thin body ideal in the Soviet Union during 1970s-1980s, it seems that the participating mothers experience themselves as overweight also due to one more factor they mentioned only briefly—the influence of American mass media with their extremely thin beauty ideal for all ages.

Subtheme D: In America being beautiful means being thin (mothers)

The participating mothers reported their preference for thinness in their youth in the Soviet Union. It seems that American media contributed to their dissatisfaction with their mature bodies. Maya reported liking "athletic women" in her youth, but stressed that during her formative years she experienced less pressure to be thin than her daughter does now, "Our generation had fewer problems than our children do now. All the commercials, everything, everything is based exclusively on attractiveness." Maya mentioned a TV show that attempted to promote self-acceptance for larger women, but concluded in an assured tone of voice, "Here the ideal of beauty is a thin slim body."

Marlena said that that she "always liked thin women" and added, "I liked them in Russia, too." Nevertheless, she referred to the TV show *Sex and the City*, especially to Sarah Jessica Parker to describe the ideal body. Margarita spoke about *Victoria's Secret* models and stressed their influence on her daughter's tastes. In spite of insisting that a "totally skinny" ideal existed in the former Soviet Union during the time of her youth, Margarita demonstrated a more relaxed attitude toward weight, defying the American expression, "a woman cannot be too rich or too thin." She said, "There is one Hispanic model, I don't remember her name. She is so beautiful, face and body. The only thing I think is not so good is her legs; I think they are too thin."

Marina also reported her desire "to be trim" in the Soviet Union, but her major stress was on the new demands for thinness she experienced in the United States:

> In the Soviet Union, we wanted to be trim, but we did nothing to achieve it. I always wanted to look good, but there it was not so significant as it is here, you would get a job anyway. And here the significance is in obtaining and keeping the job and that a person should look good for it. And since you are being compared with well-groomed and trim Americans, you also want to look as good as they do, you have your goal in front of you.

For Maya, looking good was "pleasant," but not a high priority. Yet she reported feeling immersed in the thinning culture, "One can see it everywhere—a woman is walking with a sports bag, and everybody is trying to work out, to be thin, and so on.... You get it from your surrounding, from the culture itself." As reported by Maya's mother Greta, her daughter Daniela also exerts strong pressure on Maya, "My granddaughter yells to me, 'Grandma, look what she is eating, she gained weight again!' She is suffering because her mother is plump."

All participating mothers appeared to consider weight gain a normal part of aging. Marlena said:

> In Russia, it was considered like this—if you are forty or forty-five, you have the right to be heavy. This was normal, and if you were thin, it was considered strange, like something is wrong with you, like you are sick. And here it is different.

Describing her mother as "overweight," Marlena said, "I think that for her age she is not that fat." Margarita reported that almost all her former classmates gained significant amounts of weight in their thirties.

For the participating mothers, change in the attitude toward weight and age seemed to be very closely connected. They reported their preference for thinness in their youth and considered weight gain a normal part of aging. The need to be thin regardless of age appears to be a new cultural demand they face in the United States.

Subtheme E: Age categories are different in America (mothers)

Attitude toward age and aging seems to be at the root of the participants' attitudes toward themselves and others. All participating mothers appeared to agree that in the Soviet Union people experienced themselves as mature much earlier than their American peers. Margarita said, "I was a teenager then, 18 years old. It is here called a teenager, but there we considered ourselves adults, and here one is a teenager until 20." At forty, she reported feeling that her youth was long gone, "Years ago, I considered twenty-five the limit of youthfulness, and now it is thirty-five. After that a woman becomes middle-aged; life is life. I am older than thirty-five, so I consider myself middle-aged, of course."

Maya's sense of being middle-aged was similar to Margarita's. She recalled being laughed at when she shared this view with her American peers. Her account of this cultural clash symbolized the difference between two attitudes:

First of all, there is an absolutely different attitude toward age categories here. For example, when I came here, I considered myself a middle-aged woman. I was 34 then. ... When I said it in my English class... I remember these astonished looks, because for Americans middle age is after fifty. So the time frames are so disparate between two cultures that a significant gap has formed.

Comparing two cultures, Maya recalled the traditional attitude toward age in the Soviet Union, "A woman after certain age would not take much care of herself. Not because housekeeping responsibilities left no time for it, not only because of it—it was a custom." Marlena concurred with Maya in defining the "certain age." She also pointed to the reflection of the societal attitudes in the retirement laws:

Here it is different, it is considered that a person should look good at forty. In Russia, forty-forty-five was considered a woman at sunset, fifty is a grandmother, and that is it—all the woman's interests must be in grandchildren, and she has to forget about her own life. Here a person is supposed to look good at forty, and at fifty you are still a woman. You have to work till I don't know what age here, and the retirement age there was fifty-five.

The participating grandmothers did not mention their attitudes toward aging, but their comments suggested that they have internalized the cultural norm of moving into the background for the sake of younger generations. Greta spoke about her peers, who "get no attention from their children or all juices are squeezed out of them and they are thrown away as unnecessary garbage." Galina's story contained an example of a mother who keeps "placing herself under her daughter's feet" despite her daughter's maltreatment. Nevertheless, Galina's mindset was similar to that woman's attitude, "If I could sacrifice myself to spare my child, I would do it right away." This cultural norm appeared to define the participating grandmothers' choices and actions.

Subtheme F: Dieting is for when you are older (granddaughters)

It was interesting to note that all the participating granddaughters denied their investment in being thin. They reported their enjoyment of eating and reluctance to adhere to diets. Dina said, "I don't really watch what I eat, not right now. I should, well; I am going to, soon. But not now, because when you are a teenager, your metabolism is faster and as you grow, it slows down." She reported her critical attitude toward models she sees in fashion magazines, "It is just too much work to keep a good figure. They look really skinny, like, most of the time they don't look like healthy, so I feel that I don't really care too much about that image." Dina sounded unperturbed by the possibility of weight gain connected with childbirth, "When I am going to have a baby, I am going to get, like, more, not overweight, but gain more weight with the baby. It usually happens, unless you exercise, like extremely active." She concluded with resolve, "I imagine, I don't really care." At another point in the interview, Dina sounded like she did care about her shape, yet she reported using her friends' opinion, not fashion magazines, as a basis for self-evaluation:

I really have no problems with my body, like I try to make myself confident about my body; I don't think anything is wrong with it. I feel secure about it, and everybody tells me, "Oh you look perfect," so that helps me out, too.... If somebody told me, "Oh, you look fat," I would take it into consideration, but I would not think that myself, because I just believe that I look OK. I compare myself with other people around, not with models and stuff, I never do.

Daniela who was described by her grandmother as a "top model," also spoke about media as a source of overly thin body ideal, "My body could stand to be better when you look, like, at models and stuff. You look at yourself as being fat, but among others, yes, I am fine." Her attitude toward media images was similar to Dina's, but she went further, defending the need to widen the acceptance of various body shapes:

I think that media should not be so focused on this one stereotype of the body, because all people probably have all kinds of genes and different faces. Media should not be so focused on this, like drilling in children's heads that this is the way one should be, not to make this kind of pressure.

Dosia, who reported wearing size 1, said that she liked slim actresses, but when I asked her about her own figure, she said briefly, "I am satisfied with my body." At another point of the interview, she responded to my question about her plans for the future, "I want to be... a lawyer. And about looking—I don't even know. I never thought about it." Dana reported wearing size 7 and feeling that she needs to lose weight, yet her position was, "I am still a kid, and I think that dieting is for when you get older."

Several grandmothers insisted that their granddaughters watch their weight and limit their eating. Greta reported that her granddaughter "absolutely stopped eating dumplings" and "eats no sweets at all" while her granddaughter Daniela spoke about eating doughnuts on a regular basis and "loving" traditional Uzbek dishes made of meat and dough. Golda said that Dora "watches her weight" while her granddaughter Dora spoke at length about her tendency to overeat. This contradiction can be explained by at least two factors: the power struggle between the grandmother and granddaughter around eating and the difference in their perceptions of "watching herself"—

what is "shapely" for a grandmother, is "good and plenty" for her granddaughter.

Four participating granddaughters spoke of their peers' attitude toward weight. These stories seemed to have relevance for them in providing a backdrop, against which they measured their own perception of themselves and their eating behavior. Daniela said, "My best friend, she is not fat, but she got big bones, so she always complains and she is constantly on a diet. This girl would eat an apple for lunch, and that's it. I can't be like this." Talking about her peers, Daniela described the teenage culture she is immersed in, "Everyone complains about her body." Dina spoke about her attempts to give emotional support to her seriously overweight cousin, "We always talk about that because I always make her feel better, like I tell her, 'It's OK, it's not the end of the world.' I usually give advice, like, 'You should exercise 3 times a week, eat healthier." Dina also spoke about other girls who "starve themselves," but said that she is not able to follow their example and "go hysterical" about gaining weight.

Dora's report about other Russians had a negative tone, probably due to the conflict between her desire to be "a perfect 10" she sees in fashion magazines and her determination to spend all her energy on professional achievement. She said, "They are very showy, but usually they are not even skinny. Usually they just worry about their weight, and worry, and talk about it, and they make other people feel bad." Dana described her Korean friend who pretended to be anorexic to attract attention, but "stuffed her face with pizza" at home.

Being brought up by former Soviet women with their higher tolerance for body curves, the participating teenagers spoke about their body change in puberty in neutral or positive tones. When asked about her feelings about her changing body, Dosia dismissed the issue as irrelevant, "I don't feel any difference. I know that I am older and everything, but it is not that important. I am different—like I think about different things, about college, what career I want to choose." For Dosia, career and college seem to be much more important than the way she looks. Dana welcomed and celebrated her body change:

> I was really skinny when I was young, I was really puny, and
> then all of a sudden I got really fatter, and fatter, and fatter,
> and I was growing breasts... It felt good because when I was
> little, I used to see my older cousins and my older friends, and

I was just, "Oh, I want to look just like them." And when it finally happened I felt good because I finally lived up to their expectations, or to mine, really.

Daniela and Dina reported similarly positive attitude toward body change. Daniela said, "I think I started developing even before I got my period. Yeah, I was kind of anxious because you see all the older girls and stuff and you want to look like them." Dina said, "I started developing before everybody else in my grade, so... It made me feel kind of good because nobody else had breasts, and I did, so I felt really special."

The American preoccupation with thinness appears to cause much conflict in teenagers brought up in former Soviet families. The participating teenagers are caught between the values and demands of two contradicting cultural traditions and are conflicted about their abilities to negotiate them successfully.

Taking Care of Self

Subtheme A: I would like to love myself, but I don't know how (grandmothers)

The internalized norm of giving herself to her family completely, to the point of neglect of her own interests and pleasures seemed to permeate every participating grandmother's report. Gita recalled her love of swimming in her youth and said that she also enjoys exercising now. Nevertheless, she looked baffled by my "American" question about her involvement in sports in the Soviet Union. She said, "No, never. You understand, with three kids, and your own plot, and keeping the house... I used to have some ducks, some chickens, some piglet, some other stuff... It was inconceivable... All my time was spent on this." For Gita, taking care of her family completely eclipsed her desire to exercise. Greta reported similar considerations:

In my youth I was a sportswoman, I had a high rating in gymnastics. Even when I had a daughter, my coach met me and asked me to return and train, but it was impossible to combine work, two children, two elderly parents, and sports.

Golda's voice acquired an accusatory tone when she juxtaposed herself against American grandmothers, "Here grandmothers are such that they don't even want to come and touch the baby. They love themselves. I am not like this, I give myself completely, yes." Galina's description of her relative was colored by the same negative judgement with a shade of jealousy:

> My daughter's mother-in-law is not so fat because she does not pay so much attention to her children. I think it is good in some ways. ... It is her great luck that she can control herself and take care of herself.

Genya elevated her sense of self-denial to the level of a philosophical system, "What for are we living in this world? A person should do things for other people's good. I feel this need, if I haven't done anything useful, then why am I?" Trying to downplay her self-sacrificial stance, Genya insisted that she loved herself, too, "I don't want to say that I am not selfish. I do love myself; I love doing things for myself. I am not an exception, all the mothers I know do as much as I do." When I asked Genya to elaborate on her "being selfish," she tried for a long while and, finally, came up with a single example, "I take my medicine on time." When the source of her confusion became obvious to her, she concluded with a sigh, "I would like to love myself, but I don't know how to." Genya was at a total loss when pressed for one example of her "loving" herself.

Galina reported that she disliked herself in her youth. She recalled her deep inner pain of feeling bad looking, "I kept thinking that I was ugly, that my body is ugly, that I had this and that wrong. I always cringed when I was in a group." Galina believes that her bad marriage was a result of this low self-esteem and sense of inferiority:

> I even married the way I should not have to. Good and handsome men wanted to date me, but I thought that if I marry one of them, he will cheat on me or that I won't be able to keep him. I was destroying myself.

Having suffered from low self-esteem all her life and blaming herself for passing it to her daughter, Galina sounded uncomfortable reporting Marina's efforts to bolster her daughter's self-confidence:

> Now she tells her daughter too much in the opposite direction. ... She says, 'I don't want her to be like me.' She is a happy child, yes, but to keep telling her without an end... When

somebody tells her, 'You are smart,' she answers, 'I know.' So maybe at times it is not so good...

The concept of "loving oneself" as "bad" appears to have been internalized by another grandmother, too. Greta's disapproving tone suggested her discomfort about her granddaughter's upbringing, "She should be prepared for life. Not everybody will keep telling her that she is the most beautiful, the smartest."

Since the formative years of all the participating grandmothers occurred during periods of scarcity, their sacrifices were necessary for the family's survival. Thus "loving yourself" appeared to be a negative concept for them. Their reactions to people who did not follow the tradition of self-denial for the sake of the family ranged from angry judgement to confusion and even envy.

Subtheme B: I want to look better, but I have other priorities (mothers and daughters)

All the participating mothers appeared to have internalized, at least to a degree, their mothers' cultural norm of "family first," giving their own interests the lowest priority. This attitude seems to continue to direct their choices and decisions in the United States, where their sacrifices are no longer necessary for family survival.

Marlena believes that, as a Russian woman, she was brought up not to value herself enough to make caring for herself a priority. She reported her self-concept as being not good enough inside and out, despite receiving proof to the opposite. Recalling the compliments she gets from others, she sounded and looked uncomfortable:

We brought it from there, I am sure—this undervaluing oneself. Personally I—no matter how many times people tell me, "You are smart, you are, let's say, beautiful, you are this and this..." Anyway, at the bottom of my heart I don't believe them completely because I perceive myself totally differently. I believe them, but anyway I have this feeling I am hiding inside—undervaluing myself.

Marlena reported feeling unsatisfied with her body, wanting to be "thinner, slimmer, taller," but lacking time and motivation to exercise. She described her attempt to establish an exercise routine with her daughter:

We went with Dina and walked for half an hour, it was last week, and that was the end of our walking. Then she was busy, and I did not feel well, I wanted to lie down, in general the same laziness. Excuses... I feel a lot of respect for women who can force themselves, not force, but to do it like one brushes her teeth—to go for a run, for a walk, to go to a gym—whatever it takes. I cannot organize myself this way—I am lazy."

In her youth, Marlena enjoyed all kinds of sports. She said, "I played volleyball when I was Dina's age, soccer, ice hockey, did ice skating in the winter, everything you want," regretting her present sedentary lifestyle and explaining it by the lack of free time. At the time of the interview, her athletic activities were limited to swimming in the summer. Even though she appreciated the benefits of exercise, "naturally, I feel much better when I swim," Marlena said with a sigh, "In general, I don't exercise. I am trying, take walks with Dina once in a while, but in general—no, I feel very sorry that I don't, but no." Talking about a diet she learned from her friend, Marlena admitted that taking care of herself is not a priority for her:

My friends have lost weight on a good diet, but one has to cook to be on it. This is an American diet, and it is very acceptable. They read some book, and in the book it was connected with health problems. But when it is connected with the desire to look better, it depends on priorities. And I simply have no time to cook separately for my family and myself, because they would not eat the dishes from that diet.

Contemplating how "good" or "bad" it is to love oneself, Marlena talked with admiration about her mother-in-law:

My mother-in-law lost weight, she watches herself very carefully. She has changed her diet, according to her doctor's advice. From our entire family, she tends more toward American food, like fat-free, cholesterol-free. She understood it and she listened to her doctor, and she has the willpower, she takes better care of herself, and she is right to do it, and one can say she loves herself. And this is very good. In our country to say that she loves herself sounds like an insult, how can a person love herself? And here, I think, it is the most important thing—to love yourself, and then everything will be fine with you. These concepts have changed, too.

Talking about her mother and grandmother, Marlena realized that these women's priorities were in feeding the family, not taking care of their health and looks:

There was no habit to exercise regularly or seriously in our family. My grandmother did a lot of manual work all her life. We had some piece of land, and she constantly worked there. Besides, she cooked dinners and did everything else. This is why they did not need any sports, I think.

At the time of the interviews, Marlena considered herself "lucky with my job from the day one," as she felt "very respected and appreciated at work." Her regrets were about not having learned how to treat herself better:

The most interesting thing is that we have learned how to work like Americans, but we never learned how to relax like they, we don't know how to do it, and it is the funniest thing that this is the big problem with us, Russians. I understood that here one has to live in a new way—to think more about yourself, to do what you want. I do not mean something bad, but in general, think more about yourself and live the way you want.

Since Dina spent her formative years in the U.S., Marlena expressed hope that she escaped internalizing the tendency to "undervalue herself," or at least that she retained very little of it, "maybe a couple of per cent points." Another mother, Marina, noted that living in the United States had a positive influence on her daughter's self-esteem. She said:

I am a typical product of my country—obedient, lacking in initiative. ... Dana was very insecure, too. This country helped her a lot. She is still not so sure of herself, but she is less uptight, less bound by conventions, more relaxed, I see a big difference. She still has something from me, but it was changed by this ways of life.

Other participating mothers' reports were similar to Marlena's on almost every point she made. All of them participated in sports or in dancing classes on a regular basis in their youth and recalled these activities with pleasure. Maya said, "I was in track and field, in basketball—a long time ago, in my student years." Marina said, "I did a lot of gymnastics before I got married." All the mothers were aware of the need to exercise for their health or for staying in shape and blamed their "laziness" for not doing enough or not exercising at all. Maya said,

"I attend an exercise group. Unfortunately, it is once a week and I know that I have to do it at least three times a week. From time to time, if I manage to go, but since it happens so rarely that it makes no sense even mentioning it, I go to the gym. I am a member. I used to go rather often, but during the summer this schedule somehow was neglected. Rather often also, was like once in two weeks, not more. I really don't know why I cannot stick to it. Probably my own laziness and lack of organization skills."

Margarita reasoned that she is unable to exercise because of her long working hours, "My work starts at eight, so I get up at six and to get up at five to exercise, I have no energy for it. I spend two hours a day on the road. Then, I probably find excuses for myself—I am tired, I want to hug the pillow." Lack of time, tight finances, intense work and other reasons were cited, but the underlying reason appears to be the same: taking care of herself is not a priority for a woman brought up in the former Soviet Union.

Two mothers reported looking around and seeing other women who do take care of their bodies, but they noted that these women are mostly American. Maya said,

There are several people in my office who take very good care of their health, attend special programs, and thanks to them I am well informed about the types of human body structure, of what one should and should not eat... Mostly these are Americans. It is expensive. They have support groups, exchange of opinions, and one has to attend the program regularly, I think once a week, so it is both financially and time-wise rather difficult to follow.

Maya treated taking care of her appearance as a desirable, but frivolous enterprise, so she concentrated her attention on health issues:

Now I am simply so overweight that I feel it too well, not only by the looks, but rather I pay more attention to it as a health issue. On the outside, theoretically, of course, I would like to be slimmer, younger, more attractive, and so on. But in practice, I understand that I do too little for it to expect it. From the medical point of view I understand that I have to do something in order to avoid getting more problems.

Maya felt compelled to further justify her need to lose weight by medical reasons, quoting her physician's joke, "Don't come for a checkup until you lose some weight." She presented more details, pushing appearance to the background, "Purely medical problems start appearing—my veins start bulging, I gasp for breath. I am not even talking about such aspects as satisfaction with my looks." She feels how different the American attitude toward self is from the one she was used to in the former Soviet Union:

Who had ever heard there about cholesterol, saturated fats, or free radicals? These problems did not occur to us. On the one hand, it is good that people pay much more attention to their health and nutrition. On the other, I think that too much attention is paid to the looks. Here people plan, trying to prevent, as much as it is possible, some illnesses, or weight gain, which is also considered a health hazard. It is in the air here. First of all, there are many TV programs about health, a lot of it is in the press, and I deal with other people's health issues, even if not with my own, and you can see how people pay attention to it and how significant it is.

Maya admitted that the old cultural model was still dominant in her life, "Theoretically I am more aware about health issues, but practically I do not pay enough attention to my health." Margarita's "excuse" for her need to be trim had a strong Soviet-style utilitarian overtone, "I like it, you look younger and more mobile. It is easy to climb four flights of stairs to the fifth floor, to carry grocery bags."

The participating mothers talked about the sources of their self-sacrificial position. Describing her grandmother, Maya admired this active trim woman and recalled how she "used to stress that she never did anything special for it, she never followed a diet or limited herself in any way." She recalled that her grandmother "always managed to look good. Somehow very unnoticeably she gave attention to her appearance." Other mothers described their mothers and grandmothers in similar tones. These women, whose formative years were spent with privations of the pre-war or WWII periods, generally did not take care of their looks. If they managed to spend a little time or money on themselves, they did so surreptitiously and with a feeling of guilt. They also denied any investment in their appearance and stressed that their looks just "happened" rather than resulted from their efforts. Margarita said:

> My mother was the child of WWII. She had a miserable childhood with struggling for a dry bread crust, so her personality, tastes, and needs formed differently. We never talked about looks. My mother never used makeup; she never had a financial opportunity to do something like this. She had a very good figure, so when she did buy something that fitted her well, then she looked very good, I used to notice it. But she never paid much attention to clothes.

Margarita, one mother who appeared more interested in staying trim, found a "legitimate" excuse for taking some care of herself—trying to find a husband:

> When a woman has no man, she takes a better care of herself. And this is a disease of all Russian women—as soon as a man appears next to them, they start taking less care of themselves. When a woman is in love, she changes her tone of voice, her gait, she starts taking much better care of herself, her skin, her body, starts trying some diets, she is all in action. And when a woman does not have a stimulus, life becomes colorless. I spent the larger part of my adult life as a single woman, so I am kind of on my toes. And when the largest part of your life is spent with a man, then a woman gets used to him and he does not stimulate her desire to be liked by him. This is a terrible mistake women make, and then when something happens, they start taking care of themselves right away. One should not do it, and this is a very Russian way.

Nevertheless, Margarita described exercise as a luxury, a rare pleasure she can afford from time to time:

My daughter and I went to the Caribbean islands for vacation this summer. Every morning I got up at six, went to the beach, exercised on the sand and swam. I was the first to go swimming and the last to leave in the evening. This vacation was like from a fairy tale.

All participating granddaughters appeared to have internalized, at least in part, their mothers' and grandmothers' attitude toward priorities in life. They reported their enjoyment of sports, not necessarily for toning their bodies, but for sheer enjoyment, yet when they were pressed for time, athletic pursuits were abandoned first. Dora, who weighed 147 pounds, described herself as "good and plenty" and expressed her desire to lose weight, "I would like to look thinner, definitely." Yet her reasons for not exercising sounded similar to those of the mothers. She said, "I attend a health club... First three weeks that I was signed up I went every day. I was so committed. ... Now I am so busy with everything, and community service, and homework, and everything, I just cannot." Daniela, who weighed approximately 20 pounds less than Dora, reported similar pressures and choices, "I don't try yet; the thing is that last year I had a very bad schedule in school. I got up very late, I did not have the time to do both my homework and to go to the gym." Dina spoke about her desire to support her mother in establishing an exercise routine, but seemed to be more influenced by Marlena's reluctance. She said:

I really don't have the time, but whenever I have a free night, me and my mom, we, like, jog around the block or walk fast. It usually lasts for a week, and then we stop, like we have other things to do, but I try every now and then, just to keep in shape.

Dosia and Dana were formally trained in gymnastics for several years, but neither of them reported any regret for abandoning sports. Margarita said about her daughter, "For three years in Russia I used to take her to a gymnastics class. Her body is perfect for this kind of sports. ... She did splits easily, other things." Dosia sounded interested in sports, but only as an occasional leisure activity:

I go to play basketball, something else, I don't remember what, but it is very rarely. And in winter I plan to attend Bally's gym. Not that I really want to... We have a lot of homework. I like running, we run for fun sometimes.

It appears that emigration, with its hardships and pressures, added a strong need to prioritize activities for the participating mothers and daughters. The attitudes developed for survival in the Soviet Union were utilized and strengthened during the adjustment period and had a significant impact on their choices.

CATEGORY IV: FOOD AND EATING

Eating Habits

Subtheme A: We had to use tricks to save ourselves from starvation (grandmothers)

All participating grandmothers talked about food shortages and difficulty feeding their families in the former Soviet Union. For three of them, starvation during WWII was still vivid in their minds. They introduced this theme on their own and it appeared that it has colored their perceptions for the rest of their lives. Wartime starvation was a daily reality for Golda. Sitting in her cozy apartment in Brooklyn, she related the story of her suffering and survival strategies with vivid details. She used strong emotional language to describe her struggle for survival:

> My youth passed during the war. I was not fourteen yet when the war broke. It was a struggle for a piece of dry bread crust... What I suffered through, I had to be under the ground already for a long time. We ran away naked and barefoot, left everything and lived in Kazakhstan fifty kilometers from the railroad. We had to cross the longest, roughest river, then three kilometers past the river, into the mountains; we walked barefoot on the dry spiky land with snakes and turtles. We had to go there to save ourselves, not to starve to death. There were wild onions there, so my mother, my younger brother, and I would collect half a bag each and also we ate some wild

berries. And then we would cook this mud in an iron pot, and we ate it—you can imagine what kind of food it was.

At the end of the war, Golda and her family returned to the Ukraine, where things slowly turned for the better, but hunger was still lurking on the horizon for a long time. She described her work on a Ukrainian collective farm and her earnings with satisfaction of a person who has finally eaten her fill:

I worked on a beet farm, so I was paid in sugar—forty pounds, and two hundred pounds of wheat. We were paid very little money, like 12 rubles a month, but we were not hungry there. We used to bake beets, potatoes in the open fire. In the fields, they used to cook soup and deliver it to the field groups, mashed potatoes, too. We did not have meat every day, but we *ate*, we weren't hungry. So we kind of hung on there, sold something, returned home—in a month we have used up everything and were hungry again. And a loaf of bread used to cost 200 rubles. And then we found a job sorting potatoes, and this is how we survived little by little. I got accepted into a training program for workers at a big candy factory. There I revived, of course...

Golda's life was full of hardships, from the post-war time until the time of emigration in the late 1980s. Her mother's culinary abilities were necessary to make meatless meals taste better or to stretch meager supplies to feed the family. Golda recalled the early 1950s:

My mother used to cook for me in the morning, there was not much to eat then, we could not afford meat or cold cuts, so she would cook a pot of hot farina without milk. And half a loaf of dark bread, this is what I would take with me to work; I swear this is the truth. And when we would come home, we would make potato *pirogi*, some kind of soup, so this is how she helped me manage.

It was a norm in circumstances of permanent shortages that women were used to getting the short end of everything, including the food they cooked. Golda described her life during the mid-1950s:

Then we were able to afford a little chicken, of course, not enough to have your fill, everything just not to starve. Dinner was like dinner—I used to cook ten ounces of meat for five people. I gave a piece to my husband, and a piece to each child, and my mother and I, of course... My mother-in-law used to say, "it is better than no meat at all. Even three quarters pound of meat, but your soup was made with meat, so it has some taste. Add some herbs for flavor, too." This is how we lived. Later, we started to eat a little better, but not much, it was hard all the time.

Golda's mother-in-law lived the same life of daily struggle, as suggested by her advice. When Golda's daughter grew up and had a child of her own, the times had changed for the better, but not so much that they had enough milk for the whole family. It was still for the child only, now for Golda's granddaughter:

I used to run out to get milk, and then I had to run to work. At six in the morning the milk lines are long—people used to line up from 3, 4, 5 o'clock in the morning to secure a spot, because there was not enough milk for everybody. One, two, three—and there is nothing left, so I used to beg the saleslady, I had just a pint jar for hot cereal for my granddaughter.

Shopping for other basics was a struggle for Golda; she had to scrape by to feed her family:

We used to buy dirty potatoes, cut with a spade, together with the pieces of soil, they used to weigh them together with all this dirt. And if you try to remove a lump of dirt, the saleslady slapped you on your hand, "hands off!" She would sell it to you the way she wanted, with all the dirt, so half of it ended up in the garbage and very little was left to eat. And the same way it was with any kind of vegetables and fruit. I was never able to afford to pay three rubles for a kilogram of... what do you call it... cherries... in the summer. I could never afford cauliflower; it was very expensive. There it was hard, very hard, all my life. And after the fall of the Soviet Union it was even worse. Meat has disappeared altogether; even at the market there were long lines for meat.

Genya's struggle for survival was very similar to Golda's, if even more tragic. She recalled her wartime childhood:

I got into a hospital with malaria. I was emaciated, with frostbitten feet. I had high fever, like my mother, I almost died there. After three months in the hospital, I was like a shadow; so weak I could not climb two steps. They discharged me into the orphanage where I almost died of malnutrition.

Eating her fill of bread once a month was an unforgettable pleasure for Genya, and her recollection of these episodes was alive with sensory memories:

> For being a straight-A student, I was getting the Stalin stipend—a hundred rubles a month. That was great—I could go to the market and spend it all on a loaf of bread, so my sister and I could have our fill of bread that day. I still remember these thick warm slices smelling of human body— the workers at the factory would sneak them under their clothes to pass the factory checkpoint.

Genya described how she managed to fill her stomach in the orphanage:

> There was a cook's aide there, she liked it when I was on kitchen duty—I used to scrub the tables real clean, and the pots, too, so she would let me come more often. She allowed me to collect the leftovers from the pots into two bowls and to give one to my sister.

A bowl of leftovers was such a coveted treasure that Genya's sister, the happy recipient of the fruit of Genya's "tricks," had to eat it under the bed. A chance to take home leftover food was the motivation for Genya's mother-in-law, a single mother of three. She took on a monotonous and exhausting job at a student canteen for her children's sake, "This work was the only thing she could do to survive with three children. She could eat there and take home the leftovers for them." Extra food was a gift of love, bestowed by this woman on Genya's sister, "She used to sneak a little extra food onto my sister's plate; she knew her before I met her son, she felt sorry for us orphans." Genya had to continue her "tricks" after the war, too. She recalled these times:

> Obtaining food has always been a horror there. We came here with huge amounts of cholesterol in our blood; I was happy

when I could buy a pig's head. I used to make head cheese, meat ravioli, I did tricks to feed the family.

Galina did not elaborate on this topic, but her laconic comments echoed Golda's and Genya's reports of continuous hunger. Talking about the postwar years, she said, "When we returned from the evacuation, maybe we had nothing to eat, but we always had music, singing at home." She contrasted permanent Soviet hardships with "being spoiled" by American abundance, "There if you got anything to eat, you were happy already, and here it is so that you eat it all and in general you want salads mostly, things like this, vegetables and fruit, and nothing else."

It was interesting to note that food and eating continued to be a deep undercurrent in the participating grandmothers' stories, regardless of their desire to control their weight. Golda reported the compliments she received from her friends and her response, "My friends tell me, 'Golda, you have lost weight.' I tell them, 'One should eat less.'" Nevertheless, Golda's responses to seemingly unrelated events suggested that food is still a lens through which she sees the world. When her friends described their trip to Odessa, she responded with a passionate speech, "I don't want Odessa's beauty, I don't want these delicacies, here we also have very tasty things, and I like everything here, but the most important thing is that America is a country of immigrants." Describing her happy life in America, Golda said, "We are so grateful to America. I am not hungry; thank G-d. I have my own apartment."

Another grandmother, Galina, talked about the positive sides of living in the United States and said matter-of-factly, "And of course, the nutrition." Gita's comparison of her life in the Soviet Union and in the United States also focused on food:

> I am better off here, and I like it. There is such a diversity of foods, and vegetables, and everything else, and I can afford it all, and there we had nothing besides three or four basic staples, like potatoes, lard and sugar. It was considered happiness if one had them, especially the times before our emigration.

Talking about her granddaughter, Gita said, "My granddaughter is such a good child. I tell her, 'My loved one, may I bring you something to eat?' Equating love and care with feeding was prominent in other participating grandmothers' stories as well.

In the United States, the abundance and availability of food as well as the freedom from the necessity of "tricks" seem to be a constant source of pleasure for the participating grandmothers. Their enjoyment of food appeared to be unencumbered by weight concerns.

Subtheme B: I eat as much as i want (grandmothers and granddaughters)

For all the participating grandmothers, cooking, eating and treating family and friends was a significant source of pleasure and connection. They considered sharing the recipes, preparing festive meals, and teaching their daughters and granddaughters to cook and to bake, to be special women's rites that united generations and gave women a sense of pride and accomplishment. Golda described the lavish spread she cooked for her birthday with pride and love for every tasty morsel, "First of all, I made gefilte fish; everybody loves my fish. I never adulterate it with white bread, farina, or ground biscuits, no, my mother taught me to make it—only fish, sautéed onions, salt, pepper, and eggs." She described all other dishes with the same detail and gusto, accompanying her menu with cooking pointers.

Gita included three recipes into her story. Sharing these with me was as natural for her as preparing a full spread for her daughter's birthday party or passing her culinary talents onto her granddaughter. She said:

I love cooking, I love guests; I love making all kinds of pies. ... When my daughter turned forty, we had a party, and I cooked very much, a lot of Russian food, and everybody praised it a lot. I do it very quickly. It took me twenty-four hours to cook a full spread for thirty people, almost all by myself. ... I also baked a lot of delicious rose-shaped pastries of sweet dough. I beat egg yolks in the mixer; my granddaughter helps me. She says, "Grandma, I don't like to cook, but I love making dessert." So to attract her I ask her to beat egg yolks and egg whites, roll the dough together, and then put the pastries the cut side up into a hot oven. They taste very good.

Reporting her love of food, Gita sounded guilt-free. Her comments about the need to eat less appear to reflect outside advice rather than her heartfelt intentions. She said, "I do not limit myself—I eat whatever I want. I like fatty food, yes. I try to eat less, but I still eat a lot of it." Greta reported her irritation over her own weight gain and reported her and her daughter's high cholesterol level. Then she moved on to give me her recipe for banana bread, complete with a hefty amount of butter. Food as love and connection was an integral part of many episodes reported by the grandmothers. Genya recalled her communication with her granddaughter:

> I bought a cake, the kind I like and she likes, so I tell her, "Dosia, come soon, because I will eat this cake all by myself, and I am not allowed to eat this much." So she says, "Just leave me a little piece." It is like our game. She came yesterday, I treated her to the cake, but said, "You are going to eat dinner at home." "Yes, yes, grandma, don't you worry."

All five participating granddaughters appear to have internalized, at least to a degree, their grandmothers' enjoyment of food. Dora talked about her grandmother's role in developing her eating habits:

> I eat so much, like when I go to a restaurant or something, I order something, and I feel like it is my obligation to finish it. When I was little, my grandmother used to tell me, "If you leave leftovers, they are going to bother you all night, they are not going to let you sleep." Oh, yeah, she always said, "Your leftovers are like what makes your brain, so if you are not going to eat them, you are not going to be smart." I got into that habit, so whenever I order food, I don't even know why, it is silly to say it is just because of her, but it's just like this, "I have to finish it, I don't want to leave any at the end..." Maybe it's an excuse... I guess it is both—my grandma and that I enjoy food.

Another granddaughter, Dina, also spoke of her enjoyment of food in general and of her grandmother's creations in particular, "I like the cakes she bakes, cookies, sweet stuff. When she makes it, I eat as much as I want because I am not going to have it for a long time. Just to take advantage of it." Dina's mother Marlena described the methods she and other women in her family used to feed the children, "In Russia, all the children were stuffed with food the same way. My mother, my mother-in-law, and I used to tell fairy tales, stage shows, and dance for them just to make them eat." At the time of the interviewing, Dina was a "good eater" and reported eating as a way of comforting herself, "...Whenever I am upset, I always eat. I guess, it is not a good thing, but it makes me feel better when I eat more." Comparing herself with her diet-obsessed friends, Dina reiterated her love of food and reluctance to control her eating:

> And one of my girlfriends, she is Russian, she is thin, but we went to a diner last night, and she just ordered a salad and coffee. I was eating chicken and I was looking at her. I guess she watches her weight more than I do, but right now I don't really care that much. If I gain weight, I'd want to lose it, but I would not go hysterical about it. I love eating out, not like those girls who starve themselves. I am so used to food, I like eating, so I don't think I am going to be able to starve myself.

Daniela's report was similar to Dina's, "Vickie is constantly on a diet, she has very high self-control. I can't be like this. If I am hungry, I can't just sit there and not eat." Another granddaughter, Dana, spoke about her love of food overriding her desire to lose weight, "When I am eating, I am telling myself, 'That's it, I am going to go on a diet tomorrow.' And I keep eating, because I really don't care, if I am hungry, I am going to eat."

Even though the participating granddaughters' weight ranged from 102 to 147 pounds, they spoke about their enjoyment of food and demonstrated a tendency to overeat or to eat for comfort. Considering their preference for fast food, it is reasonable to predict their future weight gain.

Subtheme C: I starve once a week to lose weight (mothers)

Three out of four participating mothers reported using two weight control methods, popular in the former Soviet Union—starving one day a week, and eating proteins separately from carbohydrates. Marlena recalled, "There I could lose weight by not eating one day a week, and now it is very difficult. There, everybody tried not to eat on Fridays or not to eat on Mondays, we only drank water." Marina talked about her inability to adhere to the system of separate eating, but mentioned her

friends who used it with success in both countries. She said, "I am not
dieting and I cannot adhere to any system. I know a Russian couple
here, they started separate eating in the Soviet Union, and they continue
doing it here, too." Margarita described her hunger regimen in detail:

> The only way to fight extra weight is to starve a day or two
> every week. I do it once in a while. My last meal is at 6 p.m.
> and then I don't eat the following day, only drink water. At
> about noon the next day, I eat, so altogether it is about a day
> and a half. This is not only for losing weight; it rejuvenates
> and purifies your whole body. Some famous American doctor
> wrote this book, *The Miracle of Hunger*. It was translated into
> Russian; I read it there. I remember everybody was doing it.

Margarita spoke at length about her cousin who lost a significant
amount of weight and became a weight control "professor." She said:

> She gave me all kinds of information about separate eating,
> like what foods should not be eaten together. She is a
> professor of separate eating, like meat is not to be eaten with
> starches, like bread. Red vegetables should be eaten separately
> from green ones. This is her hobby; she knows what organs
> are cleansed by specific foods. She used to fast for the whole
> week, too. When I came to America, she looked like a barrel,
> and now she is slim.

The popularity of these rather extreme slimming methods appears
to be the result of a combined pressure of scarcity and the need to
control weight in the Soviet Union. On the one hand, their cultural
norm dictated that they spend the least amount of resources on
themselves. On the other hand, a thin beauty ideal imported to the
former Soviet Union from the West demanded that they lose weight.
Starving once a week or eating starches and proteins separately did not
need any special foods or additional time. Arriving in the United States
and being even more pressured to slim down, the participating women
consider returning to these methods rather than spending time and
money on exercising or on special diets.

Changes in Eating Habits

Subtheme A: I eat healthier now (grandmothers and mothers)
All grandmothers and mothers compared their eating habits in the former Soviet Union to those in the United States and reported significant improvements. They indicated two reasons for this change—abundance of fresh produce, and information about healthy eating in the United States. Maya explained:

> One can clearly see the difference in attitudes toward food, our tastes have changed, too. Who had ever heard there about cholesterol, saturated fats, free radicals, or anything in this vein? These problems did not occur to us. People pay much more attention to their health and nutrition, and this information is in the air here. It is in the press, on TV, everywhere. I can see how other people pay attention to it and how significant it is. Changes in our lifestyle are demonstrated in more caloric, tastier and more readily available nutrition. We are trying to eat healthier; for example, we don't eat much fried food, like we used before.

Maya's mother Greta praised her granddaughter's influence on the family's eating habits:

> We try to eat more vegetables and less meat. I think it is good for us. My family loves tasty food, traditional dishes, basically made of meat and dough, pies and steamed lamb dumplings. I used to make them often, but now we stopped eating them, and the initiative comes mostly from my gym teacher and from Daniela.

Greta said that she eats "mainly vegetable soups and almost no meat," but since her son-in-law insists on eating meat, she has to cook two separate dinners for her family. She said, "Now I have a restaurant at home—what is this one going to eat, what is the other one going to eat? I cook practically every day." Cooking two dinners, one for her husband, and one for herself, was a choice of a non-participating grandmother, Marlena's mother-in-law. Marlena described this woman with admiration for her adherence to a healthier lifestyle:

My mother-in-law is a great achiever. She lost weight; she changed her diet according to her doctor's advice. She is the only one in our family who leans more toward American food, fat-free, cholesterol-free. She exercises and watches what she eats, even though her husband eats exactly the way he did in Russia. For him, she cooks fatty food, fried cutlets, dough, sweets, but she does not touch it, they eat separately.

Galina spoke about her desire to lose weight and admitted that it has influenced her eating:

> Our eating has changed a lot. I stopped cooking meat-based soups. Here… you eat it all and in general you want salads mostly, things like this, vegetables and fruit, and nothing else. I like other things, too, but I don't want to cook them, because you gain weight eating them.

Galina also mentioned Chinese food she ate in a restaurant and stressed its advantage over traditional Russian cuisine:

> I like Chinese food; it is tasty and less fatty than Russian. Honestly speaking, you have a heavy feeling in your stomach after Russian food, and after Chinese food it is not so, you feel better, lighter. You are not hungry, but without the sense of overeating.

Galina's daughter Marina also said that her cooking became healthier in the United States. She said:

> I buy low fat, low cholesterol foods, and when I cook, I try to cook with less fat. We eat mostly chicken, white meat mostly, and a lot of vegetables. In Russia I used much more fat for cooking. I stopped buying pork altogether, and I fry food much less.

One mother, Marlena, spoke with regret about her need to cook quick meals in the evening and eating fatty food as a result. She said, "What can one cook in thirty minutes? So usually I cook macaroni or some other kind of pasta, chicken schnitzel, fried food because it is quicker." Marlena's report suggested her limited familiarity with culinary shortcuts afforded by the diverse productions of American food industry and with alternative ways of food preparation, such as broiling. For two participating grandmothers, the change in eating habits appeared to be more theoretical than practical. Describing her dinner party, Golda sounded aware of the need to lower her intake of fatty foods due to her high cholesterol level. Yet her choice of delicacies defied this intention:

> I also made gorgeous jellied meat, first I cook cow feet and chicken, and then I strain it, put it in the refrigerator. In the morning, I remove all the fat from the top. Who needs this fat, I have too much cholesterol already—three hundred or more. Then I cut up the meat, warm up the jelly with crushed garlic, and pour it over the meat. Then I decorate it with slices of boiled eggs, it looks so good in big platters. Then, I stewed chicken livers with lots of onions; they taste great.

Another grandmother, Gita, as reported by her daughter Marlena, cooked traditional dishes to please her family, "If a grandmother comes, then we get different dishes made of dough, like blintzes, rolls with various fillings. ... Dina loves dough, and my husband does, too." Dina praised her grandmother's baking and reported enjoying it together with her friends:

> They like Russian food my grandma makes, like rolled dough with meat, just anything she makes—like cakes she bakes, cookies, sweet stuff. When she makes it, I eat as much as I want because I am not going to have it for a long time. Just to take advantage of it.

Overall, the participating women appeared to be more open than men in their families to the change in eating habits. They reported being informed about healthy eating, but the actual change depended on various factors, such as their openness to change, the attitude of the younger generation, and the time budget. Although the grandmothers' menus do not sound "healthful" by mainstream American standards, they still constitute a significant improvement in these women's eating habits.

Subtheme B: Cooking is not a necessity here (grandmothers and mothers)

All the participating grandmothers and mothers stressed the significantly diminished need for home cooking in the United States. Yet the actual custom of spending time on cooking from scratch did not seem to disappear. The tradition that demanded that women cook full three-course meals on a regular basis appears to have many roots in the Soviet culture. For the participating women, their cooking, in addition to being an economic necessity, had significant added value, as it symbolized love, connection, tradition, and barter for goods and services, to name just a few. Marlena talked about her mother's visits, "When she comes to me, she wants to please me and to make my life easier, so she cooks for me."

Marlena reasoned that she had to cook dinner every evening, so that her family would spend time together at least around the dinner table:

> I think that food is communication; this is the reason I keep cooking, to get the family to stay together in the evening. We eat at home only one meal a day, so dinner means sitting around the table for at least 30 minutes and talk. Otherwise, we drift apart, into separate rooms.

Marlena pondered over her contact with her daughter's friends through food as well:

> What kind of contact can I have with her American friends? We have nothing in common, and I have nothing to talk to them about, so the only thing I can ask them, is "Do you want to eat?" Dina tells me, "Mom, why do you keep asking them the same thing? They don't want to eat, leave them alone." *This is my way to make contact.* My mother is doing it, and my grandmother, and I do the same, even though I understand it is ridiculous.

Maya spoke about cooking in Russia as a way to connect with people and as a source of pride:

> It gave us pleasure, because everybody you loved and wanted to see and talk to would come... Everybody cooked very well,

everybody, and everybody had his own special dishes, …known and loved by everybody, it was so satisfying, and the exchange of recipes, how funny it sounds now. The food itself was not the purpose of this dinner, the real point was personal contact, but in addition to it, hedonistic elements.

When Marina talked about her childhood, her warmest recollections were about her grandmother and her lessons:

My grandmother was a great cook and an exceptional housekeeper. She had a great pair of hands; she could make something out of nothing. She was a Jack-of-all-trades. My mother told me that she even used to make shoes for the kids during the war. I learned how to cook from her, all the housekeeping. I remember visiting her before she moved to live with us; she made a cute little apron for me—I was very little then.

Being able to make "something out of nothing" sounds like an impressive talent in a culture of permanent food shortages. Inability to cook well was mentioned as a highly negative trait by Marina's mother as it resulted in poor nutrition for the family. Galina said about her relative, "If she boiled potatoes, she would keep them in the refrigerator for three days and feed them to her children and her husband. This is the kind of woman she was." Used to conclude a long list of accusations, this last item was uttered with a triumph of driving the last nail into the enemy's coffin.

Describing her life in the Soviet Union, Genya said matter-of-factly:

At home, my responsibility was to make sure everybody had breakfast, dinner, and supper. …. We liked to eat heartily, especially men. A man wants some first course, like borscht, then cutlets or fish with garnish, like hot cereal, for sure.

All her life Genya had to "play tricks" to stretch meager supplies and turn them into filling meals. Her husband, true to his "lordly ways," never helped her in the kitchen. She also recalled an episode of bartering her cooking for necessary services:

I remember one day we had a delivery of coal, and it had to be carried in. I called my husband at work. He said, "Two guys will come, but you got to feed them." I fried fresh flounder and made a large bowl of potato salad vinaigrette; this was my payment. I gave them an opportunity to sit down and eat in the house, not in some dirty canteen with flies and sticky oilcloth on large tables. They were young guys, without families. They had nobody to cook for them, so they valued real food, not that stinky cabbage soup and those terrible hamburgers made out of bread.

Genya's story suggests her complete acceptance of a Russian cultural norm that a man does not cook; he needs a woman "to cook for him." The younger generations seem to have inherited this cultural attitude. It did not occur to one of the participating mothers to ask their husbands to help them with housework. Every married participating mother said that her husband does not cook in a matter-of-fact manner and did not seem to harbor any hope for changing the situation. Despite their generally higher level of acculturation, the participating granddaughters did not differ from their mothers and grandmothers on this particular point of view. Daniela said, "When I am home alone or with my father and there is nothing to eat, I make myself macaroni or something. Not many men I know can cook. Most of them make sandwiches, like my father." Even though Dora talked about her desire to become a "breadwinner" in her future family, she could not fathom sharing the housekeeping responsibilities with her future husband. She sounded convinced when she said, "We still live in a male-dominated society, after everything women have been through, so we still have to cook anyway, a man is not going to be able to."

Cooking was a necessity in the former Soviet Union, for most of the women there were no alternatives. It was a norm for a woman to come home after a full day's work and cook. Galina said:

> I always had dinner ready when my family came home. I would warm it all up and serve. If I came home late from work, I would still stand at the stove and cook, so that my husband and my daughter had something to take with them the next day. I always cooked something for Marina to eat when she came home from school. We managed there.

All the participating women spoke about the poor quality of ready-made food in the former Soviet Union. Marina explained her need to bake before the emigration, "In Georgia, I used to bake very much, because one could not eat what was sold in stores—it was like poison." She reported the change, "Here I stopped baking almost completely, I bake very rarely, only for special occasions." Greta's report was very similar. She also presented her reasons for the change, "Lately I started baking less because we buy ready made cakes, especially when the weather is hot. I have no time for it and we are trying to limit ourselves." Greta spoke about eating out; emphasizing that she is the last person in her family to accept the alternatives to home cooking:

> I used to bake a lot for parties, but here everything is changing. In the beginning we had big gatherings at home, and now at times, on birthdays, we get together at home or friends visit on weekends. But now they are trying more, *even I*, we are trying not to do it at home, but to go to some restaurant because it is easier than to cook at home.

Galina sounded as if she needed to justify her enjoyment of restaurant food, "I like it, why not? It is better than to stand at the stove. If one can afford it, why not?" Margarita praised the possibility of an "easy out" in the United States, "It is so good here, if you want to, you can buy ready-made food or oven-ready stuff. In America, there is no such a dire necessity to cook as it was there."

With all the opportunities for change, however, most of the participating women reported cooking "every day" or almost every day. They do so despite their own waning interest. Their reasons for continuing to cook included the unyielding position of their husbands, high cost of eating out, and tradition. Marlena said:

> I can cook well, but I don't like it. If I had a choice, I would like to do other things instead. ... If it were up to me, we would eat out much more often, five or six times more often than once in two weeks, but the man is the head of the household.

Marlena also spoke about the change in her mother's attitude:

> She is also experiencing a change in her attitude toward cooking. Her friends and she started celebrating their birthdays at some Chinese buffet, so she finally understood that she does not need to spend her time in the kitchen, and she does not have that much of it left.

Maya's report sounded very similar to Marlena's. She spoke about her loss of interest in cooking in the new country:

> During the weekends I cook, I want to give my mother a little break. I loved to cook so much, we always cooked a lot; there were many people in the house. I used to bake great things from a thick book with hand-written recipes. Now it is lying around somewhere, and nobody needs it. We made preserves, all kinds of jams, pickles; it gave you pleasure to treat your guests to something of your own making, the family special. Now it lost its necessity. Of course, we do the cooking now, too; we don't go out that often, mostly on special occasions, not regularly. We still don't do it the American way.

Maya reported discussing this topic with a colleague, "One of my co-workers said, 'It does not make sense to spend so much time on cooking.' I said, 'But going out is expensive.'" She repeated the calculations her colleague used to help her change her mind, but sounded only half-convinced. She said:

> From this point of view, it makes sense to order food somewhere or to eat out. On the other hand, we are used to home cooking; when we have guests, we also cook. Besides, the generation of my mother and in-laws practically does not eat out. They do not eat Chinese food, Japanese food or Italian; as a result, it is better to cook what people are used to rather than to disappoint them.

While the participating grandmothers were just "discovering" eating out for themselves and the mothers were struggling to negotiate the demands of the cultural norm and the new opportunities open to them in the United States, the granddaughters appeared to have been completely acculturated in this respect. All of them reported their enjoyment of restaurant food and their dislike of home cooking. Dina said:

> I never do anything from scratch, not by myself. If my mom is making something or my grandmother, I help them out, but I really don't like cooking. I'd rather eat out or order food, like pizza or Chinese.

Even though Dina said she occasionally baked brownies or made pasta to help her mother, she still insisted that she did not like to do it. Other granddaughters also sounded totally guilt-free when they talked about their almost complete lack of culinary abilities. Dora said, "I can make an omelet and I can boil some macaroni, that's basically it." Daniela spoke about her grandmother's cooking lessons, but still admitted:

> I don't cook, probably because she cooks for us, so I don't have to. I am sure if I was alone, I would. When I am home alone or with my father and there is nothing to eat, I make myself macaroni or something.

Dana said, "I can't cook from scratch, it just doesn't turn out good when I cook." Dana's mother Marina expressed her approval of such change:

> I try to teach Dana to cook, but she has no interest in it, and generally speaking, I don't think she should. One needs to know how to cook, of course, but life here is so different. I think that the most important thing for her is to get good education, a good profession, to be completely independent. If you have money here, you can have anything you want without standing at the stove. If she is interested, she will learn how to cook later. If we stayed in the old Soviet Union, especially in Georgia, my attitude would be different. It was considered important that a woman is a good housekeeper, a good cook, the society was concentrated on it. And here you can buy anything almost ready, or order food in, or eat in a restaurant. I think that a half of American women cannot cook at all.

Other mothers appeared to have similar attitudes toward their daughters' preparation for the future. They valued education, professional achievement, "making it" in the United States and sounded unperturbed by their daughters' lack of interest in domestic pursuits. The only gripe the participating mothers had about their daughters' eating out was their disapproval of unhealthy fast food.

Subtheme C: *I cannot live without Cheetos (granddaughters)*

If American media succeeded only partially in influencing the participating granddaughters' perception of body ideal, these girls' acculturation seemed to be almost complete in the area of eating. All the granddaughters said that, given a choice, they prefer non-Russian food. Dana said, "I like American food more, I guess I am more used to it. I still like some Russian food, but American is just better, it's normal." Golda complained about the Americanization of Dora's tastes without realizing that what she calls "American" is still another cultural import, "My granddaughter does not want to eat dinner. She wants only American, everything American—either Chinese food or sandwiches. I have sorrow with her, she stopped eating borscht, soups, it is terrible." Dora added one more item to her grandmother's list, "When I first came here, I used to love pizza. I could not live a day without eating a slice of pizza." Other granddaughters mentioned candy, doughnuts, potato chips, etc., as a large part of their daily diet. Dosia said:

> Sometimes I eat potato chips, sweets. I like cheesecake. I know that I shouldn't eat it, but I eat it anyway. I know one shouldn't eat much candy or to chew gum. My friends eat more of this stuff than I do.

All the granddaughters reported being informed about nutritional value of different kinds of food, yet they preferred "junk food," probably to follow their friends' example. Dina said:

> On weekends, I am always out with my friends, so usually we eat at a diner or McDonald's. My mom does not really mind it, but if I go often, she'll say something like, "Don't waste your money on it, it's not healthy for you," because it is really not, it is all fat and processed food. I always order a hamburger and French-fries at McDonald's. ...My friends eat the same thing basically.

Dana also spoke about knowing the difference between healthy eating and "garbage food." Yet her choices were based on other considerations. She said, "Sometimes I allow myself, like, garbage food, like Wendy's, pizza, ice cream, all that calorie stuff, but sometimes I tell myself, "Yo, you know," and I just take salad." Describing her school meals, Dana also spoke about her mother's attempts to steer her away from fast food, "Today I had Cheetos, I love them. I can't live without them. My mom hates all this stuff. She says I should be eating more healthy food, but it's too bad. I eat what I like." Daniela reported trying to "improve" her "bad eating habits" with little success. She said, "I don't eat much healthy food or anything. I get, like, cravings for sweets, so I go and eat, like, a doughnut at night."

All participating granddaughters appeared to disregard their mothers' advice as well as their own better judgement and join their peers in enjoying "junk food."

CATEGORY V: LOSSES AND GAINS OF EMIGRATION

Losses

Subtheme A: My whole family was destroyed by the emigration (grandmothers)

All the participating grandmothers reported experiencing a sense of loss as a result of their emigration. They spoke about two sources of these feelings—missing the family members they left behind and their inability to learn English. Greta spoke about missing her closest relatives:

> I badly miss the motherland where I was born, where I lived all my life, and I miss the people I lost, I miss my son who lives across the Atlantic Ocean, I miss my relatives who are no longer living. I miss my nieces who are like my own children, because they grew up so close to me. My brother was so precious for me because we were very close. When I suddenly hear a melody that we used to play together with him, or if somebody starts playing *Freilechs* (a merry Jewish folk tune) and I see myself dancing with him, all these pictures present themselves so clearly. For me it is so painful.

Greta spoke about serious depression she suffered after her brother's death:

> Of course, with these losses it is very difficult for me to live. In the beginning, I started making good progress in English when I was taking classes at NYANA, but my brother's death ended all my efforts. I got stuck and can't move forward any

longer. I am like that proverbial dog that understands everything but cannot speak. It is another source of my suffering. I was so depressed several times that I needed treatment.

Three other participating grandmothers also talked about missing their family members who were left behind. Generally positive Gita recalled her son's visit with a sense of pain and longing:

My other son, who lives in Russia, came to visit with his wife. He liked everything here, of course, but his wife's family, her mother, they don't want to come here... I don't want to push them, but they are brothers, they miss each other so much. When he calls, this one is happy, and the other one is happy, too. When he was here, the other one took time off work, went with them everywhere, showed them everything, he gave them so much attention. Just the fate is such that one is here and the other one is there.

Golda seemed determined to depict her life in America in the most shiny, picture-perfect way she could possibly conjure up. Yet the word *depression* slipped through her panegyric to America when she was talking about her son, who returned to Odessa, and about her difficulties adjusting to the new life:

Of course, it is not so simple to get used to the life here. My son is there; of course I miss him a lot. The language is different, and the life is different. You have to have a lot of willpower to always keep your spirits up and not to get depressed.

Galina spoke about her close emotional connection to her brothers. For her, living apart from them and from her daughter was a source of constant pain. She lamented a miserable marriage of her oldest brother and then added:

My other brother is in Israel, and I miss him. Our family is such that if one of us is suffering, we are all suffering, and if one of us is happy, then we are all happy. This is why it is so hard for me; I am far away from them, and from my daughter, too.

Inability to communicate in English was another source of emotional discomfort for four of the participating grandmothers. Comparing her life in the United States and in the former Soviet Union, Galina concluded that her lifestyle has changed significantly, mostly for the worse. She considered "the language barrier" to be her main problem in America. Galina reported being stressed out by her inability to communicate with people or to read the mail she receives, "When I receive a letter, I feel stressed out, I cannot read it, even with a dictionary." She was afraid to use public transportation, "I am afraid that we don't get off on a right stop or won't understand what they are announcing. I cannot speak English at all and I don't get what they say to me."

As Galina considered "communication with people" to be "the most important thing in life," she missed the activities she shared with her friends in the former Soviet Union, "I had a totally different lifestyle. I could not live without going to the movies with my friends, to the theater, to the opera." Galina reported missing her favorite activity—singing, as it was a significant source of pride and enjoyment for her, "I participated in amateur groups at work. I had mezzo-soprano and I used to get so many awards and honor certificates there for my singing."

Three participating mothers also said that they felt like "guests" or "strangers" in the new country. Yet their reports were less tragic in tone, probably due to their at least partial acquisition of English. They did not talk about missing their relatives who live in other countries and in general made fewer comparisons between the old and the new culture. Nevertheless, for all the participating grandmothers, emigration was a serious stressor, and it took them much time and effort to overcome the initial shock and to adjust to the new life.

Gains

Subtheme A: I live like a queen (grandmothers)

Two participating grandmothers described in detail their terrible living conditions in the Soviet Union. Golda recalled going to court to regain her "tiny miserable apartment in the old part of the city" after the WWII was over and she returned home:

I had two small rooms, 200 square feet in both of them, not rooms, just boxes, a kitchen, and a tiny entrance hall. Of course, we had no running water there, no cooking gas; we had a water pump in the backyard. So we used to carry water in buckets, to the second floor. And then, excuse me; we carried out those dirty buckets, too. Toilet was in the backyard, too, and it was an outhouse, it used to stink not only in the backyard, but its stench reached the street. When I recall it, it is like a nightmare.

Twenty five years later, Golda fought tooth and nail to improve her living conditions when her turn on a waiting list for a new apartment came up, "So as a Jew, I got the worst apartment, on the ground floor. My supervisor moved to a better one, and I got his apartment, two walk-through rooms with wet walls, but I was happy for this, too." She summarized her life in the former Soviet Union:

> There we lived—two rooms and five people, of course, it was crowded. I slept in the middle of the room on a folding cot, my mother slept on a couch, and my daughter already lived in the bedroom with her husband, and the baby was born already, and this is how we all lived. I never had my own room; I never had my own private life, never.

Genya reported similar struggles:

> We lived in bad conditions—one room in a communal apartment in an old neighborhood, running water and an outhouse were in the backyard. It was my fate to live in horrible old houses all my life. ... We lost all our health there, used it up just for survival. I pulled my back there, my spine, carrying pails of coal, and my knee is bad.

Overall, Golda seemed to express the feelings of all the participating grandmothers, "All our lives it was hard anyway. Hard, and hard, and hard again. Very hard." Compared with what the participating grandmothers had to endure in their past, a small one bedroom apartment in an old walk-up building in America looked like a palace, and meager SSI payments allowed them to live comfortably. Golda said:

My life here is very different, I am happy with my life. I never had my own room, my own private life. And here, I am very happy and I should kiss the American ground, I swear, I live like a queen. I have a one-bedroom apartment. I am my own boss, I enjoy my life every day, every day I am happy that I am in this land, and I love my little apartment, so cozy, not so big, but pleasant.

In addition to better food and shelter, Golda reported two other gains she enjoyed in the United States—the sense of independence and the opportunity to spend a part of her time pursuing her own interests. She sounded happy and proud describing her participation in the chorus and other activities at the day care center:

I love dancing and singing, so I sing in the chorus. I live by it, and I live for my children, to see them graduate, stand on their own feet. This is a big source of happiness for me, and when they are taken care of, I can live a little for myself. Last Jewish holidays our singing coach worked with us, so we sang many songs—we always have great concerts. In the spring we celebrated Jewish holidays and the WWII Victory Day—so we chose special songs for it. Our chorus sang last New Year's Eve, and this New Year's we are going to sing, too.

Three more participating grandmothers also spoke about their enjoyment of the activities offered by the Jewish center they attended on the regular basis. They stressed that it would be impossible in the former Soviet Union. Greta said:

I have to say that I live the life I would have never had there, no doubt. I go to theaters, concerts, on sightseeing trips, and I have a possibility to read whatever I want. I live an interesting life. I found wonderful friends, we get together, have a good time, enjoy the activities. Now we are planning a trip to Washington, D.C. in November. ...I am very happy that we have a group. It is a combination of gymnastics and elements of Tai Chi; it is good for my health. I attend these classes twice a week, two years already. I go to the swimming pool, too, thanks to Gita, our water-loving duck, she kind of pulled me there. My time is fully scheduled: twice a week we have

English classes, twice a week—gym, twice a week—swimming pool.

Gita's report was more laconic, but she expressed similar feelings:

I am happy now. I found myself here. In the Jewish center I regularly go to the swimming pool, I love swimming. We attend a literary club, it is very interesting; we enjoy each other's company, meet interesting people who visit our center.

Having suffered all her life from "that damned stove," Genya spoke with appreciation about getting her apartment heated in September, "Here, of course, it is so different, more humane... Today the day was cold, so we had heating on...; we did not ask for it, but they turned it on for half an hour in the morning—very good." She sounded heart-broken and full of regret when she looked back at her life, "I left all my strength there, came here so sick and exhausted. It is so good to live here, but I have no strength anymore." Even though this conclusion seemed to throw a pall of despair on her life, Genya talked about her emotional sustenance—classical music and literature. She said, "When I have the strength, I go to the day care center, I play the piano there, I like accompanying singers, too. Probably this is my love for myself."

One participating grandmother, Galina, displayed a generally less positive attitude and reported much hardship in the beginning of the emigration period as well as at the time of the interviewing. She spoke about three benefits of her life in the United States: the improvement of her granddaughter's health, better nutrition, and freedom from anti-Semitism. Only one participating mother made comparisons between her living conditions in the Soviet Union and in the United States, "The worst basement in New York does not compare with the hut I lived in, and here I have a very nice apartment."

Subtheme B: We are safe now (grandmothers and mothers)

Three participating grandmothers identified anti-Semitism in the former Soviet Union as an additional reason for their emigration, or mentioned it as one of the degrading components of their life in the old country. Galina reported her joy over escaping the virulent anti-Semitism her family suffered in the Ukraine:

In our city, it was a horror to be Jewish, we were afraid to be seen on the way to a synagogue. There was one synagogue in the old outskirts, we had to get up very early to get matzos, and then we had to hide them so that nobody noticed, G-d forbid. The last few years before the emigration it was even worse. It was scary to be on a bus, the anti-Semitic hooligans would follow you and beat you up after you got off. When we were at home, they used to knock on our doors and windows. In 1992 it was especially horrible; I know many scary events. One woman lived right across the street from us; she sold her apartment and was getting ready to leave for America. They killed the entire family and took everything; they killed the little child, too. This is the horror we lived in.

Margarita, who lived in Crimea, related a similar story about Jewish families that were murdered and robbed of all their possessions on the eve of their departure. Neither she, nor her mother Genya talked specifically about anti-Semitism, but Genya mentioned it in her childhood recollections. She said, "The nurses were very anti-Semitic, they called me "a little kike." They often took my dinner away for a tiny misbehavior or just for nothing, they enjoyed torturing me." One mother, Marlena, spoke about anti-Semitism as a necessary evil she partially escaped due to her mixed background. She said, "Honestly speaking, we did not suffer from anti-Semitism. Of course, it existed, but we were used to it. We did not know anything else. Besides, my father was Russian, so I am a mixed breed."

For three generations of Golda's family, anti-Semitism was a daily reality. She reported being discriminated against by her supervisors and colleagues at work and by her neighbors at home. Her story about getting a new apartment contained several episodes of such maltreatment, "As a Jew, I got the worst apartment, on the ground floor. ... One bookkeeper from the accounting department said to me, 'Golda, you will leave for Israel anyway'." When Golda finally moved to her new place, she found herself in a "very anti-Semitic area of the city." She reported the neighbors' attitude toward her family, "One neighbor we had, she was such a bandit. She would yell at my mother, "Close the door, you kike!" One day, my daughter heard her say it, so she ran out and grabbed her hair through her head shawl." Anti-Semitism was a reality for the mothers, as well as the grandmothers even if they chose not to mention it.

Golda's granddaughter, praising her mother's support and understanding at the time when she was teased by her peers in America, recalled her mother's story about being tortured by her own classmates in Russia:

> Everyone used to make fun of her that she was Jewish, so it's like history repeats itself. She would probably understand me even if she did not go through that, but it gave her this extra anger inside, going through it herself. She, too, did not want to come to school, see these faces again, have them laugh at her. My great-grandmother died two years ago, G-d bless her soul, she used to come to school and embarrass her. She said a few words in Yiddish or speak like, "Minnele, come here!" They could tell by her accent, right away, that she was Jewish, so my mom tried to also, like, cover it up and say, "No, I am not, what are you talking about?" But they could always tell if someone was different.

According to Galina and Golda, grass-root anti-Semitism became more violent and dangerous after the fall of the Soviet Union. This is how Golda described the events that triggered her daughter's decision to emigrate:

> On April 20, Hitler's birthday, they were distributing anti-Semitic leaflets. We did not sleep all night because we heard rumors that there would be a *pogrom* (mass lynching of the Jews by raging mobs) on the night of the 20th. We stayed awake, all dressed up, we were afraid to sleep. They were just terrorizing us, making us scared, but we believed it, of course, and this was the last straw.

She concluded this part of her interview thus, "I am so happy that we left it all behind." Galina expressed similar feelings about her life in the United States, "Here we are safe and sure that nobody will beat us or call us names."

CHAPTER 5

Discussion and Recommendations

This study explored the emigration experience of a small group of women from the former Soviet Union who lived in the New York metropolitan area. The study focused on their perceptions of their family members and themselves in the process of adjustment to the new cultural milieu, the lifestyle changes they made in response to their new situations, their emotional responses to these changes, and the problems and conflicts that arose in the process. In this chapter these findings will be discussed, followed by practical implications and suggestions for future research.

DISCUSSION OF THE RESULTS

Social Issues

Unlike the United States, where women did not join the work force until the 1970s, Soviet women were expected to work along with men from the very early days of the Communist regime. All of the adult participants of this study considered working full time a necessity, so when they had children, they interrupted work for minimal periods of time. Working part-time or quitting the job to take care of the family was not an option for the participants. This finding is in agreement with the statistics about the work force in the former Soviet Union (Binyon, 1983). Goscilo (1993) reported that 90 per cent of Russian women were employed and that they account for 52 per cent of the labor force. Upon their arrival in the United States, all the participating mothers worked full-time and attended college or training programs to strengthen their marketable skills. They experienced their work in the United States as more intense, demanding, and stressful than in the Soviet Union, even when they practiced the same profession. Some reasons they gave for that included working in the foreign language; higher intensity of work; a different occupation, more distant and less supportive relationships with colleagues; and a significantly longer commute to work. As a result, the participants spoke of having little time and energy left for other pursuits. The participating granddaughters reflected their mothers' attitudes toward work and reported their future careers to be their major point of interest. Interestingly, three out of the five granddaughters aspired to become lawyers in their desire for upward mobility.

All the participants stressed the importance of friendship in their lives and talked about their emotional need for strong personal connections. They reported turning to friends for the functions mostly performed by professionals in the United States, such as counseling, therapy, and emotional relief, as they did not have the option of seeing a psychologist or a social worker. Several studies of the former Soviets found that friendship had a high survival value as it formed an informal support system in the absence of helping and religious institutions (Binyon, 1983, Shteyn, Schumm, Vodopianova, Hobfoll & Lilly, 2003). Four participating grandmothers were satisfied with the Russian friends they found in emigration, but their daughters reported emotional discomfort due to their difficulties forming close friendships in the United States. They cited language and cultural barriers as a reason for having no close friends among Americans. Lack of satisfying social contact was one of the factors that contributed to their reported feelings of alienation, being "a guest" in the new country. Friendships with other former Soviets appeared to be less satisfying than they were prior to emigration due to a strong overtone of competitiveness among them. The granddaughters spoke of the ease in forming social connections with peers of various nationalities. They had friends among Soviet émigrés, especially those who lived in the outer boroughs with higher immigrant population than the suburbs. Part of the reason for seeking friends of the same cultural background was the greater ease in communicating with their families.

One grandmother commented on the "new mentality" her granddaughter acquired in the United States—making her own decisions and protecting her privacy. These changes were confusing and stressful for the grandmother and she reported the feeling of being "lonely in spite of having a family." The mother of this young woman conceptualized the change somewhat differently. She said that while the Soviet educational system was aimed at bringing up a person with a collective mentality, the American system has a goal to bring up an individual.

The granddaughters spoke of the ease in forming social connections with peers of various nationalities. They had friends among Soviet emigres, especially those who lived in the New York City outer boroughs with higher immigrant concentration than the suburbs. One of the reasons for seeking friends of the same cultural background was the greater ease in communicating with their families.

Family Relationships

All the participating grandmothers and mothers stressed the strength of matrilineal ties in their families. This finding concurs with the results of other researchers that found that mothers in Russian culture have a traditionally strong role and a life-long influence over their children. (Hubbs, 1988, Engel, 1986, Remennick, 1999). Du Plessix Gray (1990) wrote that for Soviet women heterosexual love and marriage tend to recede in importance, while the far deeper bonds of blood kinship, filial responsibility, and matriarchal ties take precedence. Other researchers found similar traits in traditional Jewish family attitudes. Herz and Rosen (1982) equated maternal love with boundless suffering and sacrifice for her children. They pointed to the role of this practice in generating filial indebtedness and the children's sense of responsibility for the parents' emotional succor and physical care.

The grandmothers seemed to embrace the cultural belief that a grandmother must live with her adult daughter, for the sake of her daughter and her daughter's family, and through her daughter. In the United States, they continued this tradition and willingly took upon themselves most of the housekeeping responsibilities in their daughters' families. They consider no sacrifice too big in their efforts to help and to support them. In return, the grandmothers feel entitled to the continued strong emotional connection with their daughters and granddaughters, including the prerogative to control their lives. They reported feeling hurt when their daughters decided to live separately from them, or when their granddaughters insisted on protecting their privacy and setting limits on the grandmothers' involvement. The grandmothers were hurt by such behaviors and resented their daughters' and granddaughters' "Americanization." The grandmothers complained about their daughters' and granddaughters' lack of warmth and understanding. Another source of the grandmothers' distress was their tendency to worry excessively about real and imaginary dangers awaiting their family members. Given their history of trauma, loss, and deprivation, this tendency, described in literature (Herz and Rosen, 1982) as typical for Jewish mothers, was exacerbated by their feelings of dependency on their daughters for dealing with the English-speaking world. Participating mothers and grandmothers reported the grandmothers' deep involvement in all aspects of the granddaughters' upbringing. They expressed serious concern about future separation with the granddaughters due to college choice and marriage. The granddaughters spoke about their mothers and grandmothers with a mixture of gratitude and guilt, as they were aware of their feelings. At the time of the interviews, most of the granddaughters' desires to separate from their families were stronger than their guilt of leaving them. They indicated that the mothers' and grandmothers' support was a significant source of their resilience and motivation to succeed in life.

The majority of the adult participants expressed overwhelmingly negative feelings about their husbands, fathers, and sons-in-law. In their reports, men were described as insensitive and inflexible controlling autocrats. All the married participants reported getting little or no help from their husbands in domestic work. Three grandmothers were divorced and appeared to be better adjusted and able to better enjoy life than their married counterparts. Two married grandmothers were dragging their marriages along as heavy and unpleasant burdens they carry out of obligation and tradition. In spite of the grandmothers' hopes that their daughters would be luckier in their marriages, the reality was bleak—two participating mothers were divorced and three reported having little happiness in their married life. Nevertheless, the mothers expressed hope that their daughters marry young men from the same cultural background. This wish reflected the mothers' desire to keep strong ties with their daughters, as their information about American men was quite limited and concentrated mostly on their valuing personal independence and separation from their families. Language barrier would make communication even more complicated.

Thus, the participating mothers equated the daughters' marrying Americans with losing them completely.

The participating daughters seemed to adopt their mothers' and grandmothers' negative attitude toward men in general, and spoke about investing most of their energy into achievement in education and career. Marriage was relegated to a low priority by the participating granddaughters. In their choice of boyfriends, however, they tended to prefer young men of similar cultural background to accommodate their families.

Self

All adult participants seemed uncomfortable discussing their appearance and staying on that topic. Some of them considered it too "selfish" or frivolous and others believed it was insignificant in comparison to other issues. Based on observations and interview material, however, the participating grandmothers appeared to have a broader spectrum of acceptable body shapes than their daughters and granddaughters as they tended to define "fat" and "thin" differently. This attitude was probably rooted in their own experience of starvation and living in a culture of permanent food shortages. In three grandmothers' minds, there was still a strong connection between the granddaughters' thinness and dangerous illnesses that almost took these children's lives. This finding is congruent with the observations of Binyon (1983) and Du Plessix Gray (1990) that in the Russian culture feeding children was given a high priority as disease prevention.

All participating mothers reported a significant post-emigration weight gain and attributed it to a variety of factors. They reported their desire to taste a wide variety of new kinds of food in the U.S., chemical and hormonal additives to food, eating as a way to alleviate stress or depressed mood, lack of exercise, and aging. Two mothers said that a thin body ideal was imported to the Soviet Union during their formative years, so they tried to be trim before the emigration. Yet they stressed the new quality of the pressure to be thin as they experienced it in the United States—health concerns and the need to compete on the job market. The mothers reported being surrounded by all kinds of information about healthy eating and the need to exercise to stay healthy.

The mothers also compared the attitude toward age in the two cultures and concluded that people felt mature much earlier in the

Soviet Union. They spoke about the American pressure to remain thin for a longer period of time. In the Soviet Union women after fifty were considered "old", and were expected to concentrate their interests on grandchildren rather than on their appearance.

The participating granddaughters spoke about the role of the American media and their peers in the creation of a culture of thinness and dieting, but denied their own investment in thinness. They reported their enjoyment of food and spoke about their plans to start watching their weight when they are older, as they believed that their bodies are still growing. One noteworthy point was their positive attitude toward body change occurring during adolescence. In mainstream American culture, adolescents view these changes with alarm and become preoccupied with their rounding bodies (Sobal, 1987). The more relaxed attitude toward their bodies noted in the participating granddaughters, may be partially explained by their grandmothers' influence.

Most of the participants expressed their desire to lose some weight, to exercise more regularly, and to take better care of themselves. The main obstacle to fulfilling this wish was their tendency to ascribe low priority to these pursuits. The grandmothers and mothers believed that their "undervaluing themselves" comes from the Soviet tradition. Literature on Soviet women has found that the concept of "true femininity" was based on self-sacrifice and that this "essence of womanhood" constituted the basis of the moral order of the Soviet society (Pilkington, 1996). Most adult participants reported their difficulty transitioning from the Russian cultural norm that women are to focus on their families, not on themselves. Upon their arrival in the United States, the participating mothers worked full-time and continued to spend considerable time and effort on housekeeping, even when their financial situation permitted eating out or ordering ready-made food. Participating mothers did not consider engaging their husbands' help, probably due to the cultural tradition.

Self-sacrifice, ingrained into the grandmothers' attitudes, resulted in their inability to love themselves. Talking about women they perceived as "selfish," they sounded negative and judgmental. None seemed tempted in the least bit to change their attitude in the direction, they observed in American grandmothers. Even though only a few adult participants noted that the granddaughters "inherited" their "undervaluing self" attitude from them, all the daughters gave high priority to studying and extracurricular activities that could be used on college applications. Their participation in sports and other pleasurable activities, such as singing and dancing, were either minimal, or postponed due to a lack of free time.

Food and Eating

All adult participants praised the wide variety and affordability of food they found in the United States and juxtaposed it against permanent food shortages in the Soviet Union. Three grandmothers spoke in detail about wartime starvation, providing the backdrop for their enjoyment of every morsel of food. The participants were especially pleased by the newly discovered opportunity of eating out instead of spending much time on cooking from scratch. In reality, the cultural tradition that frowns on eating out seems to prevail, even when the alternative was obviously affordable. Married participants reported their husbands' demands for traditional three-course dinners for everyday consumption and for lavish spreads for family celebrations. One grandmother reported being pressured to cook even on the days when she and her husband attended a day care center that served hot lunch or dinner. Unmarried women tended to eat out and order food in more often than their married counterparts, probably due to the absence of the husbands' coercion.

Even though all participating grandmothers spoke about the need to limit their eating, they admitted to eating their fill of delicacies they could not afford in the Soviet Union. The granddaughters, who spoke about being almost force-fed by their grandmothers during their childhood, reported their enjoyment of food at the time of the interviews and denied limiting their eating. They also reported their enjoyment of eating out on a regular basis and almost total lack of culinary skills. The mothers seemed to be conflicted about this attitude. On the one hand, they welcomed their daughters' "liberation" from the "kitchen slavery," and on the other, they felt uncomfortable that their daughters spend money on restaurant food. Since the daughters reported craving "junk food" and patronizing fast food establishments, their mothers' negativity toward eating out can be also explained by the desire to see their daughters eat healthier and to prevent their weight gain.

Grandmothers and mothers in this study both noted that Americans are much better informed about healthy eating than their counterparts in the Soviet Union. They reported their efforts to improve their eating habits in the United States. These efforts have resulted in varying degree of success, depending on the availability of time, financial situation, and cooperation of family members. One participating grandmother reported having "a restaurant at home" and one mother spoke about another grandmother who cooked traditional fatty food for her husband and more healthful food for herself. This type of flexible accommodation was not an option for the mother who works full-time. This woman, as well as other mothers, spoke about her reliance on rather harsh weight control methods, such as starving one day a week or eating proteins and starches separately. This tendency appears to stem from the adult participants' overall attitude toward themselves— they can squeeze these regimens into their busy schedules instead of spending time and money on diets, exercise, or support groups. Since getting help from their husbands is not an option for them, they spend a large part of their weekends on cooking. On weekdays, they come home from full day at work and cook for their families, rather than ordering dinner in and having some free time for themselves.

Losses and Gains of Emigration

The ways in which grandmothers and mothers reported their feelings about losses and gains of emigration were strikingly different. The grandmothers were more inclined to explicitly compare their lives in the two countries, and the mothers were more implicit in their comparisons. While the grandmothers stated outright the ways in which their lives in the United States are better or worse than they were in the Soviet Union, the mothers reported their feelings of being "strangers" in America even though they have acquired considerably more material comforts compared to what they had in the Soviet Union.

All grandmothers in this study reported missing the family members who stayed in the Soviet Union or immigrated to other countries. Three of them mentioned being depressed as a result of these losses. Loss of old friends and old support systems, as well as the linguistic barrier that limits their ability to communicate and to fully partake in the cultural life of the new country were also cited as contributors to the negative emotional state of grandmothers and mothers. Literature on post-emigration shock has found that these feelings are typical for all immigrant groups in the beginning of their adjustment (Berry and Annis, 1974, Chiswick, 1993). However, for all grandmothers in this study, the benefits of emigration outweighed or at least balanced the losses. They cited three significant sources of positive feelings about their life in the United States—enjoyment of their daughters' and granddaughters' success, higher living standards and freedom from anti-Semitism.

All grandmothers in this study described the hardships they had to survive in the Soviet Union in harrowing details. Comparing their struggles with the relative comfort they enjoy in the United States, they praised their new lifestyle, including the opportunity to pursue their own interests.

Other Concerns

For better understanding of the effects of acculturation on three generations of Soviet immigrant women, it is essential to study other issues arising from the cultural clash experienced upon their arrival. One problem, resulting from conflicting cultural messages in the United States—eating disorders, was not noted in this particular study. Granddaughters in this study denied any investment in thinness and reported their enjoyment of food. However, they spoke about their peers who are obsessed with dieting and live on the brink of starving themselves. One participant spoke about a girl who pretended to be anorexic, and another reported having an obese cousin. Since the signs of disordered eating were noted in the pilot study participants' reports, it is reasonable to suggest that eating disorders occur among the Soviet immigrant women.

Another issue mentioned by one participant that warrants a closer look is the difference between parenting methods in the former Soviet Union and the United States. A participating grandmother described her son-in-law as an authoritarian, unyielding dictator who wants to control his teenage daughter's every step. Growing up in the country where every step of its citizens was controlled by the government has probably influenced this father and many others.

REFLECTIONS OF THE INVESTIGATOR

My belonging to the same ethnic group as the participants of this study was a mixed blessing. Separating the participants' reality from my own views and perceptions was a challenging task, and I went to great lengths to compensate for my cultural and emotional closeness to the participants. On the other hand, this process helped me re-evaluate my life experience and become aware of the extent of my acculturation in the United States. I emigrated twenty-three years ago and at the time of the interviews, I felt comfortably bilingual enjoying social connections with Russian- and English-speaking friends and acquaintances. Luckily, I came to the United States at a younger age than my adult participants. Probably this fact significantly contributed to my positive adjustment here. Even though I visited Russia twice after the fall of the Soviet Union, I have limited, mostly second-hand information about the changes that occurred there in my absence, so my participants' interviews provided me with information that was significantly different from my experience.

My fluent Russian was an asset in establishing rapport with the adult participants, as they chose to be interviewed in this language. However, our shared cultural background took its toll on the participants' ability to explicate their experience in depth. No matter how many times I explained to them that my life story is different from theirs, they kept making shortcuts with an assured comment, "You know how it was" and sounded surprised when I asked them to explain their statements.

I expected to find more overweight individuals among the women who agreed to be interviewed. During my trips to Brighton Beach or other areas with significant Soviet Jewish population, I observed hundreds of obese and grossly obese women of the same age as my participants, including teenagers. The participants of my pilot study were significantly heavier than their counterparts in the present study.

METHODOLOGICAL CONSIDERATIONS

An in-depth interview was used in an attempt to understand the experience of three generations of women who emigrated from the former Soviet Union. Through these interviews I obtained rich information on each participant's perceptions of and emotional reactions to their life experience in two countries. Most participants gave me an opportunity to interview them twice, as I felt the need to ask them to clarify or expand on some of their statements. The open-ended nature of the interviews allowed the participants to bring up material that was not anticipated and led me to the areas of their interest. As a result, the focus of this study shifted and its scope was broadened. My participants resisted making body issues the focus of the study, but were willing to discuss them as part of their overall experience. Given a chance to talk freely, they shared with me their joys and struggles in both countries. Body issues were assigned a lower priority, as the participants did not see taking care of their bodies as the way of getting a better man. The participating women brought in a multitude of themes and created a broad and rich picture of their life experience. As a result, the understanding they gave me was significantly deeper than what I sought initially. One of the unexpected outcomes of this understanding was a change I made in my own lifestyle that led to a 40-pound weight loss. I learned how to budget my time and energy in the way that allowed me to exercise five times a week. This is how this work made a full circle: my questions about body issues were answered and a better understanding of my own issues came to me when I let the participants talk freely and share their experience and thoughts with me according to their hierarchy of priorities.

Collection and analysis of data were so emotionally charged for me that in the process, I relived and rethought my entire life. I was able to look at myself through the eyes of my grandmother, my mother, and my daughter and to see them in a new light. I gained a better understanding of the reasons why I made certain decisions at different points in my life. My participants' words reopened old, sometimes purposely forgotten episodes of my past and presented them in a different light, giving me emotional relief and a sense of closure. I spent many sleepless nights recalling people and events that led me to the place where I am now. I felt spiritually connected with every participant of my study and experienced my growth as a researcher, a therapist, and as a human being as they opened their doors and their hearts to me. I felt proud when I sensed that we reached this stage, as I remembered the grandmothers' initial resistance to being interviewed and taped. I appreciated the strides they made from paranoia typical of the Soviet regime survivors, to the warmth and openness of our heartfelt connection. Every interview was a joint trip into the depths of our past and present, and on the way, we laughed, cried, and ate together, exchanged cooking tips and photographs of our children. Conducting the interviews in the participants' apartments gave me a fuller, richer picture of each woman's personality. I was able to observe their interactions with each other and with other family members. There was much to learn from an overheard tone of voice, the apartment furnishings, and the aromas in each interview setting.

After the interviews were transcribed, I realized that limiting this work to analysis of major themes supported by a collection of citations would impoverish their content. Taken out of context, the participants' words would have lost their unique character and cultural subtleties. Individual portraits were created based on verbatim material in order to convey the unique voice of each woman. Creating the portraits and recording the analysis of the participants' themes was a cathartic experience for me, and I feel emotionally relieved and elevated having completed this study.

SUGGESTIONS FOR FUTURE RESEARCH

The families in this study are not representative of the entire population of immigrants from the former Soviet Union. Four grandmothers that volunteered for this study were active members of elder care facilities and Jewish community centers. Such people are likely to be generally more active and open to new ideas and activities. Other former Soviet immigrant women might be less communicative, have different family structures or have lived in the United States for different periods of time. Length of stay in the United States is probably one of the most important factors determining the degree of immigrant acculturation as well as age, gender, educational level, and others. Longitudinal research following immigrant families would answer many questions, which arose in the course of this study. Many former Soviet immigrants are not Jewish, and literature suggests a significant intermarriage rate in immigrant families (Chiswick, 1993). Three adult participants of this study were married to non-Jews at some period of their lives. Study of other families will be most interesting, as the same type of research might provide different results with different participants.

This study leaves many unanswered questions about how the women will deal with the conflicts between the old and new cultural norms and how they will cope with the challenges presented by their new social milieu. Will the younger Soviet immigrants choose colleges in the New York area and live at home while attending college, or will they move to other cities and live on campus? How will the families of those who decide to leave adjust to this change? Upon the completion of their education, will they stay in the same city as their families or will they move elsewhere? Will they marry young men with similar cultural background or find their mates among mainstream Americans? Will their marriages be more successful than their mothers' and grandmothers' or will they repeat their ways of relating to the opposite gender? When they decide to have children, will they stay home to take care of them or manage to continue working full time? What role will their mothers play in their children's upbringing? How many children will they choose to have? An interesting study would be to follow these and similar families to try to provide some answers to these and other questions. A study of immigrant families in other parts of the United States, especially those with smaller populations of former Soviets, would be valuable. Some studies of individual adjustment of Soviet immigrants were conducted in the United States, Australia and Canada (Berry, 1983; Taft, 1984; Chiswick, 1993), but family issues in this population are much less researched (Brodsky, 1982).

Teenagers in this study mentioned their peers who appear to suffer from eating disorders and others who are obese. It would be of interest to study immigrant adolescents and to obtain data on the prevalence of obesity and eating disorders among them. One teenager reported her painful initial adjustment, involving teasing and prejudice against "Russians" in elementary and middle school. A study of immigrant school children would provide information about how they function and cope in academic and social situations.

This study also raises questions about the role of boys in the Soviet immigrant families and the particular family dynamics, which lead to the formation of their gender attitudes. It would be of interest to compare child rearing in Soviet immigrant families and in mainstream American families along gender lines. A study of Soviet immigrant men might look at the influence of acculturation on their attitudes toward their wives and daughters as well as at the changes, if any, in their overall conception of the male role in the marriage.

Literature on Soviet immigrants points out to their low rates of reproduction. Chiswick (1991) found that the average number of children in 900 families under study was 1.4 with only 3 percent with three or more children. In the present study, all participating granddaughters and two mothers were only children. It would be interesting to investigate the reasons for this tendency and to collect data about the influence of the length of the granddaughters' stay in the United States and the degree of their acculturation on the number of children they will choose to have.

Three participating grandmothers live together with their adult daughters or very close to them. The contribution each of them makes to her daughter's household is crucial for the daughter's functioning in the society and therefore, has a high survival value. Two mothers who decided to move far away from their mothers were married and appeared to have achieved a relatively comfortable professional and financial situation. Overall, they were less pressured to continue the tradition of living together. Nevertheless, these women spoke about this decision with a mixed sense of guilt and satisfaction. One mother said that she kept a room ready for her mother in case she needed long-term care. It would be interesting to look at the families of former Soviets in terms of care for the elderly as compared to that at mainstream American families.

All participating mothers indicated that their limited mastery of English was a major source of their feelings of alienation in the new culture even when they felt competent in their professional lives. College educated women, they sounded resolute in their belief that they will never know enough English to fully enjoy American cultural and social life. An investigation of the factors conducive to successful acquisition of English among former Soviets who achieved functional bilingualism may bring useful information for immigrants from various immigrant groups.

The granddaughters in this study were within a limited age range (14-16) and reported their perception of themselves as significantly to completely Americanized. They all chose to be interviewed in English and spoke Russian with varying levels of difficulty in pronunciation, grammar, and syntax. Investigation of the reasons for retention or rejection of Russian as a second language by different age categories of Russian- and American-born children of former Soviet immigrants is a potential resource of information beneficial to generations of immigrant families. Two grandmothers pointed to their granddaughters' lack of interest in Russian culture in general. A study of high school and college students from Soviet immigrant families might look at their decisions around learning to speak Russian and pursuing academic courses in Russian History, Literature, etc. Two grandmothers and one mother spoke about their granddaughters' perceived "moving away from cultural pursuits" and spending much time in front of the television set instead of reading serious literature. I heard similar complaints from many fellow immigrants who held American "materialistic orientation" culpable for this change. It would be interesting to conduct a comparative study of mainstream American and former Soviet immigrant children and their intellectual and educational interests.

One granddaughter in the study referred to the "Russians" as the people who "keep up fronts," trying to impress others, especially fellow immigrants, with their material possessions, even if their financial situation is far from comfortable. A study of immigrants' attitudes toward material possessions might shed light on one participating mother's choice to work full time and constantly worry about her daughter being left alone at home.

In his theory of "emerging adulthood", Arnett (2000) posited that it is a period, which is possible only in industrial or postindustrial countries. One of the major demographic factors leading to the formation of this self-exploration stage of human development is independent residential status. Living separately from their parents was not an option for most of the young adults in the Soviet Union, so this category was non-existent there. It would be very interesting to explore the emerging adulthood among former Soviet immigrants and its impact on the overall family structure.

RECOMMENDATIONS

Since the inception of this study, the number of people emigrating from the former Soviet Union has been steadily increasing, and former Soviets have formed sizeable enclaves in many American cities. This study was small, but if its results are representative of the larger group of immigrants, these recommendations would be useful for those who encounter former Soviets professionally or socially.

Parenting Styles of Soviet Immigrants

Based on the findings of this study and other research on European immigrants (Wehrly, 1982; Brodsky, 1982; Herz & Rosen, 1982, Chirkov & Ryan, 2001, Chirkov, Ryan, Kim & Kaplan, 2003), parents in this particular group tend to be overly involved in their children's lives and to maintain this overly controlling position for very long periods of time, well into their children's adulthood. Schools can and should help immigrant parents adjust to the new cultural norms that stress the development of individuality, independence, and respect for the choices young people make. Professionals, such as teachers and school psychologists working with immigrant children, are in excellent position to help the children to cope with the new situation and to reach out to parents struggling with defining their roles in the new environment.

Family Structure

According to this study and other research (Smith, 1976; duPlessix Gray, 1990; Litrovnik, 1993) in the former Soviet Union grandparents tend to live together with their adult children and to play a significant role in all aspects of family functioning, especially in upbringing of grandchildren. Helping professionals should be aware of this cultural norm and include grandparents in their work with families. Absence of a grandmother should be noted and questioned, since such exploration may provide professionals with information, crucial for their understanding of the family dynamics that led to the development of the presenting problem.

This study found a high ratio of divorce among former Soviets. Married adult participants described their husbands as controlling and inflexible and their relationships with them as markedly strained and unsatisfying. Outreach efforts should be made to involve former Soviets in family therapy. Helping professionals working in schools can inform immigrant parents about the benefits of family therapy while delineating services available to them and their children. Herz and Rosen (1982) found that American Jews often "seek treatment for some aspect of their children's behavior. Parents' primary concern often centers around (1) academic performance and (2) leaving home." (p. 384). Dealing with their children's similar problems may help former Soviets open up to the possibility of family therapy.

Mental Health Issues

Caseworkers and other helping professionals working with older former Soviet immigrants should be on alert for symptoms of depression in their clients. They should be aware of the newer immigrants' fear of authorities and should make every effort to create a comfortable supportive atmosphere, conducive for openness and disclosure of emotional problems. Even though three adult participants of this study reported their turning to psychotherapy to alleviate their emotional difficulties, other studies (Casas & Keefe, 1980; Brodsky, 1982) indicate low utilization of mental health services by immigrants in general and by former Soviets in particular.

Eating disorders and eating as a method of handling stress among Soviet immigrants is another mental health issue that warrants professional attention, especially when immigrant girls reach adolescence. The present study, as well as the pilot study of a similar immigrant group indicated that Soviet immigrant girls tend to react by starving themselves or by overeating when they experience the clash between the acculturative pressures in the United States and their grandmothers' influence that stresses enjoyment of food.

Efforts to promote self-esteem should be part of work with Soviet immigrant women of all generations. Support groups might be beneficial for their adjustment.

SUMMARY

This study explored and described the emigration experience of three generations of former Soviet immigrant women living in the Metropolitan New York area. Acculturation theory was described to provide a theoretical framework for the study. A review of literature on mainstream American and Russian/Soviet cultural traditions was presented and incorporated in the understanding of the experience of the participating families.

Five triads of women, their mid-life daughters and adolescent granddaughters participated in this study. A total of five grandmothers, four mothers, and five granddaughters were interviewed. The time these women have lived in the United States ranged from five to ten years. The majority of participants were Jewish, three adult participants were married to non-Jews at some period of their lives, and three participants were children of mixed marriages. Two mothers and three grandmothers were divorced. All participating adults worked full time their entire adult lives. At the time of the interviews, the grandmothers were retired and supported by SSI. All participating mothers were college educated and worked full-time. The granddaughters attended high school. Semi-structured, in-depth interviews were conducted. All adult participants chose to be interviewed in Russian and all adolescent participants chose English. The interviews were open-ended and gave the participants opportunity to introduce unanticipated topics.

In summary, as the participating women were acculturating in the United States, they had to negotiate two sets of cultural norms—those of their new surroundings and those they brought from the former Soviet Union. Each generation experienced its conflicts in the process. The grandmothers missed their relatives and friends left behind. They found themselves isolated from mainstream American culture by the language barrier and their dependency on their children for dealing with the larger world. They continued the tradition of playing the major role in their grandchildren's upbringing and taking care of their adult daughters' housekeeping, expecting close attachment and filial devotion in return. The grandmothers experienced their daughters' and granddaughters' movement toward privacy as a personal affront and felt hurt when they established limits to their involvement and control over family matters. The grandmothers' response to these changes ranged from acceptance to depression. As primary caretakers, the grandmothers significantly influenced their granddaughters and instilled in them their cultural values and attitudes, such as "career first," strong family ties, negativity toward men, and enjoyment of food. The grandmothers reported their enjoyment of new opportunities afforded by an American lifestyle—the possibility to spend less time in the kitchen and to participate in pleasurable activities.

While for the grandmothers the conflicts were on the outside—between them as carriers of the old cultural norm and their "Americanized" children and grandchildren, the participating mothers experienced cultural conflict within themselves. Bringing up highly "Americanized" children, working with Americans and being influenced by American media, the mothers juxtaposed their own attitudes against those of their American peers and became more aware of the cultural "baggage" they brought from the former Soviet Union. The tendency to "devalue" themselves, to give their interests and needs the lowest priority was a large part of this "baggage". The need to balance the demands and pressures of both cultures led to inner conflict and induced their feelings of guilt. Working full time in the new language combined with longer commutes was exhausting for the mothers. They lacked time and energy to pursue their own interests. Nevertheless, they felt obligated to continue cooking for the family on a regular basis even when their financial situation permitted eating out or buying ready-made food. The mothers were unhappy about their weight gain, but did little to fight it off due to lack of time, energy and motivation to exercise. The slimming methods they used tended to be harsh by American standards, but attractive for the mothers, as they required no special expenditure of time or other resources. Even though the participating mothers' contribution to the family budget was on par with their husbands', they continued the cultural tradition that "the man is the head of the household" and prepared full meals after a day's work.

Adolescent granddaughters' language of choice was English, they reported having many American friends and described themselves as "Americanized." However, they also experienced conflicts between the norms and values instilled in them by their mothers and grandmothers and those they learned from their peers and the media. The granddaughters reported their enjoyment of food and stressed that it was part of their family legacy. They spoke with guilt about being unable to fulfill their grandmothers' expectations of close connection and complete openness. They were also conflicted about their desire to leave home for college and their sense of obligation to their mothers and grandmothers who brought them up in the tradition of strong ties between generations of women. Dating was not a significant issue for the participating adolescent granddaughters, yet they were aware of their mothers' preference for their choice of dates within their cultural group. The mothers' and grandmothers' expectations loomed large when the adolescents had to make important life choices.

The number of participants of this study is small, so it is impossible to make wide generalizations based on its findings. However, I hope that many immigrant and American-born women will find the participants' stories both informative and connected with their own experience.

CONCLUDING THOUGHTS

Last spring, I participated in an international conference and reported some of these findings. Along with slides and magazines, I brought to the presentation a Russian tea cozy - a blonde, full-bodied beauty in an ample colorful dress. One of the conference participants looked at the doll and said, "If not for her color, she could have been from Jamaica." These words came back to me many times while I was working on this study. I sensed a strong connection between the participants of this study and women of disparate cultures around the globe. This connection is in family structure - matrilineal extended families with or without men are strikingly similar for Russian and African-American cultures, to name just two. Du Plessix Gray (1990) explains Russian "national matriarchy" to be the result of the disproportionate loss of men during World War II. Researchers of African-American family dynamics attribute this phenomenon to the consequences of slavery.

Extended family of strong, self-sufficient women connected by the sense of mutual obligation has a high survival value since all necessary supports, such as child rearing and caring for the sick and the elderly, are provided by the members. In cultures where survival is a priority, women of childbearing age are considered beautiful if they are full figured because their bodies symbolize the strength needed to carry out all the necessary functions. A thin, artificially youthful woman from a nuclear family represents a status found in the leisure class, such as a car of a single-family home. Nuclear family can function only in a society where domestic services can be purchased. Therefore, well-to-do women can afford to spend their time and energy maintaining their slim bodies, thus thinness may be equated with wealth. Upon their immigration to the United States, the participants of this study found themselves caught in transition between the Russian survival culture with its traditions and values and a desire to acculturate into the Western world with its emphasis on glamour and looks. I believe that their struggles resonate with common experience of immigrant women from survival cultures around the globe.

References

American Psychiatric Association. (1994). Diagnostic and statistical manual of mental disorders (4th ed.). Washington, DC: Author.

Arnett, J. J. (2000). Emerging adulthood: A theory of development from the late teens through the twenties. *American Psychologist, 5*, 469-480.

Bellafante, G. (2001, January 16). Where the belles of Brooklyn shop. *The New York Times*, p. B8.

Berry, J. W. (1984a). Cultural relations in plural societies: Alternatives to segregation and their sociopsychological implications. In N. Miller & M. Brewer (Eds.), *Group in Contact*. New York: Academic Press.

Berry, J. W. (1984b). Multicultural policy in Canada: A social psychological analysis. *Canadian Journal of Behavioral Science, 16*, 353-370.

Berry, J. W., & Annis, R. C. (1974). Acculturative stress: The role of ecology, culture and differentiation. *Journal of Cross-Cultural Psychology, 5*, 382-406.

Berry, J. W., Kim, U., & Boski, P. (1988). Psychological acculturation of immigrants. In Y. Kim & W. Gudykunst (Eds.), *Cross-cultural adaptation, current approaches* (pp. 62-89). Newbury Park: Sage Publications.

Berry, J. W., Trimble, J., & Olmeda, E. (1986). Assessment of acculturation. In W. J. Lonner & J. W. Berry (Eds.), *Field methods in cross-cultural research*. London: Sage Publications.

Binyon, M. (1983). *Life in Russia*. London: Hamish Hamilton.

Bordo, S. (1993). *Unbearable weight: Feminism, western culture, and the body*. Berkeley: University of California Press.

Brezhnev, L. I. (1979). *Prospects for Soviet Agricultural Production in 1980 and 1985 with special reference to meat and grain.* Paris, Organization for Economic Cooperation and Development.

Brodsky, B. (1982). Social work and the Soviet immigrant. *Migration Today, 10*, 1, 14-20.

Bulanda, R. E. (2004). Paternal involvement with children: The influence of gender ideologies. *Journal of Marriage and Family, 66, 1,* 40-48.

Bulik, C. (1987). Eating disorders in immigrants: Two case reports. International Journal of Eating Disorders, 6(1), 133-141.

Casas, S., & Keefe, S. (1980). *Family and mental health in Mexican American Community.* Los Angeles, CA: Spanish Speaking Mental Health Research Center.

Cass, F. (1997). *Russian organized crime: Russian émigré crime in the United States.* Redwood Books.

Chirkov, V., Ryan, R. M., Kim, Y. & Kaplan, U. (2003). Differentiating autonomy from individualism and independence: A self-determination theory perspective on internalization of cultural orientations and well-being. *Journal of Personality and Social Psychology, 84(1),* 97-110.

Chiswick, B. (1993). Soviet Jews in the United States: An analysis of their linguistic and economic adjustment. *International Migration Review, XXVII,* 2, 260-285.

Cockerham, W. C. (2000). Health lifestyles in Russia. Social Science and Medicine, 51, 1313-1324.

Desmond, S. M., Price, J. H., Gray, N., & O'Connell, J. K. (1986). The etiology of adolescents, perceptions of their weight. Journal of Youth and Adolescence, 15, 461-474.

du Plessix Gray, F. (1990). *Soviet women: Walking the tightrope.* New York: Doubleday.

Engel, B. A. (1986). *Mothers and daughters: Women of the intelligentsia in nineteenth century Russia,* Cambridge, Cambridge University Press.

Garfinkel, P. E., & Garner, D. M. (1982). *Anorexia nervosa: A multidimensional perspective.* New York: Brunner/Mazel.

Garner, D. M., Rockert, W., Olmsted, M. P., Johnson, C., & Coscina, D. V. (1985). Psychoeducational principles in the treatment of bulimia and anorexia nervosa. In D. M. Garner & P. E. Garfinkel (Eds.), *Handbook of psychotherapy for anorexia nervosa and bulimia* (pp. 513-572). New York: Guilford.

Goode, E. (1999, May 20). Study finds TV alters Fiji Girls' view of body. *The New York Times*, p. A17.

Gordon, M. (1964). *Assimilation in American life.* New York: Oxford University Press.

Gordon, R. (1990). *Anorexia and bulimia: Anatomy of a social epidemic.* Cambridge, MA: Basil Blackwell.

Goscilo, H (1993). Domostroika or perestroika? In T. Lahusen & G. Kuperman (Eds.), *Late Soviet culture: From perestroika to novostroika* (pp. 233-255). London: Duke University Press.

Hamilton, L. H., Brooks-Gunn, J., & Warren, M. P. (1985). Sociocultural influences on eating disorders in professional ballet dancers. *International Journal of Eating Disorders, 4*, 465-478.

Harris, S. M. (1995). Family, self, and sociocultural contributions to body-image attitudes of African-American women. *Psychology of Women Quarterly, 19,* 129-145.

Herz, F. M. & Rosen, E. J. (1982). Jewish families. In M. McGoldrick, J. K. Pearce, & J. Giordano (Eds.), *Ethnicity and family therapy* (pp. 364-392). New York: Guilford Press.

Hooper, M. S., & Garner, D. M. (1986). Application of the eating disorders inventory to a sample of Black, White, and mixed race schoolgirls in Zimbabwe. *International Journal of Eating Disorders, 5(1),* 161-168.

Hubbs, J. (1988). *Mother Russia: The feminine myth in Russian culture.* Bloomington and Indianapolis, Indiana University Press.

Hurh, W. M., & Kim, K. C. (1984). Adhesive sociocultural adaptation of Korean immigrants in the U.S.: An alternative strategy of minority adaptation. *International Migration Review, 18,* 188-216.

Johnson, C., & Connors, M. E. (1987). *The etiology and treatment of bulimia nervosa: A biopsychological perspective.* New York: Basic Books.

Kilbourne, J. (1974). Still killing us softly: Advertising and the obsession with thinness. In P. Fallon, M. A. Katzman, & S. Wooley (Eds.), *Feminist perspectives on eating disorders.* New York: Guilford Press.

Kilbourne, J. (1977). Images of women in TV commercials. In J. Fireman (Ed.), *TV book* (pp. 293-296). New York: Workman.

Koval, V. (1995). *Women in contemporary Russia.* Providence, RI: Berghahn Books.

Krch, F. D. (1995). Being overweight and developing an eating disorder in the Czech Republic. *Eating Disorders, The Journal of Treatment and Prevention; 3(1)*, 20-27.

Kuh, P. (1997, March). Comrade, your table is ready. *Esquire*, pp. 96-101, 140.

Kurokawa, M. (Ed.). (1970). *Minority responses: Comparative views of reactions to subordination.* New York: Random House.

Levine, M. P., & Smolak, L. (1992). Toward a model of the development of psychopathology eating disorders: The example of early adolescence. In J. H. Crowther, D. L. Tennenbaum, S. E. Hobfoll, & M. A. P. Stephens (Eds.). *The etiology of bulimia nervosa: The individual and familial context* (pp. 59-80). Washington, D.C.: Taylor & Francis.

Levine, M. P., Smolak, L., & Hayden, H. (1994). The relation of sociocultural factors to eating attitudes and behaviors among middle school girls. *Journal of Early Adolescence, 14(4),* 471-490.

Litrovnik, I. (1993*). Middle age Soviet immigrants and their adjustment in America: Coming from the past.* New York: Yeshiva University, Wurzweiler School of Social Work.

Lopez, E., Blix, G. G., & Blix, A. G. (1995). Body image of Latinas compared to body image of non-Latina White women. *Health Values, The Journal of Health Behavior, 19(6),* 3-10.

Mamonova, T. (1994). *Women's glasnost vs. naglost: Stopping Russian backlash.* Westport, CT: Bergin & Garvey.

Mandel, M. (1970). *Soviet women and their self-image.* Paper presented in at Far Western Slavic Conference, U.S.C.

McFadden, J. (1993). *Transcultural counseling.* ACA

Mendoza, R. H., & Martinez, J. L. (1981). The measurement of acculturation. In A. Baron (Ed.), *Explorations in Chicano psychology.* New York: Praeger.

Miller, R. B., & Bengston, V. L. (1991). Grandparent-grandchild relations, in R. M. Lerner et al. (Eds.). *Encyclopedia of Adolescence (1).* New York: Garland.

Nasser, M. (1986). Comparative study of the prevalence of abnormal eating attitudes among Arab female students of both London and Cairo Universities. *Psychological medicine, 16*, 621-625.

Nasser, M. (1988). Eating disorders: The cultural dimension. *Social Psychiatry and Psychiatric Epidemiology, 23*, 184-187.

National Statistical Compendium (1992), Moscow.

Newman, W. M. (1973). *American pluralism: A study of minority groups and social theory.* New York: Harper & Row.

O'Bryan, K. G., Reitz, J. G., & Kuplowska, O. M. (1976). *Non-official languages: A study in Canadian multiculturalism.* Ottawa: Government of Canada.

Osvold, L. L., & Sodowsky, G. R. (1993). Eating disorders of White American, racial and ethnic minority American, and international women. *Journal of Multicultural Counseling and Development, 21*, 143-154.

Paniagua, F. A. (1998). *Assessing and Treating Culturally Diverse Clients.* 2nd Ed., Longwood.

Parker, S., Nichter, M., Vuckovic, N., Sims, S., & Ritenbaugh, S. (1995). Body image and weight concerns among African American and White adolescent females: Differences that make a difference. *Human Organization, 54(2),* 103-114.

Pilkington, H., 1996 (Ed.). *Gender, Generation and Identity in Contemporary Russia.* London: Routledge.

Polivy, J., & Herman, C. P. (1987). Diagnosis and treatment of normal eating. *Journal of Consulting and Clinical Psychology, 100, 55,* 635-644.

Pumariega, J. A. (1986). Acculturation and eating attitudes in adolescent girls: A comparative and correlational study. *Journal of the American Academy of Child Psychiatry,* 25, 276-279.

Redfield, R., Linton, R., & Herskovits, M. J. (1936). Memorandum on the study of acculturation. *American Anthropologist, 38,* 149-152.

Remennick, L. I. (1999). Women of the "sandwich" generation and multiple roles: The case of Russian Immigrants of the 1990 in Israel. *Sex Roles, 40, 5/6,* 347-378.

Rosenhan, M. (1977). Images of male and female in children's readers. In D. Atkinson, A. Dallin, & G. W. Lapidus (Eds.), *Women in Russia* (pp. 293-305, Stanford CA: Stanford University press.

Rothblum, E. D. (1994). "I'll die for the revolution but don't ask me not to diet": Feminism and the continued stigmatization of obesity. In P. Fallon, M. A. Katzman, & S. C. Wooley (Eds.), *Feminist Perspectives on eating disorders* (pp. 53-76). New York: The Guilford Press.

Rotkirch, A., & Haavio-Mannila, E. (1996). *Women's voices in Russia today.* Brookfield, VT: Dartmouth Publishing Company.

Rucker, C. E., & Cash, T. F. (1992). Body images, body-size perceptions, and eating behaviors among African-American and White college women. *International Journal of Eating Disorders, 12(3),* 291-299.

Sanderson, S. & Sanders Thompson, V. L. (2002). Factors associated with perceived paternal involvement in childrearing. *Sex Roles, 46,3/4,* 99-111.

Silverstein, B., & Perdue, L. (1988). The relationship between role concerns, preferences for slimness, and symptoms of eating problems among college women. *Sex Roles, 18,* 101-106.

Silverstein, B., Perdue, L., Peterson, B., & Kelly, E. (1986). The role of the mass media in promoting a thin standard of bodily attractiveness for women. *Sex Roles, 14,* 519-532.

Simon, R. J. & Simon, J. L. (1982). *The Soviet Jew's adjustment to the United States,* New York: Council of Jewish Federations.

Singh, D. (1994). Is thin really beautiful and good? Relationship between waist-to-hip ratio (WHR) and female attractiveness. *Personality and Individual Differences, 16,* 123-132.

Smith, H. (1976). *The Russians.* New York: Quadrangle/ The New York Times Book Co.

Smolak, L., & Levine, M. P. (1994). Critical issues in the developmental psychology of eating disorders. In L. Alexander & D. B. Lumsden (Eds.), *Understanding eating disorders* (pp. 37-60). Washington, D. C.: Taylor & Francis.

Sobal, J. (1985). Students' health concerns; Junior High school teachers' and students' perceptions. *Youth and Society, 17(2),* 171-188.

Sobal, J. (1987). Health concerns of young adolescents. *Adolescence, 22(87),* 739-750.

Sobal, J., & Stunkard, A. J. (1989). Socioeconomic status and obesity: A review of the literature. *Psychological Bulletin, 105 (2),* 260-275.

Shteyn, M., Schumm, J. A., Vodopianova, N., Hobfoll, S. E. & Lilly, R. (2003). The impact of the Russian transition on psychosocial resources and psychological distress. *Journal of Community Psychology, 31, 2,* 113-127.

Striegel-Moore, R., & Smolak, L. (1996). The role of race in the development of eating disorders. In L. Smolak, M. P. Levine, & R. Striegel-Moore (Eds.), *The developmental psychopathology of eating disorders: Implications for research, prevention, and treatment.* Mahwah, NJ: Lawrence Erlbaum, Ass, Inc.

Szapocznik, J., Scopetta, M. A., Kurtines, W., & Aranalde, M. A. (1978). Theory and measurement of acculturation. *International Journal of Psyhology, 12,* 113-130.

Taft, R. (1977). Coping with unfamiliar cultures. In N. Warren (Ed.), (Vol. 1). London: Academic Press. *Studies in cross-cultural psychology.*

Taft, R. (1986). The adaptation of recent Soviet immigrants in Australia. In I. Reyes-Lagunes & Y. H. Poortinga (Eds.), *From a different perspective: Studies of behavior across cultures.* Lisse: Swets and Zeitilinge.

Taft, R. (1988). The psychological adaptation of Soviet immigrants in Australia. In Y. Kim, & W. Gudykunst (Eds.), *Cross-cultural adaptation, current approaches* (pp. 150-167). Newbury Park: Sage Publications.

Tiret, L., Ducimetiere, P., Andre, J. L., Gueguen, R., Herbeth, B., Spyckerelle, Y., Rakotovao, R., & Cambien, F. (1991). Family resemblance in body circumferences and their ratios. The Nancy family study. *Annales of Human Biology, 18,* 259-271.

Van Ranst, N., Verschueren, K., & Marcoen, A. (1995). The meaning of grandparents as viewed by adolescent grandchildren: An empirical study in Belgium. *International Journal of Aging and Human development, 41(4),* 311-324.

Vasilieva, L., (1994). *Kremlin wives.* (L. Vasilieva and & C. Porter, Trans.). New York: Arcade Publishing, Inc. (Original work published 1992).

Wardle, J., & Marsland, L. (1990). Adolescent concerns about weight and eating: A social-developmental perspective. *Journal of Psychosomatic Research, 34(4),* 377-391.

Wehrly, B. (1982). Cultural and social influences on career guidance. *International Journal of Advanced Counseling, 5,* 131-140.

Wilfley, D. E., Schreiber, G., Pike, K., Rodin, J., & Streigel-Moore, R. H. (in press). Similarities in eating disturbances among Black and White women. *International Journal of Eating Disorders.*

Wooley, O. W. (1994). *And man created "woman":* Representations of women's bodies in Western culture. In P. Fallon, M. A. Katzman, & S. C. Wooley (Eds.), *Feminist perspectives on eating disorders* (pp. 17-52). New York: The Guilford Press.

Index